TO SEE A WORLD IN A GRAIN OF SAND

RECONCILING THE SAINTS TO DARWIN AND EINSTEIN

DIVORCING THE SAINTS FROM SMITH AND LINCOLN

Loyd L. Fueston, Jr.

Wipf & Stock
PUBLISHERS
Eugene, Oregon

Wipf and Stock Publishers
199 W 8th Ave, Suite 3
Eugene, OR 97401

To See a World in a Grain of Sand
Reconciling the Saints to Darwin and Einstein,
Divorcing the Saints from Smith and Lincoln
By Fueston, Jr., Loyd L.
ISBN: 1-59752-648-7

Publication date 5/15/2006

What benefit is it to anyone to win the whole world and forfeit or lose his very self?

Jesus: Luke 9:25

[T]he scope of reason must be enlarged again. We have to come out of the prison we have built for ourselves and recognize other forms of ascertaining things, forms in which the whole of man comes into play. What we need is something like what we find in Socrates: a patient readiness, opened up and looking beyond itself. This readiness to look at things, in its time, brought together the two eyes of reason, Athens and Jerusalem, and made possible a new stage in history. We need a new readiness to seek the truth and also the humility to let ourselves be found.

Joseph Cardinal Ratzinger: page 158 of *Truth and Tolerance*

Contents

Preface

I don't see how I can exist as an individual apart from the universe into which I was born. I'm made of the stuff of this universe. My very prayers consist of brain-events and movements of my vocal chords just as my most dutiful movements towards God consist of muscular contractions and relaxations that allow me to stand and then kneel, to chew and swallow the very body of God Incarnate. Fresh stuff flows into my body from the universe and poisonous or superfluous stuff flows out to return to the waterways and soils. I'm a physical creature unconvinced of the desirability of a mind or a soul made of some stuff not to be seen or smelled or heard. The mysterious and the miraculous should not be obscured by implausible conjectures. Modern Christians, along with many others, hold, as if settled beliefs, highly speculative conjectures about mere creatures, empirical beings, having such components as souls separable from the body and possessing such divine attributes as immortality. These beliefs shatter the unity of God's Creation by claiming that mere creatures, men, are not fully a part of that Creation, having components and attributes which lie beyond detection or measurement by empirical means. We err in the intellectual realm by over-ruling evidence with our preferences, blurring the difference between metaphysical being and concrete entities, and we risk committing blasphemy, blurring the still greater difference between God and man.

I'm a confirmed member of the Catholic Church, and I believe in the resurrection of the body into a New Creation. I am, I hope, destined for life without end in that New Creation. If that happens, I'll still be made of stuff, but rather the stuff of a new universe not subject to the corruption and decay of this universe, nor will that stuff be subjected to the relentless pressures of development which seem to be part of God's plan for this phase of Creation.

I'm a creature of an all-powerful and all-loving God. I don't deserve to exist, nor do I deserve to be resurrected after death – if God rescues me from the death that lies in the flames of the crematorium or within the gentle, satiny embrace of the casket. My existence and all else that I have, or might have on the other side of the grave, are gifts from God.

I'm not afraid of Charles Darwin or his dangerous ideas. Evolutionary biology has produced a surprisingly powerful narrative explanation for human nature. It seems to me that evolutionary biology is more compatible with Biblical views of man than any of the anthropologies which depict man as having a component which is godly or angelic. Abraham and David are not presented as other than flesh-and-blood animals. More than that, I fear that evolutionary theory tells us how it is that an all-powerful God was able to grant some measure of freedom to His embodied creatures. Moral and natural evil are not problems imposed on this world by rebellious angels nor are they tests to select those pure enough to go to Heaven; they're by-products of a world and developmental processes which have allowed, to such a small extent, some amount of freedom from the laws which govern the stuff of our bodies.

I'm not afraid the Universe is riddled by chance and randomness nor am I afraid the Universe is haunted by demons. I consider chance and randomness to be superstitions as much as demons are. It's likely that what we perceive as chance and randomness are effects of God who, having first created a universe of pure created being, then shaped that pure created being, imposing aspects of a particular nature which we perceive as facts. Without a fact-like world, we could not have evolved as rational, self-aware creatures with some limited freedom. So far as I can see, a world less factual, more elegant and more tightly designed, would have given rise to creatures too well-defined to allow any real freedom. Whatever possibilities are open to God, human beings have become moral animals with some freedom by way of sometimes nasty development processes occurring in factual jungles.

And, yet, vaguely do I see a coherent world, perhaps a world that's also unified and complete. My respect for these qualities in this universe created and particularized by God and my feelings of creaturely humility lead me to be open to the results of empirical investigation. In a sense, it's a matter of indifference to me whether God created the first man from a puddle of slime or whether He created a world in which man's ancestral line is smeared over generations of apish creatures. Then again, simple respect for God and His generosity in creating this world mandates that I accept what He has done. It's also a matter of great importance to me to find a way to talk of concrete things emerging from the sort of abstract being which can be handled by metaphysics, the quantitative aspects of that abstract being are studied by modern theoretical physics. Metaphysics and theoretical physics are like all other human fields of thought and study in that they're valid only when subjected to the constraining influence of empirical knowledge. Only revealed knowledge is, by definition, not fully founded upon empirical facts and empirical knowledge, but, even there, God Himself can only communicate with human beings by way of physical events such as changes to brain-cell states or hormonal flows. More than that, revelation would make sense to us only if it were consistent with our knowledge of empirical reality. To a large extent, this book is an attempt at what might be called experimental metaphysics, an effort to create a narrative which makes sense of both empirical knowledge and Christian belief.

My reading of the Bible and contemplations upon the nature of the universe tell me that I'm a small part of a huge and magnificent creation which takes precedence over each of us, over all of us, because we are but part of it. The Bible does not encourage us to believe that man is some sort of god-like creature who fell into this world of blood and dirt, nor does it encourage us to believe that the world was made for us. We can speak plausibly of human beings as the crown of creation, not less than the crown but not more. We need to remember that the crown exists to glorify and complete Creation. Creation does not exist for us but for God's pleasure. We also exist for God's pleasure and not for ourselves.

The universe comes before any and all men. Even Jesus, the Word made flesh, came within the world, willingly subjecting Himself to the powers and thrones and dominions of His own Creation. He came to heal the breech made, not by a rebellious god-like Adam, but rather by God Himself. We can speculate all we wish about how God could have made a better universe for us, but we can only know that we ourselves are products of the upheaval and restless movement of this universe and its creatures, as all of Creation struggles through its birth, through its efforts to exercise a measure of freedom. God created a universe with a large amount of pain and suffering because He loved us before we were even in our mothers' wombs, loved the universe itself before He formed it from some prior stuff which I'll call the Primordial Universe. In the obscure language forced by attempts to understand evil, we should be grateful to God who loved us so much that He made us rather than making better creatures in a better world.

I readily accept the claims of traditional Christian metaphysics that created being is an image of the Creator, a manifestation of certain ideas held by God, though I have my questions as to the translation from abstract being to concrete things. Man seems to be a concrete being inside a universe that flows like a narrative; man does not seem to be a direct manifestation of a metaphysical essence, nor does he seem to have any component which is such. Concrete men cannot be explained by metaphysical principles nor by the equations of quantum physics nor by those of relativity theory. Nor can a star or a galaxy be explained by such. The ambiguities and abstractness, the very elegance and beauty, of metaphysics and mathematical physics are a sign that they cannot explain the messiness of higher levels of concrete being; nor can they explain the narrative flows of our lives or the physical universe itself. They give us tools that allow us to understand the most fundamental properties of matter and they also give us tools to tell the story of the life of a galaxy. This is a lot different from reducing a galaxy by merely 'explaining' it. Similar but stronger statements can be made about the power and limitations of metaphysics or science when it comes to understanding living creatures.

I readily accept the Patriarchal stories and the stories of the kingdoms of Israel and Judah, the prophecies of those who saw God and the prophecy of He who was God. Most of the Bible seems to be a story of men trying to hear God's words. Those words of God did not always retain much in the way of clarity or plausibility after being shoved through the thick skulls of those all-too-human prophets and kings and priests, those weak and frail Apostles and evangelists. At that, the authors of the various books of the Bible were honest observers who depicted man as if he were...

Well, as if he were a self-centered apish creature who often sacrifices himself only for the purpose of leaving great numbers of descendants. The sociobiologists would say that Abraham and the other patriarchs were creatures whose behavior was shaped to propagate their genes for the very reason that the genes that survive are those of creatures who behaved in such a way that they propagated their genes.

It's all as logical as it's circular and fact-driven.

We're embedded in a physical universe that's more than dead matter but seems to have little in the way of spirits and gods and angels. The universe is not living but has something vaguely life-like about it as if it be charged with potential but not actual life.

With some contemplative effort, this universe can begin to seem unified and coherent and complete, that is, it can begin to seem a world. It's not something that's perceivable by creatures in the ordinary course of living in their natural environments. The world must be actively perceived, must be brought into focus, by specific acts of intelligence, mostly moral intelligence, analogous to that act by which it was created and is still being created. Moreover, those acts of intelligence seem to be powered by a willingness to see a loving Creator behind all the volcanic explosions and viral epidemics as well as behind all the lively young children and beautiful sunsets.

Physicists have discovered properties of matter and energy and fields that make it more plausible as the stuff of intelligence and life. Fields generated by the brain, electromagnetic and stranger, have many of the aspects that people have attributed to mind-stuff and soul-stuff, god-stuff and angel-stuff. Fields – such as those generated by electromagnetism – can move weightlessly as if they were not physical entities. From such movements would come the illusion that minds and souls have some immaterial substance rather than being functions and aspects of physical stuff organized in appropriate ways. The stuff which God created and which is accessible to human senses – aided by human ingenuity, seems sufficient to form me and any creatures I've ever met.

Man is not a fallen god but rather an ape often dragging its knuckles.

An ape in communion with God.

An ape which has moved out of his environment that he might live in a world.

Animals are born into environments and live in such locations all their lives. Man has the potential to look beyond his environment and perceive the world. Do all men act to realize that potential? Do some men remain human animals inhabiting one or more environments?

Man is an ape. A cousin to the chimpanzee, a somewhat more distant cousin to the gorilla.

The Son of God was incarnated as an ape? He must have loved us a lot to take on the nature of an ape. Or maybe apes aren't such despicable creatures? Whether apes are despicable or not, we better purge ourselves of our Promethean pride and realize that dictionaries and philosophers and theologians are splitting imaginary hairs when they would separate the race of man from the family of apes. We're a rather unique species of ape, but we are a species of ape.

How to pull together all these various pieces? Can it be done?

We hear much of the power of narrative, some even claim it's necessary to human understanding of the world. Can this be the right tool of understanding? Is the world a story being told by God, a story we struggle to perceive?

Perhaps, thought I in a moment of optimism, I might produce a simple series of narratives that pulls together all the pieces, or at least enough to bring a world somewhat into view. To steal and somewhat re-imagine a scene that James Joyce depicted in *A Portrait of the Artist as a Young Man*, I could have a Jesuit professor of biology standing on a stage, right hand on the Bible and left hand on the *Origin of Species*. The left hand rises and index finger points downward before he speaks in a resonant baritone voice: "This is the book that tells us how we, and chimpanzees and wolves, came to be what we are." The left hand drops as the right hand rises and another index finger points downward to say, "This is the book that tells us of God's offer to make of us more than what we could be by natural means, more than what we could be by our own inherent powers."

Perhaps it's time to see if the two narratives can really be seen as the same story. Is the tale of the evolution of life on Earth really enfolded in the tale sketched in bare outline in the Bible?

Courage and a willingness to experiment are of the essence.

Let's cook it a while and then throw a glob against the wall to see if it sticks.

Introduction

The reader should approach this book as an experiment in pulling together Christian beliefs and some plausible framework of empirical knowledge, as of 2005, to create a coherent worldview, a view which presents a world unified and complete as well as coherent. I should qualify the phrase "as of 2005" by noting that much of my reading in cosmology and other fields of physics was done in the early to mid 1990s, followed by several years of readings in evolutionary biology and neurobiology, and then followed by several more years of contemplation on these matters while I was writing, or re-writing, a handful of novels which have not yet found their publishing homes. My contemplations on the universe and on my own efforts to see it as a world have reached a point where I might help others in the modern world who are trying to make sense of modern science in the light of traditional beliefs of some sort, or perhaps trying to make sense of traditional beliefs in the light of modern science.

This book is largely free of scholarly apparatus such as footnotes, though you might see one or two if the mood strikes me. I'll use footnotes when it might not be obvious that my text is relying upon a particular book or a well-known author. Occasionally, I'll use a footnote to make an important side-comment which would have disrupted the flow of the main text. If the reader wishes to pursue matters a little further in one direction or another, to see what helped to form my thoughts, he is, of course, free to browse the bibliographical essays at any time. Except for an occasional reference to a work readily available in many editions, those essays and the bibliography itself will point to specific editions, sometimes the only editions, of good books that provide entry to the literature of a specific field of human knowledge. I do occasionally refer to a well-known thinker without a bibliographical reference if his works are readily available to the interested reader.

The bibliography and bibliographical essays are not not intended to be a complete guide to the literature written for the non-specialist, not for physics nor for biology nor for philosophy. I've simply presented short discussions of books which have played a role in forming my views of God's world and those which have played a role in sharpening my understanding of God's words and God's Word.

The trick to finding good and accessible books on any topic is to find one good book on that topic or a related topic and then use the recommendations it contains as guides for further reading. There are so many bad books being published, even by people with seemingly solid credentials, that a smart reader will spend some time thinking about what he really wishes to read.

Bad books have always been with us and always will, but the marketplaces of our age both aggravate and respond to the desires of morally disordered people who have little respect for their own minds or souls. This has resulted in an extraordinary decline in the esthetic and intellectual content of our books, as well as a nearly total disappearance of works appealing to a human being with a healthy imagination. As I'll explain throughout the book, this decay in our minds and our imaginations matches up with a decay in our moral reasoning and moral habits. All of this decay can be seen as a result of a conspiracy of the invisible hand sort; we have all decided we'd rather have nice cars and large-screen television sets than healthy minds and souls. As was predicted and advocated by the founder of scientific management – Frederick Taylor, we have found that it's easier to be highly productive for the sake of being highly productive if we dumb ourselves down. The family of ideologies which shape our minds and our social, political, and economic relationships teach us that we're somehow thrown into this world as pre-formed agents, rather than being creatures made of the stuff of this world but only partially formed. They say this even while the entertainment industry and the school systems shape children to the needs of the gods of the marketplaces.

Our proper role is to engage in as many public-square transactions as possible rather than worrying about the proper formation of our own souls and minds or those of our children. For example, books had to be dumbed-down just so they would become ephemeral and uninteresting objects to be quickly read and then tossed out as we make our way to the mall to buy another ephemeral and uninteresting object.

Vote early, vote often.

Produce early, produce often.

Consume early, consume often.

With that advice to the man of the world, I'll leave you to enjoy, or despise, the efforts of one Christian to form a worldview which considers the results of modern, empirical knowledge. Christians claim to have faith in God the Creator of all. Perhaps it's time for us to realize that faith should lead us to be more open to the world as it is and as it has been according to the testimony of the fossil fields of the Dakotas or the testimony of Homer and Herodotus, Naipaul and Lukacs.

Acknowledgments

My parents – Loyd and Dorothy Fueston – provided support of various sorts even as I was approaching my middle-years, a failure in this land of opportunity. My sister Meg Mastriana opened her house to me while I was writing this book. My brother Richard Fueston and my sister Susan Wilson provided more spiritual support than they can realize.

After finding my way back to Christianity through a church in Atlanta that considered itself non-denominational (associated with the Church of Christ), I discovered the history of Christianity and found myself forced to examine the claims of the ancient churches. When I moved to Stamford, CT, shortly afterwards, I impulsively wrote a note to William F. Buckley, Jr., telling him of my situation and of my fears of the Catholic Church – some heretical priests with very strange ideas were prominent at the time. Mr. Buckley put me in touch with a young priest named Kevin Fitzpatrick. Father Fitzpatrick straightened out a number of misunderstandings and also introduced me to the liturgy; I'd been called by God in a strange way that didn't lead me to so much as attend a Mass before I decided to enter the Catholic Church. It also helped greatly that I re-established contact with a friend from a prior job, Phil Borba, who encouraged me in entering the Catholic Church and also sponsored me. Sadly, I've lost contact with both Father Fitzpatrick and Phil.

At a crucial period of my life, when I was very much a partially formed Catholic, I happened to meet Father Cyril Karam, OSB, founder of St. Mary's Monastery in Petersham, MA. Father Cyril was a man who made mistakes when he was young, being excommunicated during his participation in the Feenyite movement. After returning to the Church, he became a monk and priest and eventually founded St. Mary's, dying in a car accident on his return from leading a parish mission. I've met some wonderful Christians but Father Cyril was the one to whom I'd most readily apply the term 'saint'.

After moving from Petersham, I stopped practicing my Catholic faith, returning to communion with the Church a few years ago at St. John the Baptist Church in Ludlow, MA. Father Homer Gosselin is a wonderful and often over-worked priest at a parish which would have at least a second priest if there were not a shortage of vocations. We can only pray that his fine example will help to inspire young people to enter the service of the Church though they've been raised in a society that teaches them to be live in the marketplaces and not the sacred places. Much of the finalization of my thought occurred when I was becoming more active, attending daily Mass on a regular basis in addition to Sunday Mass. I've also been participating in a prayer group made up of devout Catholic Christians: I thank Normand Grondin, Rosemary Boucher, Sherry Meyer, Joanne Goddeau, Charlotte Doiron, and Kerry Bardon for their prayers and support. I also received great support from Regina and Arthur Lourenco in *Sonrises Bookstore* in Ludlow. Arthur and I came to an agreement that this world would be a better place if a local bookstore could afford to stock the writings of the Church Fathers – oh, for the time and money to take on a study of the works of Augustine and Athanasius and the Cappodocians. When we moved on to doom and gloom, Regina was there to remind us that this is God's world and a tempered optimism is the right Christian attitude.

Over the past two years, I've been in sporadic but sometimes heavy communication by mail with a fellow who has the courage of his Christian convictions, Stanley Hauerwas, the theologian at Duke University. Stanley follows through to unpopular political, social, and moral positions if he feels those are the positions consistent with the life and teachings of our Lord Jesus Christ. While I'm just beginning to study his writings, I've already learned the importance of a true Christ-like compassion without any of the squeamishness and sentimentality which have corrupted our thoughts and feelings and behaviors. I also owe Stanley dearly for taking the time out of his busy schedule to write to me when I was nearly ready to give up my efforts to write about the damage we modern people have done to ourselves with our wrongful ways of living and thinking and feeling.

Stanley's interpretation of St. Augustine's thoughts, expressed in his books and in some articles not yet published, have played a major role in refining my views on human nature. My later readings of my own book along with a re-reading of Stanley's Gifford Lectures, *With the Grain of the Universe* have convinced me that my thoughts have been re-structured by paying attention to his arguments that theological thought and religious practice must be centered upon God – to a frightening extent, modern Christianity is man-centered. It's the presence of God which should be the starting point and ending point of our thought and the greatest of modern Christians are likely those, such as John Paul II and Dorothy Day and John Howard Yoder, who are primarily witnesses to that presence of the God of Jesus Christ. Stanley is another faithful witness to the presence of the God of Jesus Christ. There's no better compliment to give a Christian.

My belief in the plasticity of the young human brain leads me to see the strong influence that my Great-aunt Minnie, Wilhelmina Cameron, had upon the formation of my brain. She spent a lot of time with me in my third and fourth years of life, teaching me how to read at that young age, though I would be nearly eight before I could confidently recite the alphabet. Aunt Minnie from Montrose and Arbroath helped form my insides – at least partially – to Scottish standards of the Victorian Age. I think we can do still better than those standards if we learn to care for what is important but I also believe those Scottish standards of the Victorian Age to be superior to American standards of the Disney Age.

Part I

Preliminaries

1 What Am I Up To?

I'll try to bring into focus a Christian worldview that pays proper respect to modern scientific knowledge though I'll be considering what little I know of the history of human thought and human history in general. That which I've learned about human nature from literary works will also come into play. A more complete discussion of the relationship of a Christian worldview to all forms of empirical knowledge might be desirable but it would be more than could be accomplished in this book.

I intend to show that a Christian worldview built on foundational ideas from St. Thomas Aquinas can quite readily make good sense of this dynamic universe of evolving things. This does not mean that I suggest we return to Medieval styles of argumentation for that's not necessary to the foundational insights of Aquinas. Nor do I suggest that we adopt all his conclusions or even his specific schemes for organizing knowledge. That also is not necessary for those foundational insights which have to do with the nature of human knowledge and with the importance of the act-of-being.

By showing that modern science can be easily absorbed into a Christian worldview, I hope to cast a light upon the ideological interpretations of scientific knowledge found in many works of popular science as well as in the curricula of our school systems at all levels. At the same time, the reader will see that I don't consider distortions of science to be at the heart of the problem – scientific and scientistic thinkers have not been so important in the development of the modern ideologies as some believe. The scientistic thinkers, even those who were also legitimate scientists – such as Carl Sagan – are followers, mimics who apparently don't realize the lack of creativity in their ideologically deformed versions of evolutionary biology or their advocation of process-centered physics in which substance and substantial entities disappear.

Specifically, I'll claim that the writers of most popular science-books are, like Karl Marx and many other modern prophets, standing upon the shoulders of Adam Smith. This is a simplification, to say the least, but it's useful in that it provides a focused point in place of an historical blur. And that dour Scotsman is likely the most important of the founders of the main and most successful family of modern ideologies – liberalism. Smith used his vast learning and his knowledge of literature and rhetoric to mount an eloquent defense of the eighteenth century belief that human life ideally and essentially consists of a stream of transactions in the public squares, commercial and political. He didn't originate this foundation of so many modern ideologies, but he was brilliantly obtuse in ignoring the Presbyterian moral and social discipline that led the profit-seeking individuals of Glasgow to limit their behavior and form morally well-ordered marketplaces.

We've lost our Christian traditions and all other traditions. Traditions keep people in their homes and neighborhoods and their churches. The gods of the marketplaces prefer that we live in the regions they control. It was Adam Smith who eased the transition from societies ordered by Christian traditions to societies kept in a state of moral and social turmoil that serves those idols we prefer to worship.

Adam Smith joined the elite group of dangerous thinkers who helped to destroy traditional ways of life and thought while also making sure that modern men would imagine that economic and political freedom could be had with no effort on their part. Under the spell of this illusion, men proved themselves to be cattle, easily herded into the public squares, commercial and political. In Biblical terms, Adam Smith taught modern men to turn from the God of St. Paul and to accept the principalities and angels and height and depth as the true powers of the world, powers which can well-reward their faithful worshipers and slaves. He depersonalized those powers and renamed them as the 'invisible hand'. It was appropriate to depersonalize at least some of those powers but not appropriate to advocate that we cede our moral responsibilities, including our duties to God, to the operations of those powers.

The scientists who argue that the world is really just processes are true to their upbringing as entities whose lives consist of streams of transactions; they're whirlwinds moving fitfully around the public squares. The human being is assumed to be some sort of pre-formed agent, a center of desires and a possessor of some sort of magical will which decides upon the proper bundle of goods and service to meet a particular set of desires. Against this view, I'll argue that human nature is a bounded but plastic entity. We shape ourselves by the way we live and the way we think.

I'll try to convince my fellow human beings that we hold salvation, by any substantial definition or understanding, at a distance so long as we remain under the spell of the modern ideologies. We need to construct a worldview more appropriate for Christians, a worldview which considers all that has been learned about men by historians and literary men as well as what has been learned about all living creatures and the physical universe by modern scientists.

A second-best alternative, but far from the best, is to re-adopt some of the older worldviews which include the revealed truths as well as some of the moral truths which are extrapolations from the better human instincts. This is far from the best because it ignores all that modern empirical thinkers have learned about the physical world and about physical creatures – including human beings. Those of us who are Christians have to regard service to God as our primary duty, but we have important secondary duties which come from that primary duty. Those secondary duties include proper stewardship of those goods and creatures from God's world which are placed under our care and also an openness to the truths which we can see in that world. God's world is not something which can be fully viewed or understood by any human being, partly because it includes all of the limited worldviews of human beings who make the effort to hold, or even form, such views. In the terms used by some modern scientists: human beings cannot gain a God's eye-view of physical reality. But who, other than some modern philosophers and some ancient magi, ever proposed that we could gain such a complete and absolutely true view of anything?

And, yet, in principle, we can gain something of a God's eye-view of physical reality. I'm not speaking pseudo-Zen to obscure matters. Rather am I endorsing the claim of Aquinas that, in principle, the human mind can comprehend the universe but, in fact, no actual human mind can fully understand so much as a flea. This is the proper response to the ponderings of some of the more philosophically inclined of modern physicists: Why is it that when confronted with a locked door in the natural world, we not only find the proper key on our chain but we find it very quickly? There's nothing mystical in this if we're willing to accept the fundamental truths of physical reality which underlie the ignored insight of St. Thomas Aquinas: the human mind has been shaped by physical reality. The mind-shaping process which was intuited by Aristotle and sharpened a bit by Aquinas took place over three billion years or so of biological evolution. And it takes place in the life-time of an individual human being.

We can be taken in by wrongful ideas, such as Aristotle's biological metaphors in physics or the idea that the natural world is filled with spirits which move planets or cause our illnesses. Most wrongful ideas which have taken hold in human minds do so just because they're related to some true insights. We wrongfully see immaterial spirits in physical movements just because the universe is dynamic in a way that has made life possible. In my worldview, this is due to the actions of God in placing specific constraints and conditions upon a homogeneous and chaotic Primordial Universe which is being both constantly created and constantly energized by an act-of-being possible only to God. Pure created being with its raw dynamic qualities has been shaped to make a concrete universe possible and God chose to shape it in such a way that living creatures of certain types are possible. This is not something God did once fifteen billion years ago, but rather something He did fifteen billion years ago and is still doing even as I type these words.

But what do I mean by a worldview which is supposedly preferable to modern ideologies? It's the sort of explanation that's better encapsulated in the doing, the act of bringing a world into view as, analogically, God brought a world into existence. A worldview can be defined as follows:

> The best available empirical knowledge about the physical world subjected to moral ordering. It's clearly by way of that moral ordering that the world can become a Christian world, which is God's world perceived by a frail human being. And, to a Christian, it's that moral ordering which comes from Christ which is the most important immaterial element in this universe. In this context, immaterial refers to the partial but substantial revelation from God about His ultimate purposes in creating this universe and telling a story in which the human race appeared.

In narrative terms, the Christian world is more a story than a place. it's a story in which metaphysical being plays a necessary role in forming the stuff of the characters and the stuff of the settings, stuff which has its own basic properties. In this sense, God's revelations, especially those which were the life and teachings of Jesus Christ, cover aspects of God's world but they're immaterial only because they're prefigurations of aspects of that world which a creature living in time cannot see. Those revelations are apocalyptic in the true sense of the word. The Kingdom of God is already here though we cannot see it and have to accept its presence on faith.

The metaphysical view-point and that of (very fundamental) theoretical physics overlap greatly. As I view the divisions of human intellectual work, physics at a conceptual level can be seen as a case-study of the quantitative aspects of abstract being. Experimental physics deals with this particular universe. I'll use the term Primordial Universe for the abstract being created by God and Particularized Universe, or more simply – universe, for the concrete being which came from the Primordial Universe as a result of God shaping it. The Creator constrained pure being, subjecting it to what physicists and mathematicians would call initial conditions and also subjecting it to various 'arbitrary' law-like rules which are clearly arbitrary or ad-hoc only in the sense of not being necessary, that is, not implying or being implied by the truly fundamental quantitative laws underlying the stuff of our universe. Without that process of constraining, the universe – as a particular thing and containing particular things – would not have come to be.

A worldview provides the foundations for philosophical contemplation, for literary exploration, for the practical work of pragmatic men. A worldview provides a starting point for both metaphysics and for theoretical understanding of concrete reality. One might say a worldview provides a potential person with a greater context, a way to see a universe and to see it as being unified, coherent, and complete. We're creatures of this universe, images of the image of God and are called to see that universe as having those properties, as being a world.

Unfortunately, most of the more plausible and more profound efforts to produce a Christian worldview lie well in the past, and those efforts are instructive but are no longer convincing. It was St. Thomas Aquinas who pointed out that the first science, metaphysics, uses the more specific sciences, such as physics and biology. The Thomistic metaphysics, the abstract layer – or systematic statement – of an entire worldview, worked very well in a technical sense though philosophers trying to recover a sense of the tradition, such as Etienne Gilson and Alasdair MacIntyre, tell us there were very few who understood some of the most important of St. Thomas' insights, such as the importance of the existential act, the act of being which, roughly speaking, brings us to exist before we become specific beings and continues to bring us to exist even while we're specific beings.

Later, I'll suggest a slight modification of Aquinas' understanding of the act of existence to account more directly for modern understandings of a universe which isn't stable but rather develops towards unknown and unknowable states. But the primary thrust of St. Thomas' insight, which still holds fully, is: God is His own Act-of-being. There's no divine substance as we understand substance to add to that Act-of-being. This means that God is not good because there's no divine substance, in a creaturely sense of substance, of which goodness can be an attribute. Rather is goodness an aspect which finite and fallible human beings perceive in the Act-of-being Who is Himself. Not just an example of an insight under-appreciated, the existential act stands as being very likely the most important component of any Christian metaphysical system and hence any Christian worldview. It was Aquinas who first understood God's self-revelation to Moses. God is "I-am" not essentially but rather existentially.

Etienne Gilson has argued, in several of his books, that not only have there been few to appreciate, or even to see, the importance of the existential act in Thomism, but there have been few philosophers who considered that act of coming into existence – existence was reduced to an accident of an essential being which was the object of study for philosophy as essential being is the object of study for the specific sciences such as physics and biology. For example, that essential being might be a human agent in the marketplace.[1] If we forget that the stuff of which we're made is constantly coming into existence, we forget that we're not only contingent beings but also beings subject to ongoing formation, which formation is made possible by an ongoing act-of-being. But it seems to me to be far better to speak of our underlying stuff as constantly coming into existence rather than to speak of our own beings as constantly coming into existence. Our beings are made of stuff which is a direct object of God's act-of-being but our own beings develop in the way of characters in a complex story. The latter way of speaking will discourage the belief that we come into the world as pre-formed agents, even as pre-formed persons. At the same time, we should remember that it's a fiction of a sort to make it easier to talk and think

[1]It's hard to tell the story of the degradation of our views of our own selves in the interests of making ourselves citizens of marketplaces. We don't acknowledge Thomistic existentialism but we have also thrown away the valid insights of the older views in which essence was primary and existence was an accidental property of a substance. Human beings are now no more than some strange and vaguely defined focus of desires and an incoherently conceived free-will. We're ghosts having neither essence nor existence but only desires under the control of some mythical free-will.

about difficult issues. God creates all that exists, not only the stuff of which we're made but also our very beings.

In modern scientific thought, a concept roughly corresponding to the existential act has been correctly brought to the level of the universe but then corrupted into the idea that a extrapolation back in time of the expansion of the universe points directly to God's act of Creation. There's a certain trivial truth in the idea that a movement back in time would point towards the beginning of time, and the cosmological models are a tribute to the wonderful work by astronomers, astrophysicists, mathematical physicists, designers of observational equipment, machinists who built that equipment, and so forth. All of this business about the Big Bang and related matters can also be quite beside the point so far as the act of Creation is concerned. Moving forward in time from that so-called Big Bang, the universe in this phase of its existence became more particular and more thing-like by what is called breaking of symmetries and also the imposition (at unknown times) of constraints imposed on top of the fundamental properties of matter. Running that film in reverse takes us back towards a simpler, more elegant, and more homogeneous phase of being, symmetrical and also lacking the fact-like constraints. I'm calling that phase of being the Primordial Universe, pure created being.[2] In my telling of this story, it was the Primordial Universe which was created from nothing by God and our universe resulted from God's acts of shaping and constraining that Primordial Universe to make it a Particularized Universe.

I'll delay any discussion of those fact-like constraints until the chapter about the Particularized Universe, but I'll digress for a couple of paragraphs to try to define what is meant by 'breaking symmetries'. Moving backwards in time, physicists and astronomers have discovered some remarkable facts about the universe. Most people nowadays know that the universe began with all its matter and energy and fields packed in so densely that all the galaxies we know about once occupied less space than a single atom in the current state of the universe. What they may not know is that extremely high temperatures go along with those densities. Some important stages in the expansion of the universe after the so-called Big Bang involve temperatures far higher than any that can be reached in either laboratory

[2]In the final phases of writing this book, I discovered that Georges Lemaître, Belgian priest and co-discoverer of the Big Bang model, had made a similar proposal using the term 'primeval atom' where I use 'Primordial Universe'.

experiments or in any possible events in the universe in its current state.

Without getting into the details, it turns out that matter, energy, and fields melt away at those extremely high temperatures. At relatively low temperatures by the standards of the Big Bang, protons and neutrons melt down into their constituent particles, the quarks and the gluons which bind quarks into neutrons or protons. We can conjecture that there are sufficiently high enough temperatures where all of those constituent particles melt down into the same basic components that are lacking the particular properties of electrons or protons or gluons or muons or whatever. What seems still stranger at first is that the same thing happens to forms of energy. Electromagnetic force and fields melt away as do the forces which bind protons and neutrons into the nucleus of atoms – the weak nuclear force. It turns out that electromagnetism and the weak nuclear force melt into the same sort of stuff at a temperature which can be modeled by theoretical physicists. Amazingly enough, there is, by conjecture and by the work of theorists, a temperature at which all matter and energy and fields – except for gravity – melt into one sort of being. Since gravity can be seen as a particularized form of the metaphysical property of unity, or even self-identity, I've my doubts as to whether gravity melts down the same way as electromagnetism or protons. I can imagine gravity being 'purified' to a metaphysical property while other forms of matter and energy and fields melt down along with time and space , but that's a pure speculation on my part.[3]

Let's take that one example of electromagnetic force and weak nuclear force and reverse our direction in time. When the universe was expanding, it was cooling down from tremendously high temperatures though it would be many years after the Big Bang before the average temperature in the universe dropped below that of our sun. When the temperature cooled down to a certain point, the stuff of our universe went through phase changes much like that of water cooling down and suddenly becoming a different state of matter – ice. In the case of what is called the electroweak force, cooling caused it to change state so that it partially froze into the hotter, or higher-energy, weak nuclear force and the cooler, or lower-energy, electromagnetic force. One specific symmetry was broken.

[3]If my speculation is correct, it would mean that gravity is a form of some metaphysical property which is necessarily more fundamental than space and time while any effort to develop a theory of quantum gravity assumes the opposite since quantum theory is, at least currently, defined in terms of space and time.

Symmetrical entities have fewer particular properties. A circle is more symmetrical and less unique than the shape a young child makes when first trying to draw a circle. The electroweak force was also more regular and had fewer unique properties than either electromagnetism or weak nuclear force. This breakdown of the electroweak force into more particular and less regular forces is a breaking of a symmetry. One important aspect of this and other broken symmetries is that the behavior of the more particular forms of matter and energy involve constants which might be random in the strongest sense – the digits of those constants have to be calculated one by one by way of experiments. If that holds true for an indefinite number of digits, it would mean those constants are random in the true sense – without any sort of pattern. It's possible that the digits of those constants can never be predicted but only calculated one by one on the basis of painstaking experiments. I'll later argue that only God can make a true random number and will explain why this is so.

The important claim I wish to make now is that the trip backwards in time towards the so-called Big Bang does not necessarily move us towards a moment of creation. It moves us towards a preceding state of the universe where all the particular properties of energy and matter and fields have disappeared. In fact, energy and matter and fields have melted down to a very strange stuff, homogeneous and lacking in particularity to a point where I'm comfortable speaking of perfect homogeneity. I call this earlier state the Primordial Universe and consider it to be a form of stuff which has been melted down to no more than some sort of embodiment of metaphysical properties such as self-identity and a resistance to contradiction. I use the term Particularized Universe or simply universe for the thing-like place in which we came to be and in which we develop, or fail to develop.

I'm not claiming unique insights here except possibly for seeing that it would be useful to look at the discoveries of cosmological physics in the light of Thomistic views of the nature of metaphysical being and the nature of concrete entities. I'll add that I relied heavily on Gilson's description of those Thomistic views. For my views on the so-called Big Bang model of cosmological physics, I relied upon the accounts and analyses of Stanley Jaki, Joseph Silk, John Barrow, and Marc Lachieze-Rey. It was Jaki's emphasis upon the particularity of this universe that drove me to contemplations lasting years. Those contemplations culminated in ideas which are my responsibility. Father Jaki and the astrophysicists upon whom I relied might well not agree with my efforts to insert the Big Bang model into a

Thomistically viewed world.

This earlier stage of physical being, the Primordial Universe, would be weird by the standards of a common-sense suited to the current state of the universe. The Primordial Universe, as I've said, would be perfectly homogeneous and perfectly symmetrical meaning that it would look the same from all directions in space and time. Turn around if you will, but you can't, for all around you is the same no matter which way you face – there's no way to face but one. Hence, space and time don't really exist in that Primordial Universe which is defined only by some basic metaphysical properties such as self-identity and a resistance to contradiction. It's when such an elegantly frightening homogeneity is broken that space and time, hence – things, can exist. Time and space might have been created as the first and greatest of the acts by which this perfect symmetry was broken in this entity that I call the Primordial Universe.

And this points back to a claim of the sort made by Aquinas and other Christian theologians who advocated what is called negative theology. Specifically, if there was an earlier phase of the universe, the Primordial Universe, which had no time or space dimensions, that would indicate God's being is far more strange than that. We can only understand God's form of being by analogy with what we know of created being, but God will always be beyond that, stranger than any sort of being that we can perceive or imagine. As some have said, God is the absolute other, but there are ways we can speak truly and intelligently of our Creator, largely because our minds are shaped to those of His effects I call the universe but also because He dwells inside of us as St. Augustine told us in such a masterful and authoritative way in various writings.

From our current position in this universe, I'll later argue it's best to speak of God as occupying all possible moments of time and all possible locations of space, but, in fact, God's being is beyond either time or timelessness, beyond either space or spacelessness. Time and space might well be something specifically created that this Particularized Universe might come into existence. Because of our limitations, we can speak piously of God as being timeless or of occupying all possible moments of time, but – as St. Thomas Aquinas relentlessly asserted – God's being is so different from any sort of being we can perceive that we have to be very careful to realize we can only speak analogically about God. We speak carefully about God in terms of aspects of created being – concrete or metaphysical, but such ways of speaking point to an Act-of-being that is Himself. We have to always bear in mind the radical strangeness of God's form of being, and I've misspoken for God has not being but is instead His own Act-of-Being, the Supreme Act-of-Being. Human languages don't have the grammatical structures which could allow us to point to God without implying that He has substance of the sort found in creatures. It seems likely they don't have the structures just because the concept would be utterly alien to the brain of a creature – a being which came to be within a universe and draws its being from the stuff and properties of that universe. Given this, our ways of speaking of God should always work to the task of minimizing the errors induced by the spirit of the age.

The revelation of the difference between God's being and the being of creatures allows us to transcend pantheism, which Stanley Jaki has quite plausibly argued to be the highest state of religious belief without a direct revelation as to the nature of God. As we're told that God is different from His creation and He is the source of all being, we can begin to understand that the universe does not exist by its own inherent powers or nature, nor do any of the creatures in it. The fate to which we were born is a true animal death in a universe itself being mortal. All that's not God is continually being brought into existence by God. God gives true life when He resurrects, but even that life will not be inherently ours. Rather will it be as much an ongoing gift from God as our current existence is.

But what is this world?

First of all, I'll claim that only God perceives the world. The rest of us can adopt a tradition which presents us with a worldview, a provisional view of God's world, or else we struggle to see a universe in our environments and then a world in the universe. Then again, we can choose to remain just human animals inhabiting environments.

The stuff of this world can be seen as forming the stages and backdrops for the story God is telling and the stories He encourages us to tell, but that's only a way of working towards a true way of speaking. Stars exploding into supernova glory or imploding into the dark secrecy of a black-hole are as much a part of the story God is telling as the human march across the earth and across the bodies of other humans. We're not even separate from this stuff that forms the floor-boards of the stage and the ropes that manipulate backdrops. Our feet merge into the boards upon which we walk, giving a certain sense that we move about upon a tar-pit as we struggle towards God or away from Him.

That's not quite right either. To borrow from and expand upon a metaphor used by the biologist C. H. Waddington to discuss development issues, we travel channels – I tend to use the blunter term of 'ruts' – in our physical development and in our lives. Professor Waddington was interested in describing genetic development and especially the way that an organism can travel so many different paths to reach the same general state of, for example, healthy and complete whale-ness.

I wish to expand that metaphor to consider all narratives about physical development and about moral development, in terms of ruts. These ruts are inside of us as much as they're outside of us. In fact, our insides are not private in the radical way claimed by liberal ideologists. They're images of the environments in which we live, the nurturing we received from parents and teachers and religious leaders, and our own decisions as to the thoughts and dreams and experiences we nurture in ourselves. Our innermost depths are shaped one way if we sit in front of the television watching Terminator movies and VH1, another way if we read the Bible and Melville novels and take the trouble to learn how to make our own music.

We have a responsibility to guide our own moral development and that of our children and we modern people willfully ignore that responsibility. We watch displays of gratuitous violence, we set infants down in front of such displays, and we think nothing of it.

It seems to me that our Christian ancestors could first ignore their moral responsibilities in matters of forming their selves and the selves of their children just because they believed that they were born with these components labeled as 'immortal soul' and 'free-will'. They thought they could flirt with dangerous forms of thought and behavior and their 'true selves', their souls, remained what they were at their births and would still be when they fly off to Heaven. At most, some thought their souls would go to Hell if they commited very serious sins. This view might have made sense given the static view of this universe which Christian thinkers inherited from certain pagan philosophers, but the current empirical knowledge of the universe and all it contains should be moving us toward developmental views of human nature. We now know we develop in this world to become suited to live as God's companions for time without end, or else we don't develop to such a state.

In fact, we're physical creatures of a plastic sort. We're formed by our experiences. By viewing evil in a movie, we take that evil into our own minds and souls just because that experience is forging new connections between brain-cells and also forging new habitual responses by our adrenal glands and other components of our bodies. And so we form ourselves to be that evil, though the amount of deformation to our bodies might be small with each viewing of a Terminator movie or a movie glorifying the feats and adventures of a cannibal.

If we had a better understanding of our creaturely nature, our physical animal nature, we would have to face up to the need to turn ourselves into God-centered moral persons. The virtuous pagans of the Roman Republic understood the need for moral formation and worked hard to toughen their moral fibers and those of their children. Even wolves act as if they understand this truth about animal natures. The mature adults in a wolf-pack work hard to teach both hunting skills and cub-rearing skills to their young adults. Some scientists even claim that the adult wolves will manage to delay reproduction by young adults for at least a year after maturity to ensure they've learned these skills. In this, wolves are apparently doing better than many segments of American society.

We are our bodies though our bodies generate fields which might provide us with a feel of immaterial being. In any case, there's no reason to speak of men as being beast and angel. It is – in my opinion – equivalent to saying that a man is so radically fragmented as to prevent him from becoming a person in the Christian sense. It's important to realize that human nature is not a topic God is likely to raise in His revelations other than to remind us we belong to him. Human nature is the nature of a particular type of creature. As such, human nature is subject to empirical investigation. We're no different from the fish in the seas or the stars in the sky in that regard. It's the Incarnation of the Son of God as a man and the promises He has secured from the Father that make us truly different from our cousins the chimpanzees. It's time that we Christians realize we're bound to practice a higher form of honesty, one where we must see our situation, as a race and as individuals, as truly and as clearly as we can given our limited perspective and our limited understanding. If the empirical evidence indicates human beings are a form of ape, then we Christians must acknowledge this to be God's doing.

We're animals with physical bodies and we have promises from God even to an offer of true life after the grave. Why do we need souls? The ancient and Medieval thinkers thought we needed souls to add some dynamic qualities to inert matter, but we now know that matter is a low-temperature form of some very dynamic stuff which can also take the form of energy and fields. Why do we need soul-stuff or mind-stuff? Unfortunately, most

Christians cannot ask such questions since they've confused these matters of human speculation with revealed truths. Those speculations came from human beings in response to questions which we now know to have been based on erroneous understandings of empirical reality.

It's most certainly not just Christians who have been guilty of mixing speculations or outright guesses with more certain knowledge. Many people throughout history have thought to ignore or deny one aspect or another of the universe in order to justify a set of ideological beliefs. We need to see clearly enough that we can perceive the truth that may occasionally be buried in some ideologically deformed work of empirical fact-gathering and analysis. In particular, we should admit that, on his way out of Christianity, Charles Darwin might well have discovered how moral freedom has arisen in men and other animals. We don't have a moral nature implanted directly by God but rather a moral nature which has developed over the eons, especially the more recent 10 or 20 million years when the evolution of social, placental mammals has accelerated. Later in this book, I'll speculate on God's reasons for letting moral creatures evolve rather than creating them directly but I can't say authoritatively why He did. I can say there's a growing body of evidence that moral creatures, blue whales as well as men, did evolve by way of physical processes which were downright nasty at times.

The most ideologically corrupted of the Darwinists make a serious error by claiming the amorality of the underlying processes of evolution tell us that moral creatures cannot arise in a natural way. In fact, the empirical evidence is that moral creatures are surprisingly common. This is a hard situation to deal with, but here's a try:

> Moral nature is a factual matter, its specifics depending upon the more general nature of a species under observation. Moreover, it's somewhat an anthropomorphic concept because we call 'moral' that behavior which is proper to species which are organized into families, tribes, or packs for the care of slowly maturing young. Sometimes the animals in those species form live-long bonds between males and females. Both characteristics, monogamous bonds and forms of life revolving around care of young, are certainly plausible results from an amoral, chaotic process of evolution.

> Ancient and Medieval thinkers had little reason to believe men had evolved from other creatures, though some had intuited general evolutionary processes. More recent thinkers have sometimes preferred the misguided anthropological beliefs of various traditions when it seems quite possible to explain much about the moral natures of animals by straightforward facts. Human morality was split from its true home in our embodied natures as highly social, placental mammals. Some wished to see human moral nature, human nature in general, as coming down from the Heavens, made of better stuff than hormones and brain-cells and physical habits. To a large extent, the modern skeptics have taken up this line of reasoning by unwise Christians, merely pointing to the evidence that there's no such soul-stuff or mind-stuff and therefore our moral natures are illusions. Other Christians and non-Christians have used a wrongly spiritual view of human nature as an excuse for ignoring the proper care of their bodily natures and those of their children.

Our ancestors separated what has to be one. While the person who is the Son can take on two natures, we mere mortals cannot. It's our natures which develop person-like characteristics as we try to become better images of God. If our natures were radically and inherently split, this process could not proceed. But we've gone beyond the errors of our ancestors. Though most human beings in the world today probably have at least a suspicion that we're fully physical animals, we have adopted a form of moral disorder in our societies such that we're no longer merely two radically different stuffs pasted together. We're collages, paste-ups of all sorts of beings, each of which functions differently and separately in the various marketplaces and other places of our lives. This has led to such silliness as the attempt to see an inherent division between thought and practice, between what is useful and what is morally good. This fragmentation has resulted from efforts to live out the erroneous liberal ideas which give the wrongful sort of unity to human beings, conjecturing us to be autonomous agents attached only accidentally to our biological natures which are members of specific families, ethnic groups, religious traditions, and so forth. Cast out into the marketplaces and told that we're free-standing individuals, we modern human beings fragment as we try to deal with different aspects of our lives. We consider ourselves wrongly as agents who face no dangers when we choose to watch a Terminator movie on Saturday night and then go to church on Sunday morning. In fact, this behavior fragments our being in radical and dangerous ways.

There's a related division between utilitarian and idealistic social views which is plausible but is, in fact, caused by nurturing our disordered desires so that we don't see that our greater good is secured by our own moral order and that of our families and other communities, with the Christian Church – the Body of Christ – being the ultimate and most important of those communities. In fact, no human being will be perfectly well-ordered in his moral nature – other than Jesus Christ. That means that no human society will be perfectly well-ordered. Even a society of morally well-ordered human beings would see disorder arise as a result of miscommunications and other problems caused by our limited natures. Still, there have been societies in past centuries which showed strong signs of moral order, telling us that an appreciable portion of the population of those societies were morally well-ordered by some reasonable definition if only that of virtuous paganism. Adam Smith observed a reasonably moral economy arising as a result of the free interactions of morally well-ordered Scotsmen, Presbyterians for the most part. That moral order was not perfect and maybe was already decaying into the moralism which so bothered Robert Louis Stevenson and others in the 19th century. But no society is perfect and the dynamic nature of human interactions tells us that any society will likely be increasing or decreasing in moral order. Still history indicates that a certain exploitive stability has occurred in some morally disordered societies, such as the Roman Empire or the Inca Empire. Unfortunately, it looks as if the American Empire has joined the ranks of those morally disordered societies which have a certain order based upon slavery and exploitation.

The issues of political and economic freedom are important to human beings during their lives on Earth but a Christian thinks of them as being important primarily in their effects upon our ability to form church communities and to integrate others, including our children, into those churches. Currently, most practicing Christians seem to regard these political and economic issues as being more important in their effect on our living standards and our supposed rights to do things morally well-structured people wouldn't wish to do. We live our lives as if God doesn't exist or at least as if He doesn't care about us. We live as atheists and to live as atheists is to be atheists even if we formally pronounce our belief in God each Sunday in church. My current view on our situation, developing late in the process of writing this book, considers three overlapping and interdependent historical processes by which modern man became an atheist. The first two processes are described in readily available books:

1. In *Denying and Disclosing God*, Michael Buckley tells us how well-intentioned but unwise Christian theologians made atheism more intellectually plausible by proposing that we can prove the existence of the God of Jesus Christ without bothering with the historical revelations of that God in Jesus of Nazareth, the human nature taken up by the Son of God. In this year of our Lord 2005, Christian theology can be done without the need to believe in the God of Jesus.

2. In *Without God, Without Creed*, James Turner tells how religious leaders tried to fit God into the modern world in various ways, most of them involving an overestimation of what modern empirical knowledge can tell us. In this year of our Lord 2005, Christians can worship and engage in their other ordinary activities without holding the specific beliefs of the Christian creeds.

3. In the sections of this book which deal with ideology, I'm describing how Adam Smith and his followers taught Christians and ex-Christians alike how to make our livings and how to govern ourselves as if the God of Jesus Christ doesn't exist. In this year of our Lord 2005, Christians can form communities which are organized around secular principles and not around the commandments of our Lord Jesus Christ.

In summary, we Christians have been given ways to think, worship, and form our communities as if the God of Jesus Christ doesn't exist.[4] We've adopted those ways as our own. As a people, we of the modern West – especially in the United States – are atheists no matter how faithful some of us might be in attending church on Sunday, no matter how many pious words are spoken by our politicians and our prominent clergymen.

Let me return to my absurd effort to restore Christian beliefs to Christianity. . .

---

[4]I'm not speaking directly to the parallel problem that many Christians have taken these ways as good reasons to become ex-Christians, but the underlying discussion would be similar. I should also note that Turner covers the same ideological distortions as I do, in a different way and with rich, historical detail.

It's not only God's original acts in creating the Primordial Universe and constraining it to become this universe, but also His ongoing acts of creating this universe that make order possible. We can't describe this mysterious act of bringing something to existence from nothing. We can't even state the concept in a grammatically correct sense because God didn't bring the Primordial Universe, and then the universe, to existence from nothingness the way that we can bring a table to exist where once there was only a pile of lumber and metal hardware. Nothingness is not the building block of something, no matter how many quantum philosophers might talk about universes forming from random fluctuations in nothingness. Empty space inside an existing universe can give rise to such fluctuations in created being, but that empty space is most certainly not nothingness. It's a spatial point in an existing universe and that point is alive with a form of potential energy.

The inability of most human beings, even some very intelligent scientists and philosophers, to understand that nothingness is radically different from any emptiness inside of Creation, is clearly one reason for the difficulties that Aquinas had in bringing the concept into clear view. As Gilson tells the story[5], even St. Augustine, who was not lacking in his appreciation of God's difference from creatures and His immanence in those creatures, had trouble escaping his Platonist assumptions, or at least phraseology, where an act of existence would be at most an accident or attribute of a substance.

If we think about God in terms of a divine substance, then that divine substance has to be made so transcendental that God is no longer able to directly interact with His own creation. The traditional chain-of-being model cannot resolve that difficulty since the greatest of angels would still be a creature and no closer to God than we are.

That's perhaps why St. Augustine, in the quote provided on that page of Gilson's book, inserted an angel between God and Moses in that Old Testament event which seems so clearly a direct confrontation of God with a man. To be fair to St. Augustine, I should note that Gilson acknowledged him as a rock solid Christian theologian but said he reached that level despite his inadequate philosophical understanding of being. As a theologian, St. Augustine was well aware that God is immanent as well as transcendent, inhabiting our own beings so that He knows us better than we could know ourselves. As a theologian, St. Augustine understood the psychological as-

[5]See page 85 of *The Christian Philosophy of St. Thomas Aquinas.*

pects of human nature better than any other human thinker just because he understood that God is present in each human being.

Modern physicists often hold a very dangerous version of that Platonist belief that stuff provides for its own existence. Then, because of their atheism – implicit in some and explicit in others, they make the error of thinking that contingent being needs no Creator. Modern physicists think that a description of the quantitative aspects of stuff can be treated as if it were an explanation of existence. In truth, those descriptions of quantitative aspects of stuff are not even equivalent to the stuff itself let alone the act of that stuff coming into being.

> A mathematical equation in physics is a description of some quantitative aspects of physical reality; it's not equivalent to that reality anymore than the dreams of shamans or the poetry of Gnostic magi are equivalent to that physical reality.

The existential aspects of stuff certainly cannot be captured in any equation. There's no conceivable equation that can describe an act-of-being, not that Supreme Act-of-Being which is God and not the lesser acts-of-being which He initiates and in which we participate in our very limited ways. By this I mean that our acts of understanding God's world, our worldviewing, are analogous to God's acts of bringing the world into existence. This is how we become better images of God whether our efforts, such as mine in this book, are abstract worldviewing or whether our worldviewing is the acceptance of an existing concrete tradition as we're lighting candles in front of an image of the Mother of God.

It's not only physicists, but those in all fields supposedly empirical who, often unconsciously, impose strong metaphysical assumptions upon their gathered information, sometimes distorting the resulting knowledge into one ideological monstrosity or another. I'm not opposed to metaphysical assumptions – they underly our understanding of concrete being, are necessary for all abstract thought, and naturally emerge as a worldview is constructed or adopted. However, unconscious metaphysical assumptions can be dangerous even when they are coherent.

And I wish to repeat that the underlying metaphysical assumptions of scientists are not what they themselves imagine. Darwin was able to flee the Christian God so rapidly because he was running down a path cleared and smoothed by Smith and the French Physiocrats and Malebranche and others who had foreseen men dwindling to mere nodes, however mobile, which were connected by various sorts of transactions – or processes if you prefer. Creatures reduced to this state are not capable of even realizing they're the brothers and sisters of Jesus Christ. Worst of all, those nodes are oddly independent of the universe in which they lived. I say that because we know God through the physical universe – as Aquinas emphasized relentlessly, and a person who has a distorted view of God's universe is going to have a very hard time accepting his proper relationship to God. Pretending to be somehow independent of God's universe, we become separated from God.

Nodes are not so evocative of our current situation, and so I'll state that we're widgets one and all, who think of ourselves as free individuals because 'free' has been re-defined to cover only activities agreeable to the gods of the public marketplaces of the modern world. This should seem surprising to those who have read much in the fields of anthropology and history and evolutionary biology and brain-science – it's pretty well-established that we're descended from creatures evolved to live in small-scale human societies and to live lives balanced and integrated between various sorts of activity, including religious ritual and community parties and family activities and, of course, making a living in local economies. This means that our character traits are those proper to those sorts of life. And yet our natural desires can be inflamed so that we run away from families and local communities and churches to enter those public marketplaces, some desiring to exploit others and many willing to be exploited in return for illusions of safety and security. Of course, we have developed various ways to pretend that we value the family which has been stripped of all roles but breeding future widgets and that role is now under attack.

Science and medicine provide a number of clear examples of this process of stripping away old attachments and old moral beliefs that we might better serve the gods of the marketplaces. Over the past fifty years, medical doctors and biological scientists – though not only these human beings – have modified their moral positions on a variety of issues so that now activities once despised or feared are positively encouraged. Abortion is a respectable business. Geneticists argue for the freedom to modify all sorts of organisms used to feed human beings as well as other creatures. We speak in neutral terms of 'research on embryonic stem-cells', meaning that scientists are preparing to conduct experiments upon embryos at various stages of development. These are activities worthy of a Nazi doctor. As I'll later discuss, human babies at birth are embryos – experimentation upon embryos at earlier stages is no more than preparatory to turning human beings at all stages of life into materiel for the use of the wealthy and powerful in our societies. But we accept these despicable and evil activities because we're told that we'll be cured of a variety of painful and life-shortening conditions. The very fact that we have such stocks of frozen embryos is itself a comment upon our morally disordered state. We've advanced rapidly in our efforts to turn the defenseless into means to our greater health and wealth.

Yes, we're an enlightened people not imprisoned by the prejudices of the past. But, then again, maybe not. It seems to me that all the changes in the moral beliefs and practices of medical doctors and scientists over the past half-century have been in the direction of increasing their income and the income to their institutions whether hospital or university or corporation or government laboratory. They're able to present these changes, to themselves and to others, as a form of moral enlightenment because those changes appeal to our moral cowardice, specifically our fears of dying or suffering. Scientists also soothe their own already stunted consciences by telling themselves that research as such is good. It's unclear why this is so until we realize that what's good is to increase the number of transactions which involve data acquisition. The GSDP, the Gross Scientific Data Product, is ever rising to shouts of acclamation of those little different from the Wall Street financiers who cheer every rise in the Gross National Product. One might think that if science were to be a truly moral enterprise, it would be subjected to moral guidance, which moral guidance might even be one day called wisdom. Wisdom seeks morally appropriate knowledge, not mere data, just as wisdom seeks a better human life and not just higher levels of marketplace transactions.

No one can deny that certain specific acts of science can be immoral and no one can deny that specific acts of investing or acts of governing can be immoral. But Adam Smith taught us that marketplaces will magically move to a state of good moral order if any old mob of people enter that marketplace and begin to satisfy their self-interests. In fact, history indicates that corporate capitalism and its master, the nation-state, were parasitic upon Christian societies in Europe which were at least somewhat well-ordered.[6] By 2005, corporate capitalism and the nation-state have al-

[6]To avoid clumsy language, I'll speak of a society with significant moral order as being morally well-ordered without qualification. The historically and spiritually aware

most destroyed any possibility of Christian moral order in the interests of profits and military power.

Some historians and philosophers have tried to teach us that corporate capitalism is sustained by positive laws and government programs (such as social security and unemployment benefits which 'free' human beings from their natural forms of attachment); those laws and programs work to the interests of the central governments of the modern nation-states. At best, a system of modern nation-state and corporate capitalism allows interstices of freedom which a pure state socialism will try to eliminate. Abraham Lincoln, himself made wealthy by serving various corporate clients, started the process of rationalizing corporate organization and taxing laws and did it for the purpose of supporting the first of all modern wars, which wars seem necessary to sustain the nation-state and its system of corporate capitalism.

We have distorted the true lesson underlying Adam Smith's analyses: markets can be self-organizing because decision-makers can stabilize markets in a form which suits their purposes – without aiming at such a global result. Adam Smith observed a Christian society in which these markets were morally well-ordered and told us that this sort of moral structure will arise naturally in any society where decision-makers in the markets freely pursue their self-interests. In fact, there have been plenty of societies in which human beings have freely pursued their own interests, in the political marketplaces and the commercial marketplaces. A morally well-ordered marketplace, political or commercial, rarely results. A morally well-ordered marketplace, and society, might result if the self-interested decision-makers are themselves morally well-ordered. In a morally chaotic nation-state such as the United States, the natural and normal pursuit of one's own interests will result in predatory behaviors in the commercial marketplace and the political marketplace alike.

Skeptical readers might be thinking I'm caught up in a muddle. I'm saying that creatures of moral nature can arise from the amoral processes of biological evolution and I'm denying that morally well-structured economies can arise from the interaction of decision-makers who are not morally well-ordered. My first defense rests simply on facts. Creatures with moral natures have arisen during the amoral processes of biological evolution. Morally well-structured economies have arisen only in societies where the decision-makers are themselves well-ordered, though there's a certain im-

---

reader can supply the proper qualifications and the proper clumsiness of thought.

moral but stable order achievable in slave societies or other exploitive societies as long as the exploiters are morally disciplined to some demanding and sustainable standard – such as those of certain warrior societies. In addition, I would point out that the amoral processes of evolutionary biology can bring creatures of moral nature into existence but those creatures are not born morally well-ordered – they must act to bring moral order to their own insides, to their societies, and to the environments they inhabit.

How could we have come to believe that there's some magic that'll convert the interactions of morally disordered human beings into a morally well-ordered society? It doesn't seem a belief that an intelligent thinker could even consider, but lots of clever human beings manage to hold that belief as if it were coherent, as if it corresponds to history. I don't have the learning to trace the development of this glorification of a superstition, but the true pioneers of this line of thought have certainly been the economists and political scientists. There are a host of highly regarded scholars in these fields, some of them Nobel Laureates, who continue to appease the established powers by trying to tell us there's some sort of magic that turns a mob of morally disordered human beings into a morally well-structured democracy, that turns their economic activity into a morally well-structured commercial marketplace. And scientists follow along in the wake of these social thinkers. Scientists and doctors are different only in the fact that their technical efforts are subject to peer-review and verification or denial by those trying to repeat experiments or to follow lines of analytic thought. This gives the illusion that the scientific enterprise itself is inherently moral. It's not. Scientists have been, as a group, just as willing to advance evil causes as other groups have been, even groups of MBAs or lawyers or politicians.

Yet, the need of fallen Christians to feel righteous and pure is too strong. We have shed the humility which is more proper to Christian belief and more conducive to moral order and, yet, we can't be willfully evil in the manner of Adolf Hitler nor even self-centered in the disciplined manner of Genghis Khan or Napoleon Bonaparte. We've retained just enough of our Christianity that we feel a need to be pure, washed as white as snow. So we need to justify our moral disorder, to see it as some sort of moral enlightenment. Easing the suffering of human beings with damaged spinal cords or with Parkinson's is a good justification for carrying out research that's allowing the gods of the marketplaces to turn human bodies into an exploitable resource, but only the bodies of those who will have no credit cards nor the right to vote. Hannah Arendt told us that the nice, middle-class human beings who staffed the bureaucracies of the Nazi Reich had families to support and careers to advance. We're no different.

The emperor has no clothes, folks. We're in it for the money, or rather for a high volume of economic transactions, because we and our parents turned our souls and minds over to be formed by the gods of the market-places. We act to increase the GNP rather than to increase devotion to God or the amount of goodness in His world and we manage to convince ourselves we're wonderful people. The criminals are all of us because we all act within the constraints dictated by the needs of the gods of the market-places of the modern world. We happily march to the beats of the various versions of the modern ideology. And those ideologies are destroying minds and deforming souls as power is increasingly centralized though we delude ourselves into thinking we're free individuals. We Christians delude ourselves into thinking we serve God, that we care what God has said to our ancestors. We certainly have blocked off any possibility of hearing anything He has to say now. God whispers tales of our damnation and we hear Him not over the blare of *The Battle Hymn of the Republic.*

Centuries ago, St. Augustine said: "We do not sin, we are sin." I'm saying that we're not agents suffering from disorder imposed upon us, we are that disorder. If we nurture that disorder, we can become irredeemably disordered, we can become sin to the deepest parts of our beings, we can become evil.

I think we might almost be wise to banish the concept of 'will' from moral theology and moral philosophy – it's a tool of misunderstandings far too often. So many of the people of our time who do evil and are evil, such as those who experiment on human embryos, do their evil and become evil, while willing another, unrelated good, such as the cure of Parkinson's disease.

> If we're to presume anything about our afterlives, it's safest to presume that Dr. Jekyll will go down to Hell with Mr. Hyde.

I digress often because digressions are a part of creative thinking. It's hard for people formed by textbooks and by life in a bureaucratic society to deal with digressions. Our imaginations are every bit as stunted as our minds and souls. A healthy imagination, well-tuned to reality, would lead us to question our belief that we can truly make rather than interpret laws given by God and God's nature. A healthy imagination would lead us to see the dangers in our efforts to reshape our moral principles to our perceived interests – which are usually those of increasing transactions in the political and commercial marketplaces.

Even if we were to suddenly have the moral vision and courage to confront the damage we're doing to ourselves and those around us, our lack of imagination would make it impossible for us to so much as choose a direction in which to head from our current moral wasteland. We should not expect any leadership from scientists any more than from politicians – they're both morally corrupted as a group and are corrupted by the same ideological delusions. And, so, I'll end this digression on the degraded moral state of modern people, including scientists, to return to my discussion of empirical science.

Empirical science has advanced greatly during recent centuries, producing piles of raw facts, only some of which have become piles of truer facts by those circular processes which go from fact to theory and back again. There's much to be digested in order that one or more Christian philosophical systems can be built to stand up without a lot of ad-hoc props, which situation is the most obvious sign that the current Christian philosophical systems are grossly defective, though the basic insights of Thomism provide a good foundation for building better systems of thought. Of particular importance are the Thomistic theory of knowledge and the Thomistic understanding of the act-of-being. The defective parts of Thomism are all superstructure. That superstructure is still useful for pedagogical purposes, but, for those wishing a Christian philosophy which considers modern empirical knowledge, the superstructure can be razed that new construction can use the solid foundation. Any attempts to preserve Thomism in its original form will do nothing but obscure the foundational truths of Thomism. It's time to start the process of building with the new materials provided by the sorts of careful researchers, thinkers, and artists that I mention in my bibliographical essays.

Let's start with this claim:

> Einstein provided the first explicit definition of what this universe is. By doing this, Einstein seems to have shown that the most conceptual levels of theoretical physics are a branch of metaphysics.

I speak of theoretical physics intruding upon metaphysics for a simply stated reason: as cosmological physicists and particle physicists have expanded out the implications of the General Theory of Relativity, they've developed means of describing aspects of the universe prior to the imposition of the constraints and breaking of symmetries which made it a particular thing and allowed particular things to develop inside of it. When theoretical physicists deal with the universe prior to those events they call breaking of symmetries, when they speculatively penetrate to levels of matter where time and space seem to have ambiguous existence, they're dealing with certain aspects of more general or abstract being. Like metaphysicians, they're dealing with being and not with things – which are the daily bread of most physicists, all chemists, and all biologists.

Theoretical physics at those fundamental levels can be important in understanding the important quantitative aspects of our universe and the Primordial Universe from which it comes. The nature of pure being, before it was constrained to be our universe, plays a fundamental role in defining the behavior of matter and energy and fields in the current state of the universe, but we need to remember that pure being had to be shaped and constrained to become concrete being.

We should also remember that pure being has very general and abstract properties which could have been the foundation of universes of an infinite variety – in laws and not just in particular history. But it's our universe that God brought into being. We should be grateful that He made that choice and our faith should be placed in God and His promises; human speculations are necessary but always provisional. We should be willing to discard our most favored speculations when empirical evidence or deeper understandings of revelation cast doubt upon them. The evidence from empirical investigations supports the proposal that human beings are physical creatures with no other stuff, though there are some respected scientists who feel that our minds are made up partly of electromagnetic or even quantum fields. Such fields would account for our sense that our minds are not of quite the same stuff as the 'ordinary' parts of our bodies, such as our livers and stomachs.

Some philosophers and theologians, starting with the great thinkers of ancient Greece, had reasons for positing an immortal human soul, or at least one which was not made of the same stuff as the human body. They also had good reasons for believing that God was so removed from this universe that He needed messengers as well as various spirits to move the planets and keep the rivers flowing. Both reasons are in conflict with Christian beliefs now that we have a plausible understanding of what a universe is. In the Aristotelian cosmos, mundane matter and ethereal stuff co-existed and were contiguous, separated by the moon's orbit. The Einsteinian universe is more self-contained and more homogeneous than that – the most distant objects are assumed to be made of the same stuff as our bodies and are subject to the same physical laws. It's Einstein and his successors, including Pere LeMaître, who have banished immaterial entities from our universe, not Darwin nor the atheistic philosophers nor the skeptical theologians. Some might feel this has taken a bit of magic out of the world, but there's no reason to believe that Jesus of Nazareth inhabited a world of magic. Why should we imagine ourselves to be in such a world? Why should we want to be in such a world? Aren't the miracles which God brings us with every baby, every litter of puppies, every meteor shower, good enough for us? Aren't the promises of a resurrection if we return His love worth more than any immortal soul?

We have some insights from physicists into the actions God takes in shaping this particular universe. More than that, we have some insights from evolutionary biologists into the processes God set into motion to allow primitive living creatures to evolve to a state where they have some freedom of a moral sort. I would go beyond the developmental models of evolutionary biology and cosmological physics to claim:

> God continually creates contingent being, else it would cease to exist, He does so in the manner of a story-teller who participates in His own story to power it that much more strongly, but not in the manner of a story-teller who overrides his characters or the general flow of events. This freedom which we have and which even the physical world has to some extent is one of the greatest miracles in God's Creation.

2 Some Peculiar Definitions

2.1 Universes of All Sorts

I use the term 'Primordial Universe' to refer to created being in the abstract, that is, without particularity, without thing-ness. The term 'Particularized Universe', or simply 'universe' means created being, or a certain self-contained portion thereof, after it has been constrained so that it becomes a particular thing containing more particular things. Immediately, it becomes clear that particularized being comes from some sort of abstract being but abstract being comes from the concrete God of Jesus. In other words, there's no abstract set of possible gods from which the God of Jesus Christ happens to be chosen – He is the ultimate reality standing above all other actualizations and above all possibilities. We know a God apart from and above the universe because He had revealed Himself to us, directly by way of signs and words given to our physical senses and indirectly by way of His effects in the physical universe.

If we're to understand our relationship to God, we must have some plausible understanding of our relationship to this world in which we have been borne. Such an understanding can use factual, verifiable data of the sort beloved by physical scientists but there must be a tale of some sort, a narrative that speaks of an origin and an end to give meaning to the middle of the story where we live. Mortal men can only tell this sort of tale in a provisional way – for all of the brilliant work by modern scientists and their helpers, we still have only an obscure view of the beginning of the expansion of the universe. We have barely a clue what might be the ultimate fate of the physical world. I can only argue that this matters less than we might think by actually constructing a narrative corresponding to the world which only God can see truly or completely.

We cannot see the event by which God created something out of nothing, but we now know much about some aspects of the events by which God shaped this Particularized Universe. This tale of the constraining of the Primordial Universe so that it became particularized can be told in a dangerous but useful way by using the Big Bang imagery, much of it distorted but...

We should actually forget the so-called Big Bang in the sense so many intend it. We don't know, and cannot ever know from inside the universe, what really happened at the very instant that something began to expand. Nor do we, nor can we, know with any certainty if that beginning of the expansion can be called the 'moment of creation'. Physicists have discovered much about what happened even during the early fractions of a second of that expansion fifteen billion years ago or more. They've also discovered what the unknown something became: matter and energy and fields. The stuff of our universe emerged out of the events of those early seconds. The universe passed through a series of events that physicists call 'breaking of symmetries'. After one of those symmetries was broken, certain types of particles and their associated forces, such as electrons and electromagnetism, coalesced out of a stuff too vague to be called matter or energy or fields.

With our over-active imaginations and our contemplative visions, we can move backwards towards the so-called Big Bang. That extreme contemplative movement results in a vision of what seems to have been pure created being, a thingless sort of being with little or nothing in the way of attributes beyond very basic metaphysical properties. We arrive at the thought and the vision of a created being so abstract and so undifferentiated as to be nearly a metaphysical essence – a pure abstraction. But it's the journey that's important because it tells us much about the shaping of that primordial stuff into our universe with its particular stuff. Of equal importance: it tells us something about the power of the human mind, however defective and provisional the best of our thoughts are.

If our minds can be broadened to be receptive to the universe in a wider sense, then we can see our minds as being images of what the universe is. Our minds seem to be story-telling entities, though using rational tools when good and plausible stories are told. But this would imply that the universe which shapes a more highly developed mind is itself shaped as a story with rational underpinnings. I emphasize the universe is a story, physical stuff passing through various stages of a coherent narrative stream. The universe is not an engineered setting for human beings passing through.

Human beings are embedded in the story being told in this universe. Human beings are formed by the roles they play in this story.

The Primordial Universe is a specific entity from God's point of view though it's pure being of the vaguest sort to men, invisible to our perceptions – for it's still here even in the Particularized Universe – and subject to only formal investigation by metaphysicians and theoretical physicists. It was abstract and non-specific simply because it had no insides, no time, no space, no things. It could still have become any of a multitude of universes but God shaped it into this universe, as we're told, because He loved us before we were born, before the universe itself was born.

2.2 The Particularized Universe

For convenience, I'll refer to the Particularized Universe as simply the universe. After all, it's our universe.

The universe is peculiar and particular, it's concrete. The universe is specific and not abstract in the way of the Primordial Universe. It's a thing of a very special sort, to be sure. It also contains a multitude of things. In general, it's right to talk as if the universe has the same properties, at least the same sorts of properties as its parts (intervals of space and time) or the things which are in it. At the same time, we should remember that the universe is different, at the very least, in being the primary concrete entity formed by God from the Primordial Universe which He had created. The universe has primacy over the things it contains. Moreover, though a contingent entity, it's necessary from the viewpoint of any creatures which are born inside of it. The Primordial Universe forms the very foundation of our being and the backdrop of the events of our lives as well as the foundation and backdrop for a star being born or a planet being molded by tectonic processes.

It's the universe which came into concrete being, by way of God imposing conditions upon the Primordial Universe or pure created being – as I tell the story. Any telling of the story must recognize that though the universe does not exist necessarily, its existence precedes the existence of the entities to which it is home. This allows it the appearance of necessity which may lie behind the beliefs of pantheists.

We must see the universe correctly if we're to see God even through a glass darkly. If we see God as absolutely transcendent because we think of the universe as running freely after God had created it, then we shall become Deists. If we tie God to His universe by chains of necessary reasoning, then we shall become pantheists. There are groups of Christians and others making each of these errors even as I write. These spiritual or moral errors are far more damaging than any errors in understanding the nature of physical forces. Errors of this sort can damage not just the details but the very structure of the story we must all tell to make sense of our lives and our relationships to God and His world.

And the universe is a world from God's point of view. It's unified, coherent, and complete. The universe can be perceived as a world by men who are morally well-structured. And these limited and particular worlds are not illusions or delusions. They're real because they correspond to those stories we can tell about our lives when we try to bring moral order to those lives. That leads to the interesting claim that God sees a world enriched and made more complex by virtue of these worlds brought into being by the moral perceptions of human beings. The universe, very good to start, becomes better by a minuscule amount as human persons add their limited and defective views of that which is accessible to our senses and our minds. In encouraging us in such acts, God is almost like a parent pleased with any act of creativity on the part of little Missie even when she's drawing stick-figures on the living-room wall.

2.3 Worldview

A worldview includes at least pieces of a metaphysical system, though that might be a very slight system, perhaps based on the minimal belief that God and creatures have different sorts of being. Also, the metaphysical components of a worldview might well be implicit. The average Southern Baptist or Italian-American Catholic doesn't know much about the metaphysical beliefs underlying their specific worldviews.

It hardly matters because a worldview is more a story than a metaphysical system. It's populated by entities which are concrete, obeying metaphysical laws but not being directly derivable from those laws or other abstract principles. A worldview is a moving picture, *Dr. Zhivago*, rather than a flow chart. A worldview provides places where we can stand to look towards the realms of metaphysics and theoretical physics. To most of us, it's more important that it can provide the foundations for a way of life. A true worldview, one which sees the physical universe through morally ordering perceptions will bring into being a true world, unified and coherent and complete. This is dangerous from the view-point of those abstract, mythical beings that I'll name as simply the gods of the marketplaces. While the gods of the marketplaces have only a literary existence, their viewpoint is horribly real and has been adopted by most of the dominant thinkers in the west from the 1700s on. Even now it's being defended by hordes of philosophers and economists and politicians, bankers and janitors and car mechanics.

In fact, most Christian thinkers, and pastoral leaders, have shown themselves ready to live by the rules of those gods. They keep their mouths shut when it comes to the activities of those acting in the name of those gods. They've even chosen to re-organize their hierarchies and their charities to better match up with the institutions which serve the gods of the marketplaces. Most dangerously, they've chosen to play by the rules which compartmentalize the human person into a marketplace participant – the largest piece by far, a family member, a religious believer, etc. A world-viewing creature cannot be compartmentalized in this way. As soon as you allow a radical separation of work-places, homes, local communities, and places of worship, you've constrained men to be no better than animals moving from one environment to another. Since the human mind is formed by interaction with its environments, minds will be formed to expect and even welcome a radical fragmentation that will prevent them from seeing a universe, let alone structuring it as a world. In terms I've already used, a fragmented human being lives most of his days as if the God of Jesus Christ doesn't exist and becomes an atheist.

2.4 Ideology

The modern world is founded upon a closely related group of ideologies where an ideology is a stunted and deformed worldview. These modern ideologies are centered around the liberal view of man as an individual only accidentally bound to family or church or local political community or physical environment. Of course, a man could never be bound to God by anything but a voluntary and revocable decision. Liberals, right-wing or left-wing, see man as a pre-formed agent who is no more and no less than a decision-maker choosing from the options of the political and commercial marketplaces. Most aspects of human nature are effectively suppressed in favor of the marketplaces, commercial and political. Go to church as much as he will, modern man has separated himself from God. Go to sea-shores and national parks as much as he will, modern man has also separated himself from the universe which he inhabits. Modern man has willingly turned himself into a strange creature who is primarily a loyal employee and customer of the corporate servants of the modern nation-state. Public morality, hence private morality for the most part, has become a matter of faithful service to the gods of the marketplaces.

So far as I can tell, even a distorted worldview, an ideology, cannot be imposed upon a people the way that you can impose a new operating system upon a computer. The efforts of Lenin and Stalin led to nothing but the crippling of countries which had been limping to start with. Mao's efforts seem to have collapsed into some sort of coal-powered revival of Confucian bureaucracy from the imperial past of Beijing. The ideology of the West took hold just because it grew up from the efforts of countless numbers of shop-keepers and small-town politicians as well as the efforts of Nobel Laureate economists, corporate tycoons, and national politicians, all of them at least as morally ill-structured as the butcher, baker, and candlestick-maker. We Americans have seduced ourselves with unfulfillable, in fact – undesirable, promises of safety and security. Now many other peoples are getting in on the fun.

So what happened to the old truths? What happened to even the platitudinous moral truths which Kipling called the gods of the copybook headings? Why would I think worldviews would disappear if they're the sorts of things held by French-Canadian Catholics, Norwegian Lutherans, Scottish Presbyterians, and other people who used to have more sense than philosophers and politicians and corporate executives? There are some human beings, from some ethnic groups, who have made an effort to morally shape their young even in recent decades. Are they now raising their children to become academic philosophers or corporate executives? The melting-pot nation has proved its ability to melt down minds and souls and to reconstitute them as entities of rather odd shapes which fit the holes available in the American marketplace.

We have brainwashed ourselves and our children in the interests of the gods of the marketplaces and there's no way to deny that we did know what we were doing, at least on some level of our minds and souls. Everyone – bishops and ministers and religious instructors, violinists and poets and medical doctors, carpenters and short-order cooks and school-teachers – have seduced themselves into a state of moral cowardice. The modern ideologies encourage people to consider security and safety, comfort and long life, cash incomes and externally supplied entertainment, to be the minimums of a human life. We have all of us, especially our leaders, become fat, dumb, and happy. We all serve the gods of the marketplaces, not just businessmen and politicians but also religious leaders and particle physicists. We're as unified and as self-regulating as any slaves those gods have ever had. Our minds and bodies and spirits are filled with bloated desires for the goods and services of the marketplace economy, so there's no room left for a true worldview, Christian or otherwise. Still many of us convince ourselves that we remain Christians because we have come to associate this life of prosperity and putative security with Christianity.

But now I seem to have reversed direction, writing as if modern man is materialistic after having claimed that we have etherealized things away in the interests of mere processes or statistics about processes.

Are we materialistic or idealistic? Are we money-grubbers or spiritual creatures?

Modern man has gained such a high degree of control over the modern world as to blur the distinction in his own mind. This, combined with the genuine accomplishments of modern theoretical science, has perhaps led to an intuition that some pre-modern thinkers erred greatly in splitting mind and body, spirit and matter. We have public squares from which churches have been banished but we also have an oddly insightful form of moral corruption that blends the spirit and matter which were separated, somewhat legitimately by ancient and Medieval thinkers and wrongfully by Descartes, Kant, and other modern thinkers.

Despite their ultimate unity, the spiritual and materialistic concerns of physical creatures have to be addressed separately in this world. So the modern blending of the spirit and matter is not so much an insight as an error which is useful in allowing us to see ourselves as unified marketplace agents before fragmenting ourselves in far more dangerous ways.

If we forget our creaturely status or willfully distort our understanding of physical reality, then we can feel righteous and chosen by God as we go about our business of seeking material prosperity and comfort and security. Modern human beings have etherealized God, sometimes retaining the name but making Him no more than a vague spirit of history, the ghost of Manifest Destiny. This perverse way of thought and feeling was born in many regions of the world during the 1800s as believers refounded their faith on worldly ideas and attitudes. This process of mistake leading to decay was particularly noticeable in New England where the Congregationalists, the church of the Puritans, renounced adherence to any Christian creed in the 1860s. The misguided refounding of Christian belief first appeared in New England in the early 1800s in the writings and preachings of Protestant clergymen who wanted to be up-to-date without having the courage or the creativity to actually restate Christian truths to consider the facts and theories of a rapidly expanding base of empirical knowledge. In other words, some men tried, probably with the best of intentions, to construct a Christian worldview allowing for modern science and modern historical discoveries, but soon enough they proved themselves to have more faith in Charles Darwin than in St. Paul, more faith in the United States than in the Church of Christ. The Holy Trinity and the incarnation, death, and resurrection of the Son of God were lost in efforts that were quite incompetent even in their understanding of physics and biology.[1]

But that doesn't explain why it is that we confuse matter and spirit rather than re-uniting them in an intelligent manner. In the life and the thoughts of Ralph Waldo Emerson, we can find hints about the motivation for taking this wrong path. In various writings, some unpublished in his life-time, including marginal notes in books by Emerson, Herman Melville claimed that the spirituality of Emerson and like-minded thinkers masked a great concern for comfort and security.[2] Some provocative quotations from Melville and others on the subject of Emerson, along with a variety of references to other materials, can be found at http://www.melville.org on the Internet. As Melville and Nathaniel Hawthorne and Henry James, Sr. saw matters, Emerson had confused spiritual and material issues in a very dangerous manner that threatened the very foundations of moral belief and behavior. In my opinion, Emerson confused spiritual and material issues because he had begun to think of himself as a self-subsisting individual and not as a creature of God. He had turned himself into a plaything of the gods of the marketplaces.

Emerson and others of like mind carried out a great service to those gods by confusing our understanding of the human condition and also by the

[1]See James Turner's *Without God, Without Creed* for the account of the popularization of atheism in the United States upon which I relied.

[2]See Stephen Matterson's foreword to the 1990 Penguin edition of Melville's *The Confidence Man.*

related obscuring of the very subject matter of religious thought. American prosperity was not to be easily separated from spiritual claims. In fact, they're not separated in the minds of most Americans and many others around the globe in this year of our Lord 2005. The confusion serves our disordered desires and our self-righteous need to secure our own salvation by associating American prosperity and goals with some vaguely defined spirit of which the greatest prophet was Abraham Lincoln.

My story gains nothing by considering Emerson instead of simply attributing all of the confusion to the guiding light of liberalism – Adam Smith. The Scotsman was a much better thinker than the New Englander, and also much the better stylist.[3] He was a very dangerous man just because of his talents, but he provides a convenient antagonist to the telling of my story because he allows me to simplify the development of the modern ideology in a plausible way. We should also give Adam Smith credit for depersonalizing those processes by which systems organize themselves, processes seen by many people as being evidence of specific demons or angels. And so I've chosen to regard Adam Smith as the most important single spokesman for the emerging spiritual disease which lies underneath the modern ideologies. In fact, it's the form of the individualistic viewpoint so beautifully and enthusiastically stated by Adam Smith that has played such a major role in tearing us free from the tradition which is necessary for the telling of the Christian story.

2.5 World

A world is the object of a worldview which I've already defined as follows:

> The best available empirical knowledge about the physical world subjected to moral ordering. It's clearly by way of that moral ordering that the world can become a Christian world, which is God's world perceived by a frail human being. And, to

[3]For all my disagreement with some of Adam Smith's ideas, I find his pre-modern style of writing, with all of its commas and subordinate clauses to be quite pleasant to read. Emerson's writings are, to me, gobbledy-gook and I have to gather up my strength to tackle each murky sentence. When I hear some of my fellow human creatures claim they enjoy reading Emerson, I'm not quite sure if I should admire them or pity them. In Emerson's writings, I see the foundational beliefs which would be more clearly stated in *The Gettysburg Address*, the founding document of modern fascism.

> a Christian, it's that moral ordering which comes from Christ which is the most important immaterial element in this universe. In this context, immaterial refers to the partial but substantial revelation from God about His ultimate purposes in creating this universe and telling a story in which the human race appeared.

In all that I say, I use the Einsteinian definition of the universe even when I speak of those like Aquinas who thought in terms of the cosmos of Aristotle. Under the Einsteinian definition, we assume that the entire physical universe is made of the same stuff, or at least the same sort of stuff, and the same laws apply to that stuff throughout the universe. In Aristotle's cosmos, there were two different types of stuff, earthly stuff below the orbit of the moon and heavenly or ethereal stuff outside the orbit of the moon. This heavenly stuff was presumed to be purer than the dirt and water and blood of this earth.

I assume that there can be multiple particularized universes shaped from the Primordial Universe, one example is this universe and another might be the universe of the resurrected. The universe of the resurrected is made from the same pure created being as God used to shape this universe, but it's radically different in being stable and peaceful and inherently well-ordered rather than being a place where development occurs as a result of conflict between order and disorder. I also assume that each particularized universe, if there's more than one, are fully separated from each other. Neither ghosts nor angelic beings, if there are any, could pass from one realm of being to another unless God Himself were to move that entity.

2.6 Person

Plainly and simply, as I use the term, a human person is a human being who has a worldview, a human being who has acknowledged the truths of empirical reality in light of some sort of coherent moral order. A human being who does not have a worldview remains a human animal inhabiting environments, sometimes a large number of environments in our world of jets and cross-continental highways.

There's a strong and highly focused narrative description of a Person given in the Bible, the entirety of Chapter 4 of the Gospel of Luke where we read of the temptation of the Lord Jesus Christ by Satan. Likely the result of a contempation by one or more communities of people trying to understand the sheer incorruptibility of Jesus Christ as He met up with the forces of disorder in this world, it becomes for us a warning of the price to be paid by any human being wishing to follow his Lord but that powerful chapter also points towards the glories to be gained by paying that price. We form ourselves by giving ourselves over to our Lord and we too will become well enough defined, by way of borrowed strength, that we can bear the same burdens that the Son of God bore during His earthly life.[4]

[4]I don't think it's possible for us to even describe, let alone understand or bear, the pain endured by the Son as He continued to exist as His human nature died. It could be argued that, of all entities, only the Son of God has truly experienced death for only He continued to exist as He also died, truly died in the way of a mortal animal. This unimaginable pain seems to me to be far more important than the gory details of the torture of the human body of the Son of God.

3 Getting Used to It

Science and philosophy and every other mode of human thought or action have their little transitions which are brought about only by people getting used to a new idea, or at least a different idea. There's most certainly no guarantee that people will only get used to ideas which have some relationship to truth.

It's the plasticity of the human brain that leads to the get-used-to-it phenomenon. The human mind is shaped by its environment. We have some instincts about reality which seem to be inborn, but not many. Some of those instincts correspond to metaphysical truths, such as our general resistance to contradictory ideas or suggestions of contradictions in physical things. Other instincts correspond more closely to the nature of this Particularized Universe and might not be true in other possible universes. For example, very young infants can be shown to believe in the constant existence of a toy which has disappeared momentarily behind a screen. There's little reason to believe there to be an inherent tendency for continuous existence on the part of things. There are any number of ways in which things, or living creatures, could be destroyed without warning. Moreover, all things could be melted back down into the pure and abstract being of the Primordial Universe. Yet, it's generally an advantage to act as if our environments, made largely of the half-frozen stuff we call matter, contain mostly stable things. We seek a reason if something disappears behind a tree and does not emerge when it seemed it would continue moving on. In any case, our brains assume a few metaphysical truths and a few basic contingent truths which apply to this Particularized Universe.

The question I would ask is: how did we Christians come to hold so strongly the pagan belief in an immortal soul? It's not that the belief is wrong just because the pagans first proposed it. Plato and Pythagoras and Aristotle and many others proposed plenty of good ideas, but only some of those are true. The immortal soul is not found in the Bible. As I'll later note, some of the most important of the early Christian Fathers considered the idea of an immortal human soul to be absolutely wrong and fully in opposition to a Christian understanding of God's promises of a resurrection.

I'll start by asking: Why did the pagan philosophers find the idea of an immortal soul or mind, separable from the human body, to be attractive, even necessary? Those thinkers were trying to reconcile the experience of abstract thought, nearly weightless in a sense, with their false belief that physical matter is inert, not at all dynamic. Aristotle, in particular, did not believe there to be any physical organ in the human body which was plastic enough to allow the formation of the concept of 'dog' after the observation of only concrete doggish creatures. This is essentially why St. Thomas Aquinas conjectured the subsistent rational soul, though he was a good enough observer to know what any death-bed watcher knows: most human characteristics, including our ability to love, are part of physical human nature and get stripped away as the body is dying.

We now know that matter is a low-temperature form of a highly dynamic complex of matter and energy and fields. We now know just how plastic the human brain is, dangerously plastic in an exploitive and morally ill-structured society.

There's no longer a good reason to advocate a human soul which is separable from the human body and is immortal at that. As a body of believers, Christians over the centuries came to accept a provisional and speculative idea which is probably at odds with more fundamental Christian beliefs. Those interested in the history of Christian doctrine can read the first volume of Jaroslav Pelikan's magisterial *The Christian Tradition: A History of the Development of Doctrine* for discussions of St. Athanasius and other early Christian Fathers who were strongly opposed to any talk of human beings having souls which survive our bodily death by way of powers or attributes inherent to those souls. Opposition to the pagan doctrine of immortal souls even played a prominent role in the efforts of Tatian, considered to be the first theologian of the resurrection. At the same time, the careful reader should bear in mind that many of those opposed to the immortal soul, such as Athanasius, and those with a very limited definition of an immortal soul, such as Aquinas, spoke often of the soul in a context where they were clearly referring to the Aristotelian animal soul, the mortal form imposed upon mortal flesh and blood.

As a pastoral matter, an acceptance of the physical foundation of the entirety of human nature makes it far easier to understand and deal with brain-damage victims and Alzheimers patients who sometimes become violent in mood and sometimes even in their physical actions. When a human being's hormones or brain-chemicals go completely out of balance, when brain regions are being destroyed, the patient will typically shed some of her human characteristics. These are hard facts about this world that we have to accept. Typically, we do accept these and are appropriately tolerant to people whose brains are being destroyed by disease or the after-effects of an accident. After observing the tight link between human attributes and the human body, we often go back to pretending that we have immaterial souls or minds.

R. B. Onians wrote a book titled *The Origins of Human Thought* which traces the development of soul- and mind-related words and concepts in the ancient Greek civilization and also the ancient Roman civilization. A few other civilizations are also discussed in less detail. It's a hard-to-read book for someone like me who has so weak a background in languages, but it's still a worthwhile struggle to pick out bits of sense without being able to read direct quotes from *The Iliad* or other classical works. This is my attempt at a simplified story-line:

> Early man seems to have developed words to refer to aspects or functions of human nature without necessarily having explicit concepts to go with those words. For example, there would typically be words for life force and for reproductive force. Those words were reified[1] in the process of contemplation and story-telling. The life force was given the name 'thymus' by the Greeks and the reproductive force the name 'psyche'. Reification, essentially the same human fault as literalization, attached the thymus, or life force, to some part of the trunk of a human person – Onians argues it was the diaphragm but that's an unimportant detail for my purposes. The location of the psyche is apparently more clear: the gunk in our skulls which is, more or less, continuous with the gunk inside our backbones

[1]Reification is a fancy word for the sort of process where functions or other immaterial aspects of a thing or an environment are turned into a concrete entity. A playful example would be asking a young child for some of her happiness and then holding out your hand so she can put some in there. Do you want a full pound of happiness?

> and was falsely believed to be continuous with the gunk in the reproductive organs as we now know them.
>
> There was a lot of overlap and interpenetration of these ideas but, more importantly, the process of reification had produced claims that would be shown as errors by the early Greek natural philosophers. So far as I can tell, the opposite process of etherealization[2] occurred in reaction to such insights as: the fluid of the brain and the spinal cord isn't the same as the fluids of the sexual organs. Similar insights came regarding the nature and functions of the organs of the chest and abdomen. The psyche and thymus somehow became the mind or soul. The ancients and many modern Christians could not think in terms of physical organs having functions and aspects not material, at least not in obvious ways. They thought the choice to be between a human being reduced to simple and fully determined physical processes or else a human being with an immaterial component not really part of this universe.

If you simply conjectured something which is, by definition, undetectable and unperceivable, it would seem difficult to prove it doesn't exist. Unfortunately for those who adopted this strategy, empirical investigation can narrow down the range of actions which are available to that mind-stuff or soul-stuff. There now seems to be little room left for soul-stuff or mind-stuff to do much that's important to human nature. Aquinas knew that in the 13th century and only conjectured an immaterial rational soul as a dry-as-dust entity that carried out our purely abstract thinking. Given the proper biological biases of Aquinas, he would not have made such a conjecture unless he had struggled with the question, "How do we form abstract knowledge when we only perceive particular things from the physical world?" Given the assumption of the inertness of matter and a lack of understanding of the development of the brain in young human beings,

---

[2]Etherealization is a mistake somewhat similar to reification. In this case, some function of a thing or an environment is objectified but claimed to have an immaterial substance. An example would be the tendency of human beings to see physical movements as being the result of immaterial living creatures rather than as a result of physical processes. The world might then be seen as inhabited by gods or spirits which move the planets and rivers. Biological processes are seen as the result of immaterial minds or souls.

it's understandable that he felt forced to conjecture a very limited sort of immaterial soul.

We should not be worried by the loss of a belief in the immortal soul or the immaterial mind. We now know that our physical natures, natures made of the physical stuff created by God, can do everything that human thinkers have always attributed to mind or soul.

Over the centuries, human beings have simply gotten used to various ways of thinking about important aspects, or even functions, of human nature. First our ancestors seem to have improperly associated the life force with the diaphragm (in the speculation of Onians), an illegitimate concretization or reification of a function. Then that life force was etherealized as an immaterial entity, the soul.

Immaterial souls and minds are quite beside the point now that we know that the observable stuff of this universe can carry out all functions that Aristotle or Aquinas needed for their understanding of the human mind – and that understanding is good enough to be seen as anticipating many of the discoveries of modern developmental neurobiology. I repeat: centuries of modern scientific research have revealed that matter is not inert but is a low-temperature form of a very dynamic stuff that's energy or fields at higher temperatures. This low-temperature stuff is also interpenetrated by the hotter stuff we call energy and fields. The physical stuff of this universe can do anything a Christian could properly expect of immaterial soul-stuff or mind-stuff.

To a large extent, human thought – even some which appears quite sophisticated, is merely a process of self-brainwashing, a process of getting used to some set of ideas forced upon us by empirical facts or by revelation. The process of "getting used to it" is necessary for us to accustom ourselves to our environments – it's hard to see how human learning could take place without this plasticity in some of our most basic attitudes and views of reality.

We can brainwash ourselves to accept wrongful ideas brought about by ignorance or misinterpretation of what we truly know, a process which seems likely to occur in a society so prosperous that its citizens think themselves to be free from the constraints of nature and the revelations of God. The most likely scenario involves a combination of ignorance and misinterpretation. We can brainwash ourselves to the point where we hold on to our beliefs in immaterial mind or immortal soul when there's no evidence they exist and when there's no legitimate reason for Christians to speculate they exist.

We can also brainwash ourselves into accepting slavery to the gods of the marketplace even while imagining we're Christians.

Part II

Narratives for a New Age

4 Piling Rock Upon Rock

4.1 Becoming as a Child

Ground must be cleared and it's likely that the modes of thought of academic philosophy are not proper for such action. Academic philosophers are trained to analyze. Rubble can be analyzed. And rubble is what we have in these modern cities of man. It has proved to be a relatively easy trick to tear down traditional beliefs and customs and institutions and not so easy to build replacements. We have a suitable landscape of ruins for the consenting peripatetics to engage in dialectics and other acts from which children and child-like thinkers should be protected. Analysis in the midst of piles of rubble often turns into so much rock-throwing, a childish activity to be sure and not one to be encouraged. The child-like game of piling rocks upon rocks in a whimsical manner is often the most highly moral activity in which a man can engage. Buildings, or least ideas for buildings, might emerge from such playful activities.

One must become as a child to enter the Kingdom of Heaven.

One must become as a child to think new thoughts. Neurobiologists have told us why: the human being's brain forms in interacting with the surrounding environment. We form ruts in our brains. A child has a brain ready to be shaped to proper standards.

One must become as a child and a child, if given the proper environment, will take advantage – unconsciously to be sure – of what the neurobiologists call 'windows of opportunity'. In a strict biological sense, these are usually unique periods, as when a child from birth to the age of six or so, is acquiring basic language skills. It's important that a child during this period be exposed to rich and complex adult language as well as being encouraged to speak in a manner that starts as babble and ends, in a cultured environment, with language capabilities that are moving rapidly towards a uniformly adult level of accomplishment.

The child's brain has few deep ruts and those which have been started by the purely physical processes of development are the necessary ones for inclining the child towards learning basic social and cognitive skills, language skills belonging to both categories. The process builds upon itself, as we can observe in children who are socializing and conversing in a nurturing environment.

We're organisms which form in response to what we're taught, to what we experience, to what we allow ourselves to think or feel. There's not so much of a division into content and form in the human mind as many thinkers have claimed, not nearly so much as the modern ideologies assume. Teach a child how to care for his shoes, how to care for the wood furniture in his bedroom, and you're not just teaching him some mundane skills – you're teaching him respect for the things of God's Creation. Teach a child how to play a musical instrument and you're not just preparing him for the high school marching band – you're changing his brain in ways that are still being unraveled by brain-scientists. Teach a child to be a passive consumer of entertainment, television and movies and recorded music, and you're taking away a little of his potential initiative, even a little of his moral character. Teach a child by way of rote learning from mind-deadening textbooks in a factory environment and you're taking away still more of his potential initiative and moral character. You're preparing him for life as a slave to the gods of the marketplaces.

For all their errors, Nietzsche and Foucault and other radicals, were right that human beings, in recent centuries, have been deformed by ideological systems, not formed into healthy human persons. Then again, those two radical skeptics were wrong in thinking it's not possible to see a world which is a manifestation of truths. It's possible, however far short I might fall in this effort. In fact, it's only possible in principle in the sense that all human views of God's world are provisional and will have to be re-envisioned or at least expanded as languages and cultures change, as knowledge about men and planets increases.

When a human being is forced to envision anew a world rather than being able to accept or modify a worldview inherited from his forefathers, it's necessary, so far as I can tell, that he have some fairly high level of abstract intelligence. A proper sort of abstract thought allows a pilgrim to rise above the confusions and chaos which seem to make nonsense of his environments. The universe can be first seen as all of created being, a surprisingly accessible abstraction. Yet, the most powerful of abstract thinkers cannot perceive a world at that level, a physical universe – yes, and maybe even the Primordial Universe, the pure metaphysical entity which lies behind it. He who would perceive a world must return to that seeming chaos and confusion of his environments because it's chaos which tells us much about the order which we can only dimly see at the level of the universe. Yet, those acts of abstract thought and abstract imagination allow an early leap towards the hypothesis of a world even when the immediate environment does not yet seem to make sense. And that leap takes us to an unstable perch from which our environments can be seen in a different perspective.

The universe is what it is and that does not seem to be something that can be constructed from a set of basic ideas the way that a toy crane can be constructed from an erector set. It becomes a bit clearer why the getting-used-to-it phenomenon is generally good, though it can go bad and lead to untruths and hatreds:

> The universe is what it is and it's a work of God. When our minds are shaped to fit our environments, they're shaped to the things around us, things which are reflections of some thoughts of God.

At the same time, we should remember that God created of His own free-will, the only truly free will of any entity. He did not have to create any universe. Given that He decided to create a universe, it could have been different from this one. More than that, we don't have the capacity of mind, nor the understanding of the basic properties of the Primordial Universe, to be able to truly trace back – even on a purely physical basis – to the underlying principles by which God formed this world. I've emphasized and will continue to emphasize that the chasm from nothing to that single something, the Primordial Universe, is infinitely wide and infinitely deep. There also seems to be an immense chasm between the Primordial Universe and the Particularized Universe. We can leap over that chasm but only by acts of imagination, including the mathematical acts by which theoretical physicists construct possible Primordial Universes – even when they don't realize that to be the task which they've taken on. It's the Particularized Universe which is, in principle, fully comprehensible to the human mind, but that implies the human mind can also comprehend, in a more limited way, the Primordial Universe.

So what is our universe or the Primordial Universe which lies behind it? More selfishly: Is our universe the best of all possible 'worlds'? Could God have made a universe which pleased Him while lowering the level of evil, of pain and suffering? I know of no way to even intelligently approach those questions given the current meanings attached to the words, but it doesn't matter to us, at least not to those of us who are Christians. This world and our particular existences are gifts of God, freely given and fully undeserved. Moreover, those two gifts – the world and our particular existences – are fully entangled. We're more embedded in this universe than most people seem to think. We're part of this universe and would not have first come to exist if this specific universe had not been created. We're not a collection of agents who were somehow tossed into this universe, though that's implied by most modern moral theories. We Christians believe we have a future beyond this universe, but this universe is our birth-place and our place of development, not merely a place where we're tested.

We're creatures who travel in ruts. Our physical, mental, and social development consists of being taught to dig ruts, sometimes ruts well-determined by an ill- or well-structured society and sometimes ruts we choose for ourselves during that learning process. But I wish to speculate beyond that, in a direction consistent with the Christian fear of bad habits. Our habits, good and bad, are us. Our thoughts lie not entirely in our head, but those parts of our thoughts which are private or internal will reshape us just as our external actions reshape us. A serial killer is not a good human being who happens to have some bad thoughts and some bad behaviors. He is those bad thoughts and bad behaviors. He's evil, and it's likely he became that way as he cooperated with an entertainment and news industry that makes money by displaying evil, consequently pushing it inside of the heads of those who allow themselves to be exploited and those who were exploited with the permission of their parents.

Self-deluding moral conservatives look back to earlier decades or centuries for the time when the American entertainment industry was producing movies, songs, television shows, stage shows, and books that displayed the old-fashioned American family and small-town life or urban neighborhood life or farm life at its best. In fact, those old-fashioned American families and communities were not healthy or traditional but rather the result of a desperate effort to protect children against the destructive power of industrial capitalism in its early years. Unfortunately, Daddy, as soon as he was out in the marketplaces protecting his castle back home, started developing products and services that would allow the marketplaces to invade that castle. Among those dangerous and morally corrupting products and services were those of the mass media. The very existence of the mass media was itself inherently corrupting. Daddy had become a vampire feeding on his own mind and soul and those of his wife and children back in that castle. And now Mommy has left that castle to also become a vampire feeding upon the minds and souls of her self, her husband, and their children.

Remember my demystification and redefinition of Adam Smith's true insight:

> Markets can be self-organizing because decision-makers can stabilize markets in a form which suits their purposes – without aiming at such a global result.

Our laws of business organization punish those managers who don't pursue a maximum return on capital invested in their firm, leaving them subject to criminal prosecution or to civil suits. These laws allow no exceptions for moral reasons, not that recent generations of American business leaders would have been likely to have chosen moral actions over greater profits. We encouraged a certain type of self-serving scoundrel to fill the ranks of our corporations and financial institutions, as we'd been doing in politics since the death of the Founding Fathers. Those scoundrels were ready to put on moral blinders and pursue short-term profits, as the laws of this country mandate them to do. Political scoundrels and commercial scoundrels alike re-organized American political and social and economic life to suit their desires. All of this was done though few of them had the intelligence or imagination to realize they were dismantling what was left in the United States of the traditional moral and social structures imported from Europe. Those structures were mere obstacles to those who relish a world where everyone is forced to live in the public squares, political and commercial.

In one of the most damaging attacks upon families, churches, and other local communities, television invaded the home with *Father Knows Best*, *I Love Lucy*, and even various attempts at creative and meaningful drama by the likes of the young Rod Serling and various esthetically ambitious directors and actors. Once the broadcasters became big corporations, growth opportunities began to emerge, even when it involved morally despicable content, but I wish to emphasize that those early shows were already reshaping the minds of Americans so that they would be dissatisfied with their lives that were local and concrete, and at least potentially Christian. Mass-media has trained us to be bored with the ordinary sorts of activities for which we evolved. The television networks didn't begin by broadcasting such moral trash as Terminator movies or MTV videos, but they necessarily eroded the actual and concrete foundations of human moral life by pursuing profits on goods and services distributed on a mass basis to physical creatures who only have moral lives on a human-scale. It was only after the television viewers were corrupted that they would find Terminator movies or MTV videos or the *Friends* television series attractive – just a few short years before, they would have been disgusted.

American moral foundations were already badly weakened by inappropriate moral thought and even inadequate understanding of what moral thought is, as I've already discussed regarding Ralph Waldo Emerson. Now, predators in our marketplaces could complete the job of moral destruction with the gleeful help of this mass media, and I refer not just to businessmen but also to politicians wishing to have a mobilized herd under their control. But I repeat that few businessmen and few politicians were smart enough or imaginative enough to realize they were increasing their influence by destroying the moral structures to which they paid nominal tribute. In terms introduced by that inconsistently moral thinker, the late Senator Patrick Moynihan, we'd started the process of defining deviance down and it turned out that deviance helped increase the size of the public marketplaces by enticing us to leave the more natural, more humane, and more human lives of our ancestors. As Adam Smith pointed out in his sly way, decision-makers can stabilize a system to their advantage without intending that global stability or even knowing it's coming into existence.

It's important for me to keep in clear sight the linkages between the various aspects of the developing and plastic universe which is the birthplace of us who are developing and plastic human beings. When we expose ourselves, or our children, to the predators of the mass-media, it's not that we're wallowing in a pig-sty for a short-while – we're being turned into swine whose true home is that pig-sty. Let me return to the biological foundations of this claim.

Six months or so after conception, the human brain reaches its maximum size in terms of the number of brain-cells. Those brain-cells are largely just circular little things that are not connected to the other circular little things around them. Most brain-regions have not yet formed and there's little in the way of signals passing through that largely unfunctioning but high-potential organ. In a process labeled as 'neural Darwinism' by the brain-scientist Gerald Edelman, those brain-cells begin to respond to various sorts of stimuli, from the body of that human creature and from the outside to the extent that the sensory organs are able to receive signals with minimally functioning sensory regions of the brain. Those brain-cells begin to form into glia, or support cells to provide structure and to move nutrition about, and neurons which are what most of us think of when the term 'brain-cell' is used. As the baby responds to the sounds of her environment, the hearing regions of her brain begin to form. As she responds to the coos of her mother, the language centers begin to form.

The brain-cells which don't receive or transmit a high rate of signals will die. This is sure to happen if they don't become part of an organized region or network of brain-cells, but it may happen if they play only a marginal role. Death of unused cells is about as good a way of burning deep and permanent ruts into the brain as you could think of. On the whole, the process works for the good, but it's not hard for us to imagine how it could go wrong, just as we now know how the animal urge for concentrated calorie sources can work to the harm of us and our pets. Read a biography of a serial killer or two, or watch a television bio-documentary as I did for a few – those people worked themselves into a state of evil, gradually and willfully. First, you might start by reading *Playboy* or the equally degrading magazines about celebrities, likely learning how to objectify certain human beings – perhaps pretty young women or pretty young boys. Move on to the raunchier magazines that are still displaying only submissive bodies and not yet acts of emotional or physical brutality. From there, you slide relentlessly but only inch-by-inch. If you give in completely, you might even make a few attempts to act out the fantasies which have burned their way into your brain and you might even overcome your disgust with your own fantasies, your own actions, and your own self.

Those fantasies, unconnected to reality or to the social instincts of human beings, are seizures of a sort. Those human beings suffer from a rigidity of muscles and nerves that leaves them traveling a rut that passes through regions of great disorder. Some would say those serial killers or rapists are themselves victims of those fantasies which have taken over their insides and sapped their moral wills. I would say that's true only to the extent that a creature can be a victim of his own self. Those fantasies have become parts of those creatures, just as a man's memories of killing in battle, even justly in a war he considered to be justly motivated and justly fought, will change him and stay with him his entire life. Almost everything you do or think will change your physical being.

Under the conditions of that New Stone Age, and during most of the ages of man, our desires to consume high-calorie, high-salt foods probably helped our ancestors to survive. In any case, there were not enough bee-hives or salt-licks to create a wide-spread health problem. During an era when foods can be preserved, processed, and transported so easily, many a corporation has accumulated impressive profits by exploiting those suddenly dangerous Neolithic desires. We should keep in mind that those exploitive corporations and individuals are ultimately us. Putting that aside, we see a similar situation with people who play off a cave-man's desire for exciting sights and cheap sexual thrills. The first is likely a result of our need to pay attention to the world, the second a more direct result of openness to cheap opportunities to reproduce – or, a woman's openness to finding a superior father for her children so long as her mate is not likely to discover it. Any legitimate desire, including the desire to produce healthy and wonderful children, can be misdirected. It's possible to view most sins as being legitimate desires not properly ordered, though perhaps the worst sins can be better viewed as a rebellion against all forms of order that will constrain us and remind us of our creaturely status.

> We cannot be morally ordered in a Christian manner without recognizing our humble status as creatures, limited and prone to nurturing the disorder inside of us and celebrating the disorder all about us.

We're moral creatures and we're also oriented towards keeping ourselves safe and healthy, but we definitely have strong desires that can be exploited to our harm and to the harm of those around us, the harm of society in general. If we give in to these temptations which surround us, we damage our hearts and lungs, our brains and hormonal systems. If we systematically move from temptation to more dangerous temptation, we can do a tremendous amount of damage to one or more organs. And those organs contribute to those aspects of our being we call 'mind' or 'soul'. Though the brain is certainly the most important direct contributor, the hormonal systems contribute greatly, as do the heart and lungs and liver.

We are what we eat and we modern human beings tend to eat diets that will make us diabetic, cardiac patients filled with lustful images and evil, violent thoughts.

Another way to think of this issue is by following up on what I said earlier about the way that brain development occurs – Edelman calls it 'neural Darwinism'. The processes inside the brain are similar to the messy, opportunistic, sometime nasty, processes that appear to have driven forward the evolution of life on earth. Our brains are neither the rational philosophical souls of some lines of traditional thought nor some sort of wetware version of a computer. The human brain is better seen as a miniaturized version of the physical environments in which life has evolved on earth. We have minds which rest upon a messy, evolving organ called the 'human brain'. Messiness comprehending messiness because messiness shapes itself to be an encapsulation of that larger-scale messiness.

There's substantial order and more than just subtle hints of a personal intelligence underlying physical reality, however messy it is to human perception. Even when a human thinker denies the order of physical reality, as Charles Darwin did, his mind adopts some of that order and makes its own some of those subtle hints as it shapes itself to match up well with its surrounding environment. We should remember that we are truly creatures of this world created by God and only truly seen by Him. We're embedded in it. It forms us. We can never shut it out. It interpenetrates us. The processes by which the mind forms itself in response to its environment are less those where an agent stands back and cold-bloodedly analyzes an independent process, more those of an organism which could not possibly separate itself much from the environment which provides its nutrition and receives its waste products. This organism, in its entirety and in some of its particular components and aspects, shapes itself to better fit its environment. And the process is much like those you see described so well in a novel by Tolstoy or George Eliot. Perhaps the God-centered craziness of a Flannery O'Connor novel would be a still better example.

The universe is what it is, but the universe seems to be a rather messy it, an it which is still in the process of birth. Our minds can be no better than this. This can be a justifying reason for the ideological deception that the universe is not made up of things but only processes. Many scientists seem to believe that and it's true in the sense that a fetus, a young child, and even an adult with a living mind is growing towards possibilities seen only through a glass darkly. The dimly seen possibilities of which I can speak are generally under-determined. We can change some of the details of our beings and our lives under all circumstances and we can greatly change our lives – more likely those of our children – under some circumstances.

We can even affect the shaping of our minds, or those of our children, by selecting experiences, by developing certain habits of behavior and thought and perception, by choosing amongst the various idols of the marketplace or by choosing God – or at least the pursuit of the possibility that the God of Jesus Christ exists. This is where our moral freedom lies and not in some mythical free-will of a sort never observed and not even compatible with human nature. There are some who think themselves to have free-wills when they were really formed to one or another system of virtue. Many of the Roman Patricians were formed to a rather harsh, sometimes inhumane, but very real and demanding standard of virtue. The wills of those virtuous pagans were guided and not free, guided down ruts formed during their upbringing.

In more recent centuries, the Puritan theologian Jonathon Edwards was formed in the household of his father, a rather strict and pious Puritan. He was formed to very high standards of honor, if a bit prudish in the way of the later Puritans. Edwards deluded himself into thinking that his virtue was due to a radically free-will when it was in fact, the result of a rigorous upbringing. I suspect that we see in Edwards' views on free-will a baptized version of the same view that Adam Smith held: man is some sort of agent standing aloof from his environment as he makes rational decisions. This belief is probably related to, maybe descended from, the erroneous beliefs in a human free-will and an immortal soul held by many Christians and many ex-Christians.

We're citizens of this universe in the deepest sense but we're not well-determined citizens at birth. We're formed to be any one of a number of possible creatures. For example, we might become members of a hunting tribe with brains highly developed in their sensory regions and with highly developed capabilities to mimic the thought and behavior of the species we hunt. Or we might become city-dwellers with brains that are highly developed in their literary capabilities and abstract reasoning capabilities. We become one or another as our brain shapes itself to fit in with the type of environments it perceives. Those environments might be perverse and not at all true to reality – picture a young person growing up in a household of dedicated Nazis in Germany during the 1930s. Then the brain will mal-form itself in legitimate response to a perverse environment. Under those circumstances, there's a good chance that the child will become a Nazi in his behavior and thoughts, some chance he will rebel, and no chance he will be just an aloof agent ready to shed his Nazi upbringing as soon as some good liberal government comes to power.

We travel in ruts and yet we don't travel those ruts in chains. Gravity works against us as does the steepness of the slopes to each side. If Jonathon Edwards was raised to be a Calvinist of moral rigor, his contemporary, George Washington, had far less guidance in his youth. His father had died when he was a child and his older brother was in England. As a teenager, George Washington saw a production of Addington's play about Cato, the most honored and most admirable of those who defended the Roman Republic against the imperial ambitions of Julius Caesar. At that time, that young man who would become the primary founder of the United States set the goal of becoming a man of absolutely unimpeachable public honor. By way of a life-long concentration on that goal, he became one of the few men in history who held nearly absolute power and then willingly gave it up when it was appropriate. This is not an example of free-will but rather that of a man putting forth a sustained effort beyond the strength of most of us. Most of us need an extended family and a local community and a church to help us with the task of becoming a true Christian or even a true virtuous pagan.

We're not fully enslaved to our genes nor to our upbringing but one puts limits on our possible ruts and the second places us in specific ruts which are hard to climb out of. We're moral creatures though our species evolved by way of a messy and often nasty set of processes which seem to have little or nothing to do with morality. Some would use the nature of the evolutionary process to deny our moral nature, and I don't mean only some of the literalistically minded evolutionary biologists. There are many Christians who seem afraid of evolutionary biology because they imagine that it necessarily leads to a denial of the moral nature of human beings. I've read a good number of books on evolutionary biology and largely accept the presentation of facts and theories and I've certainly not lost my faith in the most holy Trinity and in the Incarnation of the Son of God. Nor have I lost my limited faith in human moral nature. The major change in my beliefs has been the birth of a certain respect for the moral natures of other social mammals.

Open-minded exploration of books on evolutionary theory and nature-books on specific animals or environments will quickly indicate that there are other species, such as wolves and bears and elephants and whales, which have moral natures. Modern biology has not shown us that man is not a moral species but rather has it shown us that there are other species which have strong moral natures as well as many species which have some behaviors which can be interpreted as moral to some extent. Moral nature has evolved in stages just as much as the liver and kidneys have. As we might expect in such a messy process, some non-human creatures have stronger versions of particular moral traits than humans have though the overall moral natures of bears and wolves and others are less complete and more primitive in a substantial sense. For example, wolves have stronger instincts against killing other members of their own species than do human beings.

When researchers show that even some rodent species exhibit behavior generously labeled as 'altruistic', why are there so many who seem to think that makes the earth less amenable to morality? Simple voles, similar to the prairie dog, are studied often just because their genes and nesting habits allow easy definition of genetic relatedness between individual animals, and those voles exhibit other-directed behavior which becomes stronger with closer genetic relatedness. Why would people be upset by the discovery that even rodents sometimes display self-sacrificing moral behavior, especially in the interests of their close relatives? If God wished to create moral natures with that complex set of phenomena sometimes described badly as 'selfish genes', then that's God's business and we have to accept the universe and our own natures as He created them.

There seem to be many who really want to believe this is Satan's world and that men are moral creatures thrown into this world to which we do not belong, this world which is not good enough for us. Some of those would have us born as angels thrown into bodies not really ours; such creatures, essentially bloodless, would be no more willing to give themselves for their siblings than for some unknown human being on the other side of the globe. In any case, we're not such creatures but rather creatures who develop our moral natures, plastic within our limitations. We must learn how to love those close to us, those we break bread with and drink wine with. Having learned to love those with whom we press the flesh, we can learn to love, in some measure, those with whom we have more occasional contact, perhaps antagonistic contact. Some may even develop a true capacity for loving human beings in general.

We must never forget that this process by which human beings can learn to love ever wider groups of human beings is a developmental process that's probably disrupted as easily by attempts to jump to a generalized love as it is by training into jingoistic attitudes. One might even imagine the two processes moving together with advocates of each not realizing they're allies.

When we think about human moral nature, we must think in evolutionary terms over the eons when worms became frogs which became dinosaurs which became rat-like creatures which became monkeys which became men. We must also think in developmental terms over the precious days of infancy, the few years of childhood, and even the decades of adulthood when plastic human beings become St. Francis of Assisi or Adolf Hitler. Welcome those developmental processes, as painful as they are to contemplate or to endure for they're the processes which form us.

As John Paul II told us about God's world in general: Do not be afraid. We have the opportunity to live a story in which God shapes us to be companions of His, but He allows us to refuse to live our proper stories. Either way, the story is possible, as it isn't for even wolves or bears or dolphins, just because the Son of God took on human flesh. We should consider this fact in grateful wonder, giving up our habits of glorifying our apish selves. Despite the supposed instincts of ancient philosophers and mystics, there is little reason to believe that human beings are made for eternity, though there is a promise that we can be re-made for a life without end as companions of God.

These human development processes which occur at the boundaries of order and disorder can produce a St. Francis as well as a Hitler, but there are some who think that the amoral nature of biological evolution and biological development tells us that our moral natures are illusions. There are some who think that the evidence of morality in many animal species tells us that our moral natures are illusions. I guess there's a desire on the part of modern people to look for a reason to believe that our moral natures are illusions though we do have seemingly contradictory desires to see ourselves as pure and righteous. There's probably no simple motivation for this perverse desire to look for reasons that our moral natures are illusions. Perhaps it's because we've made too much of such horrors as the dropping of the atomic bombs on Hiroshima and Nagasaki even while we didn't have the energy nor the courage nor the integrity to call our leaders to account for those crimes, and many others.

If we'd wanted to discourage such crimes, we should have simply investigated what seem to be crimes. Then, if it was appropriate, we should have tried those who gave the orders to commit the crimes. If we aren't going to do anything about the crimes our leaders commit, then we become collaborators and might as well just admit our morally corrupted condition. Why lose sleep over situations we refuse to properly deal with?

Now we get to the importance of all of this to a Christian worldview:

> As leaders of a country which was once Christian, our presidents and congressmen and generals and bureaucrats should know you can't fight evil with evil. When you use evil, you become evil.

Robert Louis Stevenson wrote *The Strange Case of Dr. Jekyll and Mr. Hyde* partly as a warning of what happens when human beings try to bury their disordered tendencies rather than dealing with them directly. Such people display their oh-so Christian selves, or virtuous pagan selves, to the world while their disordered selves fester inside. I would suggest that our leaders are Dr. Jekylls when they head up charitable efforts and are thuggish, murderous Mr. Hydes when they make many of their decisions during wartime and peacetime alike. For some degenerate definition of 'personality', Dr. Jekyll and Mr. Hyde were different personalities, but they were part of but one human nature.

> If we're to presume anything about our afterlives, it's safest to presume that Dr. Jekyll will go down to Hell with Mr. Hyde.

Fragmentation rules in both the external and internal aspects of the modern human being. Specifically:

> The perceptions and thoughts of a morally fragmented human being will be at least as fragmented as those moral beliefs and behaviors.

There are practical implications to this insight which should be obvious, and they don't allow happy forecasts for the near-term future of Western Civilization, but I'm trying to view a world rather than trying to forecast that future of the West. So, I'll turn to ask: Is this overwhelming disorder a necessary state? Already, by turning St. Augustine's "We are sin" into "We are disorder," I have claimed we enter our lives in a state of a lack of order though it's not a state of willful fragmentation or nurtured disorder. What's the source of this disorder? Of course, I've already given various forms of an answer: the disorder of this universe is a factual state imposed by God Himself that a particular universe could come into existence, a universe which develops and in which life can evolve into a species capable of knowing that God exists, capable of hearing His offer of friendship.

As we tend towards an illegitimate separation of human nature into physical components and supernatural components, so we also tend towards an incoherent separation of evil into natural and moral. Our moral natures are part of our human animal natures. All evil in this world created by God, all disorder, all privation or even poverty of being, is natural. Disorder is part of the story God is telling by way of settings and characters which have underlying substances made of the matter and energy and fields studied by physicists. It's time for us Christians to stop our forced retreat from the pagan superstitions which lead to events such as the embarrassing persecution of Galileo. We were forced against our wills to admit that epilepsies and cancers are caused by physical factors. We should willingly admit that our basic moral natures are also caused by physical factors. It's the shaping of those moral natures in human communities that can raise us to a higher level in human terms, even to that harsh but noble level I've labeled as 'virtuous paganism'. It's only in our submission to our brother, Jesus Christ, that we can rise to a level beyond what's possible in terms of brain-cells and hormones and liver secretions. Yet, even there, we should remember that God's grace completes and perfects human nature – that of a particular species of ape. Grace does not replace human nature with some angelic nature.

We're slaves, and we're enslaved by our genes to some significant extent but we wear no chains and can climb out of our fated ruts with God's help. It's the ruts through regions of disorder that we travel voluntarily that can trap us in a way that God's servants on Earth cannot undo. God Himself may not undo those voluntary bindings – He has strongly hinted He will not forgive those sins for which we don't ask forgiveness of Him, those sins we don't even recognize as being sins. Our modern ideologies encourage us to travel ruts which are comfortable and well-paved, ruts that help us to shape ourselves as rather mindless moral invertebrates who imagine ourselves to be righteous and upright. But this is what we have done to ourselves and what we do to our children because we have chosen to absorb those ideologies into our innermost selves. We can no longer make any meaningful sacrifices for our professed beliefs, and we no longer even have the clarity of vision, and the allied honesty, to see this weakness in ourselves. But, digressor though I am, I don't wish to digress too far on these topics when I've so much ground to cover in this preliminary work. But it's necessary to make the point that our viewpoints on moral matters, including our fears or hopes of the amorality that some see in evolutionary biology, are tied to our acts of cutting out our own moral spines as if we were fish for the cleaning. We're spineless and some wish to believe nature made us that way; others fear that there's no possibility of recovering from our moral spinelessness. This moral corruption has led to ideological distortions in the interpretation of even our best science.

A universe of good physical order will be seen only if the viewer is morally well-ordered. But moral order comes to human beings by seeing the physical order in which we're embedded. But that physical order can be seen truly only by a morally well-ordered person. And it's time to break this silly circuit and note that the processes by which we understand this universe shaped by God and the processes by which we learn to order our moral natures are intertwined and recursive and both sets of processes begin with gratitude to Him who created us and this world. With that sense of gratitude welling up, a morally well-ordered person begins to see physical order as being the effects of God, as Aquinas told us. No matter how strong the faith of an individual might be, it's all but impossible for those processes to reach any sort of stable and sophisticated state during his lifetime and not much possible for that to happen even during the course of a particular Christian society. It took an awfully long time to create the theological and moral and literary treasures of the Christian West and we're wasting those treasures so quickly. It's so sad that the work of St. Augustine and St. Thomas Aquinas and all those who came before them has been significantly damaged and mostly by those who think of themselves as Christians. Christians have, in fact, damaged Christianity far more so than the enemies of the Church – read the books of Michael Buckley and James Turner for a wealth of supporting evidence that it was well-intentioned but unwise theologians and clergymen who laid the foundations of popular atheism.

When Christians got to work proving the existence of the concrete, self-revealed God of Jesus Christ by showing that $1 + 1 = 2$ or by arguing that an eye can see, they also converted pagan gods into various sorts of immaterial entities which moved planets or just generally dwelled in the ethereal regions beyond the moon's orbit. And we have taken those erroneous beliefs deeper into our souls than ever did we allow the Lord Jesus Christ Himself to penetrate. Step by step have we Christians been forced to purge one element or another of animistic paganism. Forced to concede that Satan doesn't cause lung cancer, we're still reluctant to give up our claim that he, and not us, was responsible for Auschwitz and our sexually perverse young people. Forced to admit the universe is an explosively dynamic entity and that matter can be seen as frozen energy, we continue to believe we need souls to compensate for some imaginary shortcomings in the physical stuff of this universe.

The major responsibility for pushing young descendants of Christians into atheism belongs to parents and to Christian leaders and theologians. Some of those leaders and theologians continue to present us with implausible and superstitious views of men and their moral natures and others tell us why an historical Jesus and a self-revealed Trinity are not necessary for Christianity. It took centuries for us to concede that angels weren't moving the planets and demons weren't causing fits. Some of us are still not ready to admit that men are apes who have received a rather unexpected invitation from God and others admit we're apes but no longer hear that invitation. Some of us are not ready to admit we have the moral natures appropriate to a certain sort of social mammal, along with a level of intelligence that allows us to draw a purer set of moral rules from an understanding of our own moral natures and an understanding of our environments and some of us imagine that creatures with particular natures can make up their own moral rules.

We do have a brother in Jesus Christ, the Son of God who became man that man might share in the life of God. We do have a Father in Heaven and a Spirit to guide us. But our God-like possibilities are not in us; rather are they in Christ so that they affect us only when we allow our Lord to infuse Himself in us.

We were given the solid foundations of traditional Christianity though those foundations came with bodies of doctrines where revealed truths had been mixed with defective or incomplete empirical knowledge. Over time, those errors became obvious but we held on to them with perhaps more energy than we held onto the revealed truths of the Triune God and the Christ who was true man and true God. We chose to turn those mistakes of empirical knowledge into divinely inspired superstitions. By doing so, we helped turn many Christians or descendants of Christians into unbelievers and we created absurd divides between empirical knowledge and Christian knowledge, allowing ourselves and our opponents to forget that a God who enters the history of His own Creation doesn't allow such divisions. We destroyed the moral order of societies at least somewhat Christian. We turned our evangelists from fools for God into simpler sorts of fools. We separated ourselves from God's world, the world which is our only home for now and our only school for learning how to turn towards God and to become His friends.

It's hard to say if any given human being was villain or victim in this complex process by which we threw away a substantial amount of our Christian faith. In the published version of his Gifford Lectures, *With the Grain of the Universe*, Stanley Hauerwas discusses the extremely interesting case of the philosopher and psychologist William James who was most certainly a man of moral integrity by purely human standards but he was also a man who could not make sense of God's omnipotence and infinite goodness in a universe which contains evil. He chose to hold onto his skepticism about God's very existence and could not take that step of seeing the chaos around him as being as least possibly a world, unified and coherent and complete. For all his moral integrity, the inability of William James to humble himself and to believe that he might understand was a moral failing. This is a common failing in the modern world and may well be the principle error of modern men. But we should be reluctant to place too much moral responsibility upon the individual because it's almost beyond human strength to tolerate that sometimes rapid and disorienting movement from the battlefield that's our own moral selves to a chaotic assembly of environments that can only be perceived as a morally ordered universe by great intellectual and moral effort. And then you realize that it's time to use that newly perceived universe to better see our place in God's story and then to come to a new and deeper understanding of our human natures. And then a recognition of Christ's role in all of this introduces the complications of our invitations into His Body, our chances to unite our human natures to divine nature without any loss of our individual selves.

Certain aspects of our loss of faith came about because of the mistakes of those well-intentioned Christians, theologians and clergymen, but the seeds had perhaps been sown even before St. Thomas Aquinas produced perhaps the greatest body of thought in history – to little effect. As Alasdair MacIntyre tells the story in *Three Rival Versions of Moral Enquiry*, Aquinas and others like him in teaching the unity of faith and reason were confronted by other accomplished theologians and philosophers who argued that a highly developed mind was not necessary for Christian preachers or teachers – all that's needed is movement of some undefined spirit though most mistakenly believe it to be the Holy Spirit. Also important was the shattering of the links between liturgy and doctrine. As a young Protestant lad, I was always mystified – in a non-mystical way – by those plates covered with cubes of white bread and the trays of shot-glasses filled with grape juice. We didn't know so much as the Apostle's Creed and our minds were leaking away those stories of the life of Jesus which are nothing more than the stuff of greeting cards when separated from an understanding of His God-hood.

So much has been thrown away. So many have died without so much as a baptism. So many others have lived the lives of luke-warm Christians. Still more have wandered away from the Church of Christ. All because of an apish stubbornness on the part of creatures who refused for so long to believe they're apes. Some of us have refused to open our minds that they might be formed as three-dimensional holograms of the world of God, a world which is a manifestation of thoughts He wished us to have. Some of us have even refused to let ourselves be found by God.

There are no Darwinian arguments nor any Jamesian doubts which truly cast the world into any basic moral disorder because the world exists only to those who have allowed themselves to be morally ordered by the commandments of our Lord Jesus Christ. At the same time, it was Darwin and James, amongst a few other modern men, who have given us the specific tools to see the true nature of order in this world created by God. Rather than being a place decaying from an Edenic state, God's world is one which develops by way of the clash of physical order and physical disorder. To be sure, St. Paul seems to have seen this centuries ago, but we can now understand his insights in the light of a better empirical understanding of the universe.

Though we're not fallen gods, we human beings are, in fact, moral creatures and all the research on rodents and all the bones to be dug out of the African soils can only fill in blank spots on the canvas of human nature. Common sense, which is more often good than bad, tells us that it's interesting when a moral creature is formed by a process that's largely amoral and unstructured at the level of human perception and conception. It's cognitive or moral incompetence that leads us to believe a moral creature is not truly moral if it was formed by such a process. If a building is being used to provide medical care for poor children, a discovery that the building was put up as a brothel has no bearing on the morality of the children's clinic and the enclosed activities. Even more to the point, a woman working at a low salary as a doctor in that clinic is the same moral creature even if we were to discover that her ancestral lines contain brutal and sadistic killers, as is true of the ancestral lines of all of us. There are a few genetic conditions which distort our moral natures, such as a form of manic-depression in some male lines of descent. The men in some of the great warrior families have been pre-disposed to loss of control, sheer brutality, under certain conditions, but on the whole, killers or saints are formed from the same basic protoplasmic stuff by a combination of environmental circumstances and personal moral decisions. We're given moral nature by our evolutionary heritage, but our moral natures are themselves unformed. We can move towards a true order or we can nurture the amoral disorder which is us at birth and which becomes a morally culpable disorder when we nurture it.

And so wander I down various byways and cross-paths as I try to work out a worldview which honors the valid truths and lesser insights of science and literature and philosophy and theology and plain common-sense. I know this much: neither a world nor a person who inhabits a world can be inherently divided or incoherent or incomplete. In practice, all of these faults will be present in any human person or in any world which forms through a human person's worldview.

Let's retreat a bit to first examine our basic biological situation. The human race evolved by a catch-as-catch-can process which has produced an erect body suited for a crouching animal. Thus there are some who are bothered by sciatic nerves rubbing against bone where those nerves pass through the pelvis – the angle of the hole is better suited to a crouching animal. Our lower backs are barely adequate improvisations on a theme – that of a crouching ape once again. Some of us have sinuses that drain improperly and that again is partially due to drainage tubes angled more adequately for a crouching animal. Given enough time, this evolution business sometimes works – porpoises are perhaps the greatest athletes in all of nature and they're patched-up land creatures.

Most importantly for this discussion: our brains are rather strange organs compared to what most thinkers imagine them to be. I would say the human brain operates in strange ways just because it's an image of the strange ways of evolution.

> The human brain, as is true of all other organisms and organs, is a product of the evolutionary process. However, the human brain has a still deeper relationship to that process than any other known organism or organ – it has somehow come to be an encapsulation of sorts of that process. Our thinking processes are a miniature version of the process of biological evolution. Our remembering processes are a reflection of the processes by which the structures and metabolic processes of ancient creatures are buried in both inactive and active genes in our bodies, and those hints of ancient apes and reptiles and worms interact with more modern structures and metabolic processes in the strangest and most wonderful ways.

A better knowledge of the best views of evolutionary biology and of the current, good views of the human brain leads – at least for me – to a deeper appreciation of God as a Creator. In fact, I'll be assuming through the rest of this book that the human brain, in the context of a formation in a morally well-ordered human community, is an encapsulation of the general development processes of the entire universe, those which shape galaxies as well as those which brought reptiles into existence. I'll leave these thoughts dangling for now though I've given hints of the reasons behind such claims. It's time to address a specific issue about God's relationship to His Creation: is it such a relationship that we can prove God's existence from inside Creation?

4.2 Proofs and Designs

Overview

Given the current sad state of human thought, including Christian thought, I've little interest in formal proofs of the existence of God. Under different circumstances, I could have much greater interest in formal proofs and I can well understand the interest of the great Medieval thinkers in such proofs, but it's important to realize that the Rabbi Moses Maimonides and St. Thomas Aquinas didn't produce formal proofs set in the desert landscape of abstract philosophy. Both of those men produced formal proofs in the context of a worldview which assumed the existence of the God who revealed His name to Moses in the case of Maimonides. Aquinas, of course, viewed a world in which the further self-revelations of God in Jesus Christ were basic facts. As Michael Buckley, James Turner, Stanley Hauerwas, and others have shown, the assumption that God's existence can be proved by abstract arguments or by arguments from the physical universe provides a variety of double-edged swords. That is, God can also be proved to not exist by arguments of the same sort. Just choose your assumptions properly to prove what you wish.

Of all beings, God is the most concrete and not abstract in any meaningful sense, though abstract arguments and proofs about various aspects of being might well be useful in theology. Let me repeat: God is concrete and not some sort of pure idea in the way of a mathematical concept. He's not ethereal fluff. Of all entities, only God truly exists and He's also the source of truths, abstract and particular. It's we creatures who are ethereal fluff, existing only as God brings us into existence by an act-of-being, moment to moment. It's abstract truths which are dependent upon God; God's being isn't regulated by some body of abstract truth and the associated forms of reasoning.

Recall what I said about negative theology. In an age when God was seen as the great Pan – as the universe, it made sense to emphasize God's transcendental aspects and to develop theologies which now seem too abstract. When God was seen as a creature of infinite magnitude, it made sense to argue for His absolute simplicity and impassivity. I'll repeat that Aquinas and Augustine and other truly great Christian thinkers, made such arguments only to make specific points about a God they knew darned well to be a God who had created the world and then revealed Himself in human history.

We live in an age where Deists more radical than those of the Enlightenment have conquered our languages, relativizing not only morality but also making their transcendent Deity into something more ambiguous than the Being of the atheistic Buddhists, which Being is also Non-being. We're a touchy-feely people who worship the great Fluff who lives in a far distant galaxy.

The very words which point to God carry ghostly connotations. To fight the dominant errors of our age, we should emphasize the concreteness of God, but that's what we were supposed to be emphasizing all along. And there's an easy way to see that this is appropriate – only God necessarily exists. One might think that a necessary being, one which is His own act-of-being, would be more concrete than a being which is made of stuff which is made, in turn, from nothing. To approach God by way of proofs, whether you're a believer or a skeptic, you're better off thinking the densest matter in the universe is fluffy compared to God's being. It's ultimately the wrong way to think of matters, but it's less erroneous than thinking of God as being analogous to a mathematical concept – which is the situation if you approach God's existence as something which can be proved by abstract means starting with a minimum of assumptions. The climax comes when we begin to speak of the God who sent His Son down to become one of us that we might share life with the Father and the Son and the Holy Spirit.

My personal view is that the formal proofs of Maimonides and Aquinas were not efforts to prove that God exists but rather efforts to show that a human being, already believing in the self-revealed God, has a mind capable of dealing with those revelations of God and making sense of them in the form of a theology. In a sense, Aquinas was not proving that God exists but rather proving that human beings are, in some creaturely sense, worthy of being companions to God.

We no longer have a worldview of the sort which Aquinas partially inherited and partially built. Abstract proofs outside of the context of such a worldview are meaningless and, in fact, pointless. Before we can construct meaningful abstract proofs of God's existence, using tools provided by modern mathematicians and logicians and scientists and historians, we need to build a more general sort of proof which will simply bring a greater unity and completeness and coherence to Christian doctrine and a plausible set of views about the physical universe. There's a test of God's existence which consists of telling a plausible human version of the story God is telling with this world He created. The Christian worldview is necessarily God-centered and retains its properties of unity and coherence and completeness only if it remains God-centered. Since we cannot truly see God by our own powers, we must remain focused upon that burning bush and, even more importantly, we must remain focused upon that Cross on Calvary.

The decay of Christian belief is a complex tale in which some leaders of the Catholic Church have played roles as villains or cowards, but the biggest problems grew during the Middle Ages and then emerged during the Protestant Reformation. It's even somewhat valid to describe the family of modern liberalisms as the Protestant Christian worldview shifted to a man-centered perspective. The Protestant Fathers were unwise in thinking that Christianity could be non-sacramental, in thinking that men could live lives in some secular realm separated from the Church of Christ and separated from the liturgical calendar which was the setting for Christian life. To a Christian, there are no true walls dividing holy places and times from secular places and times, but Martin Luther and others imagined that such could be true for a follower of Christ.

This is my claim which I consider an observed truth: our inner order or disorder will reflect the order or disorder in our environments. It's also true that our human societies will reflect the inner order or disorder of their citizens. By willingly and willfully shattering even the ideal of a well-ordered society in which a man is the same Christian at worship, at work, and at play, the founders of Protestantism put an unreasonable, and ultimately unbearable, burden upon their followers: unity could be sustained inside a man only by a charade taking vast amounts of psychological energy and intense, constant concentration. We have reached a point where most human beings don't even desire to be unified in the Christian sense.

I can tie together a few issues by pointing to the Biblical tale of the temptation of Christ by Satan[1]. If I were to try to define 'person' in a concrete and humanly accessible way, I would point to that tale, almost certainly a lesson intended to summarize the impression that Jesus Christ made upon those around Him rather than being a tale of actual events. This impression which Jesus Christ made upon human beings, and which is shown in terms of His incorruptibility, is the external evidence of a true person, or Person in that case. We should worry more about the fact that the human beings we most admire are those who give in to the forces of disorder, of corruption, in their own selves and in the environments around them. Modern man idolizes those human beings who give up any chance for healthy minds or souls in their quest for power and wealth. We should also worry more about the strange fact that we use a percentage of the rotten fruits of those quests for money and power and then label it as Christian charity, trying to bribe God with a percentage of dirty money.

> Modern Christians are producing proofs every day that Jesus Christ was not the Son of God and that He did not have the authority to place inconvenient demands upon us. Those proofs are the very lives we lead and the ways in which we worship.

Morally well-structured people certainly didn't disappear after the Protestant Reformation, but they maintained their own moral order by drawing

[1]Chapter 4 of the Gospel of Luke.

down the moral and cultural resources of their more truly Christian ancestors. The ordinary person even found it all but impossible to hold God at the center of his worldview, in his inner thoughts and feelings and also in his external behavior. This is the reason for the shattering of the human personality in the modern world, bottoming out – I would hope – in the general belief that a desirable personality is that which allows a 60 year-old grandfather to prance across the stage at a rock-and-roll concert making an utter ass of himself. We think human beings are true to themselves when they act this way, and it's an insight in a way – their disordered behavior is likely an accurate mirror of their inner disorder which is, in turn, a mirror of the disorder of modern societies. In most modern human beings, especially in those admired for their personalities, we're seeing evidence of failures to form their beings into persons. Disorder is cool. Stupidity and immaturity are profitable.

I've pointed out that the concept of 'person' is meaningless outside of the context of a Christian belief in the God who is three Persons. The authors of the American Constitution and other modern law-givers have often used 'person' as meaning either 'citizen' or 'human being', but both of those usages are no more than sounds, words with no foundational meaning. Define a 'human person' as a 'human being' and then you can define a 'human being' as a 'human person', but a 'human being' is just a physical animal of a particular species of ape. I've tried to refound the concept of 'human person' as being a human being who is a true worldviewer, one who becomes unified and coherent and complete in his own being – to some limited extent, by viewing a true world, a universe that's unified and coherent and complete under its Creator. One way of bringing this all together is to claim forthrightly that a formal proof of the existence of God makes sense only to someone who is at least moving towards a state of human person-hood, of a greater and better imitation of Jesus Christ.

Human thoughts and attention in the West have drifted from God in a natural process that would have horrified that God-centered man, Martin Luther, if he'd had the wisdom to foresee such an anti-Christian result of his actions. Without God at the center of the individual's thoughts and attention, Christian worldviews have lost their most importance characteristics, decaying into ideologies and becoming depressingly attractive to the disordered creatures who are us. The environments of modern men are no longer even potentially unified or coherent or complete and, thus, are incapable of being seen as parts of a world. The external disorder becomes part of us, to the deepest parts of our beings. Our environments are no more than the various parts of the modern marketplaces to which we have been assigned by fate or the educational system or the whims of our corporate or governmental masters. To see a world, a man has to dare to step outside of these environments. That's hard to do, especially for those having responsibility for feeding and clothing and housing children.

Under these circumstances, a Christian state of mind can be sadly maintained with great psychological effort and by rapidly drawing down our life's energies or a false Christianity can be maintained by shedding our Christian selves as we enter the public squares. Even in our daily activities, we inhabit various environments rather than a world, going from home to work and then to church on Sunday. Our minds are formed by those environments so that our minds are as fragmented as our daily schedules. We still see the effects of God, at least some of them, but they're scattered across various environments that we can't pull together into a world. Most people really can't even envision the purely physical universe of the scientists. Under our current circumstances, belief in the existence of God is not held so much as it drifts in and out of our field of thought. No stable or convincing proofs of the existence of God are possible, certainly not the existence of the God of Jesus Christ, but that points to deeper problems. It is necessarily true that the God of Jesus Christ must find us, and, as Cardinal Ratzinger pointed out: "We need a new readiness to seek the truth and also the humility to let ourselves be found." Many there are who are proud of their immortal souls or their powerful minds and few there are who train themselves into that proper state of humility. We do not wish the God of Jesus Christ to find us because we prefer to delude ourselves into thinking we can make of ourselves what we wish, to pretend we can make laws rather than hearing the laws that God has revealed through His prophets and through His world.

Proofs of the existence of God were more comprehensible to Medieval man as he inhabited a world that dominated his vision because there was a strong sense of unity to European civilization and that unity made possible a general sense that there was a true world, unified and coherent and complete, where that world was created by the God of Jesus. It's not that Europe was homogeneous, but there was a strong sense that all Europeans inhabited the same world under God. More than that, European Christians didn't have the freedom or the desire to split their selves into public and private components. Medieval men could probably not have even imagined such a perverse state of being. It's not that we should idealize that particular form of social and personal order which Medieval man realized, imperfectly to be sure but also substantially. Nor should we imagine that we could ever return to that particular form of order, nor should we desire it. Individual order and social order reflect each other as do individual disorder and social disorder. We need to work towards the realization of a social and individual order which is a reflection of the needs of a multi-racial and multi-cultural humanity covering the globe as well as being a reflection of the universe as modern empirical knowledge has shown it to be, a universe which is quite plausibly, but not provably, the creation of the God of Jesus Christ.

Contingent Truths and Absolute Truths

Many seem to regard mathematics as a vast continent where an explorer can wander from one absolute truth to another, no matter which direction he takes. Against that sort of view, I'll speak of mathematics as we normally view it, elegant and made of well-founded truths, being islands of order in the midst of an absolutely infinite sea of facts. For now, this seems the most coherent possible view of the state of mathematical knowledge, but questions remain. For example, do those islands pre-exist their discovery? Do we build them by the very process of exploring regions of that sea from the base of an already existing island? That sea exists independent of our efforts, and I believe it to have been a specific construction of the true God, the most holy Trinity. The islands might well have started to rise from the sea when God chose to create the Primordial Universe with its particular forms of order.

I'll not further address such fundamental ideas, but I'll suggest that whether these islands of order are pre-existing or built by the process of discovery, we're limited to discovering islands in those regions of the sea within reach of the islands upon which the human mind feels at home. I'll also use this general model, islands of order in a sea of chaos, to describe our physical world in its various aspects, qualitative as well as quantitative.

In addition, I'll claim that there are truths which are such on the islands inhabited by man and in the nearby regions of this chaotic sea but they may not be absolutely true across all possible regions of created being or across all possible thoughts of all possible creatures.

For example, forms of life which have evolved on earth include social mammals. I've claimed and will continue to claim that essentially all of these social mammal species, and some other species have moral natures, albeit sometimes primitive and limited to predetermined behaviors. To continue on this specific issue: forms of reproduction different from those of social, placental mammals might well involve different relationships between the adults involved (a single male and a single female are not the only logical possibilities) and also the relationships between youngsters and the adults (long-term dependency of youngsters upon adults is obviously a good foundation for the growth of moral tendencies in an evolving species, but I don't know how to go about imagining other possibilities).

Human sexual morality is customized to the needs of a highly social species of placental mammals. Human females, not so much the males, are highly specialized for acts of reproduction, and I mean the entire repertoire of acts including all those which have been partially taken from human mothers by profit-seeking corporations or government agencies wishing to gain control of the formation of young human beings. Those acts deal most prominently with the nurturing and formation of young children but also include such complex acts as those by which control is exercised over child-bearing women by the older women in an extended family or tribe. The medical industry's takeover of these birthing processes and child nurturing activities have played as prominent a role in the destruction of the extended family and local community and church as social security and welfare have.

Scientific knowledge, such as that of obstetricians, has increased greatly in the modern world, but it's promulgated widely and used in setting public and private policies only when it serves the needs of the gods of the market-places. Our squeamishness is such that we'll eliminate every possible infant death even at the cost of the souls and minds of those children who survive their births. The discoveries and plausible speculations of evolutionary biologists and neurobiologists strongly support my claims that we're creatures suited to lives centered around local and concrete attachments to families and neighborhoods and churches. All of that knowledge also supports the view that the traditional respect for human mothers is more than warranted by the specialization of human females for long and crippling pregnancies, difficult childbirths, and very long periods of nurturing and education of human children. And that knowledge also supports the view that the child-birthing ties between women of different generations in a family or local community are necessary for the formation of morally well-structured human societies. A return to biological sanity on the role of mothers and the role of older women in an extended family is necessary to form any society which is capable of living the Christian story and bringing their children, and outsiders, into that story.

The above claims, in all their nitty-gritty biological nature, are necessary for the sort of worldview I'm constructing, for an understanding of the nature of this world created by God – including the nature of human beings invited to become His companions. Morally well-ordered societies will produce a far higher percentage of citizens who are worldviewing human beings, human persons in formation. This means that such societies may produce a higher percentage of human beings who are suited to life as companions of God in the New Universe, the never-ending phase of Creation which the resurrected will inhabit. Of course, God can save anybody He wishes, completing and perfecting their human beings, but we have no right to presume this, though it's a duty of Christians to pray for the salvation of all. But our first duty is to do what we can to help bring specific human beings to Christ and to properly form those who are under our influence to any extent, including ourselves. That leads to a larger-scale duty to form well-ordered families, church communities, and local political communities.[2] And that's possible only if we structure our lives according to human nature, including the most physical and biological aspects of our nature. And that means children should be birthed into extended families and local communities and local churches.

As is true of most of our professionals and other businessmen, doctors – more recently even veterinary doctors, have a strong incentive to expand their responsibilities even at the expense of the moral order necessary to our families and other communities. This has been one of the pressures leading to the reorganization of our societies to, as they say, more efficiently and more effectively take care of our needs, even needs we didn't realize we had until some marketplace entity invented ways to satisfy those needs. Many of those so-called needs are destructive of human social order and individual moral order, but they're the inflamed desires of disordered creatures and as difficult to fight as any other such inflamed desires – such as those of a heroin addict.

[2]This process can be described by the term 'invisible hand'. The decision-makers will be dealing with particular problems in such a way that a greater social order will emerge though that's not the specific intent of the individual acts.

Our reorganization of our societies and even our moral insides in recent centuries came about as our ancestors offered up their souls and minds to the gods of the marketplaces, the two most powerful of which seem to be the nation-state and corporate capitalism. To form a worldview and consequently perceive a world, we must purge ourselves of ideologies, that is – marketplace idolatries. We cannot serve both the God of Jesus Christ and also the gods of the marketplaces. We cannot serve the political gods and the economic gods for nearly all our hours and then imagine we're God-centered people when we go to church for an hour or so each week. We cannot serve any ideological gods. There are those who might think I'm doing so with my discussions of the sexual dimorphism of the human race, but I'm not advocating that we worship the family for its own sake.

A little knowledge of human social history would let people know that the family idolized by some modern Americans is a modern invention intended to protect children against the industrial revolution. That revolution settled down into a form of economic activity, corporate capitalism, which gains most of its advantages by freeing its decision-makers from the moral inhibitions of particular and concrete human communities. Corporate capitalism has extended its reach, has expanded its economic realm, by forcing women into the public herd we call the job-force, the next step after turning mothers and homemakers into mostly consumers of corporate services. Most horribly, we allow the agents of corporate capitalism to prey upon the young people, even inviting them into the living-rooms by way of televisions.

This suburban family, in fact the suburb itself, was invented by the Clapham sect, English Evangelicals who played a major role in fighting slavery. William Wilberforce and his followers were acting out of desperation to protect what they could as the industrial revolution, even before corporate capitalism was fully formed, rolled over the traditional family and local institutions of all sorts. The suburban family displayed on shows such as *Leave It to Beaver* is not healthy, nor is it adequate for raising morally well-structured children, but it was the result of a well-intentioned effort to create at least some sort of a haven in a heartless world.[3] Despite being well-intentioned, it has proved itself incapable of providing such protection partly because young parents do not have the wisdom to see that even so-

[3]The story is told in a very accessible way in the book *From Cottage to Work Station*, Allan Carlson's summary of many of his scholarly findings.

called educational programs re-shape their children's minds and souls to the purposes of the gods of the marketplaces. Those children's minds are shaped so that they cannot re-imagine the story which is the proof of the existence of the God of Jesus Christ because it's His own revelation of His existence and of His life with the Father and their Holy Spirit.

We long ago passed the point where that suburban-style family could protect us or our children. We have no hope of living God-centered lives or raising God-centered children unless we make a more radical break with corporate capitalism and all other forms of liberalism, all of which have been so effective in destroying traditional families and communities of worship that human beings could be formed into self-centered individuals milling about in the public marketplaces. While it'll take true conversions to a God-centered worldview to save us, part of the effort will involve a restoration of our respect for that healthy, robust femininity which blossoms in a confident maternally oriented personality. Our society strongly discourages women from being child-centered human beings that they can produce and consume to the pleasure of the gods of the marketplaces. So long as this continues, few children will be nurtured in such a way as to grow into the sorts of healthy human beings who can become true persons.

We came to be in the universe created by God and we're bound by the moral rules which arise from an understanding of our physical natures and our places in this universe created by the God of Jesus. Our Lord asked, "What benefit is it to anyone to win the whole world and forfeit or lose his very self?" What benefit is it to a woman if she forfeits her maternal nature, forsaking her children, or the children she never had, that she might better serve the gods of the marketplaces? Sociobiologists, often of intelligently feminist beliefs, have noted that being a slut or a whore can be a desperate reproductive strategy for women in a society that despises them and leaves them with low self-esteem.[4] Anyone with eyes to see can

[4]The fact that babies are rarely produced by most of these women is beside the point. In the book of Genesis, the curses pronounced upon Adam and Eve assume the proxy nature of our sexual desires that have been explored by sociobiologists. Our reproductive acts are immediately motivated by feelings of personal desire and sometimes a tenderness leading us to please our sex partner, one night-stand or beloved spouse. In a sense, nature fools us, but morally well-structured societies go one up on nature by raising children with the habits of family formation. God's revelation of His plans for human beings also lead believing Jews and Christians to produce children to whom He can offer His friendship.

note the large number of girls and young women who are choosing to idolize the sluts of the popular singing and acting world when the other major role models presented to them are corporate or academic or political nerds. This corruption of girls and young women is part of the story we tell to prove that the God of Jesus Christ doesn't exist, freeing ourselves to live in the marketplaces. This part of the story is inordinately importantly since it cuts off the maternal nurturing that produces human beings better able to respond to God's call.

Let me retreat a little and address these problems from a more abstract viewpoint, that of the so-called 'natural law':

> Natural law is that structural component of moral law which can be read out of nature or the universe, though many natural law theorists seem more concerned with Aristotle's inadequate views of nature than with modern biology. The problem, even when you begin to consider a more accurate view of human nature and of the physical universe in general, is that there's still something missing. A universe viewed as an accident or a pure mystery – whether or not that's ultimately coherent is beside the point – isn't the same entity as a universe created by a God who is both all-knowing and all-loving.

Let's take a nasty example: why would Christians believe that non-Christians would view abortion as being evil? The probable answer is that we're as confused as those descendants of departing Christians who thought that the moral beliefs and behaviors of Christianity were natural to mankind raised to some minimal level of civilization. It seems strange to modern sensibilities to learn that virtuous pagans, such as the Romans of the Republic, knew abortion to be murder and allowed it to solve difficult problems. But it was a solution restricted to problems they identified as true 'hard cases'. It's not hard to see that modern human beings have a problem restricting the use of a 'solution' to hard cases. There have been those who have suggested that modern people quickly turn acts they consider necessary evils into positively good acts just because they are degenerate Christians and need to feel righteous and holy in all that they do. Such people are going to be more promiscuous in their evil acts than ungodly but morally disciplined pagans of the pre-Christian sort.

Without even considering the greater demands of revealed Christian morality, we incompetent modern Americans have proved for the benefit of future generations of pagans that moral order will be destroyed if you make laws and judicial decisions to allow nasty solutions to hard-cases without having the sort of thick-skinned attitude that allows you to restrict those solutions to legitimate hard-cases. But I'm advocating a Christian worldview and I'll return to discussing that sort of a view in the context of providing foundations even for abstract proofs such as those of mathematics.

Some of our most treasured moral truths have fallen and more will fall because they're truths in the context of a world which was created by the God of Jesus. If we give up the foundational beliefs of our moral traditions, we should expect the entire superstructure to fall but we seem to think we can save the second-story bedroom we like so much even as the rest of the structure falls down around it and underneath it. The very idea that the ordinary person is worth as much as the rich or the powerful is no longer viable in our brave, new world and will likely be violated often and brutally in the near future. It's one good example of a moral truth in a world created by a God Who has adopted all human beings, but it's only an obscure cultural accident once man-centered ideologies come to dominance. All efforts to re-found Christian morality outside of the context of a specific universe which was created by the God of Jesus Christ have failed. Kant's efforts to transcendentalize his favorite Christian moral beliefs failed as much as did Nietzsche's efforts to return to some sort of pagan warrior ethics, which efforts produced a botch that had a strong Christian aroma not quite covered up by the general smell of rot.

God gave us the truths we imagine to define the possibilities which include His existence and His attributes. Even most Christians seem to implicitly believe there to be a range of possible gods, all sharing some common abstract properties. When we prove the existence of God or try to understand the truths He embedded in this world, we retreat to some abstract world where we prove the existence of all those possible gods and then we return to history to say we believe in the God of who revealed Himself partially to Moses and then more fully in Jesus of Nazareth. But God is God. God is not just one realized possibility out of a set of possible gods. God is God. All truths are in God but He is free to create any of an absolute infinity of worlds manifesting specific subsets of those truths of which He is the eternal and ongoing source.

We inhabit the specific world He did choose to shape from the Primordial Universe He had chosen to create. Let me try to summarize:

> There are aspects of nature that can be seen only when you make the proper assumptions as to the beginning and end of the physical universe as well as the purpose for which it came to be. Many of the moral truths of the West are truths only if we assume the physical universe was created by the God of Jesus, the only God and hence the only possible God. If we fail to see the universe as a particular creation of the most holy Trinity, the moral truths of the West are degraded to cultural accidents that might be shed when it seems convenient to the power-brokers and decision-makers of our society. We might well lose many of these rights we imagine to be inherently a part of being human. We who are poor and without political power might well become materiel for the use of those who are wealthy and powerful.

The world actually became a different world 2,000 years ago because God chose freely to act in a specific way, incarnating His Son, God becoming man that man might share the life of God. Since the world is more a story than simply a space-scape and time-scape, it actually moves with more freedom than not, coming freshly alive with each event which is narrated by God and lived by one or more of His creatures, but the Incarnation of the Son of God, His life and mission, His death on the Cross, and His Resurrection pushed the story of this world in a different direction from any which man could have predicted. The Son of God became our brother and the Father adopted us all. We remain human animals but we're now marked as God's special property. When that mark is not seen, abortion becomes an option. When that mark is not seen, experimentation upon cloned human embryos becomes possible along with slavery, extermination of unwanted human beings, and countless other acts of exploitation.

I admit to a fear that maybe the radical animal rights advocates were correct all along. I strongly oppose the way we raise farm animals nowadays, though I confess to buying the cheap beef and chicken at the grocery store. I strongly oppose experimentation upon animals that causes them significant amounts of pain, but I likely use medicines and other products developed or tested with such cruel experimentation upon animals. Now I wonder if I should be opposed to the use of those dumb brutes even in psychological tests, maze-running by rats and the like. Since we're animals and the scientists doing these experiments certainly know we're animals, it seems to me that we let those scientists lead us onto a slippery ramp many years ago. Without our status as the brothers and sisters of Christ, there are no absolute barriers that allow scientists to torture rats but prevent them from torturing human children, starting with cloned embryos. Maybe God never wanted us to torture rats.

This much is true: a Christian lives in but a single world though he might see it dimly. There is but one set of moral rules imposed by God, in His original act of creation and in His ongoing act of creation. We need to consider the possibility that we have lost sight of our absolute moral obligations to the adopted children of God partly because we long ago failed to appreciate our moral obligations to any living creature which feels pain and which has a specific nature suited to a particular life – which life is unlikely to be one lived in pens in modern-day live-stock factories or in the cages of a laboratory.

Even in the best of times, our untutored instincts are not a sufficient guide for our behavior even towards other human beings. We have strong instincts against killing other human beings, but those instincts are far from absolute, as anyone knows from the morning paper or from the slightest of history courses. In fact, wolves have much stronger instincts than human beings against killing other members of their own species.

Observation tells us that members of social species, including most human beings, value highly the lives of other members of their species. But that value is far from the absolute value which Christians place upon human life, and there are some human predators who are quite willing to sacrifice other human beings for their schemes, often schemes which supposedly are targeted at a moral goal as when Roosevelt and Truman ordered attacks upon civilian populations supposedly for the purpose of defeating murderously aggressive regimes in Germany and Japan. Christians place absolute value on human life because God has revealed His plans for us and He has adopted each and every one of us. You don't touch wrongly that which God has taken as His special property.[5]

---

[5]We Americans are clearly not about to take up any radical non-violence. Our claims to be a moral country imply that we should adopt some rules of behavior such as the Christian just-war theory of our ancestors. But such a theory would condemn American actions in most of the wars against native Americans as well as our attacks, by air, upon civilian targets during World War II and most wars since then. See Yoder's *When War is Unjust* for a fair-minded appraisal of just-war theory on both intellectual and historical grounds. It's interesting that George Patton, no bleeding-heart liberal, wrote in his memoir of World War II, *War as I Knew It* that he'd argued against those

Non-Christians, and many who claim to be Christians, have no such moral insights corresponding to the commandments and revelations of Christ. Some think they do because they're still running off their Christian inheritance, as were Immanuel Kant and Adam Smith and so many others in recent centuries. Nor do non-Christians have a reason to believe that the life of a carpenter is worth as much as the life of a Senator. We have this delusion that the Christian moral beliefs of our ancestors are natural to mankind if only everyone were raised to a proper appreciation for American-style prosperity and for American-style machine politics.

Think of it in terms that Flannery O'Connor used in her masterpiece, *Wise Blood.* We have decayed into a people who think we can form a Christian Church without the inconvenient presence of Jesus Christ. We think we can turn away from Jesus Christ and keep those of His commandments which we find to be convenient in securing our comfort, safety, and prosperity. But we can't. Without a belief that the God of Jesus Christ created this physical universe, the earth has decayed to being a disordered collection of places poisoned by ideologies, places bereft of the hope given to those who centered their attention upon Jesus.

But now I return to the very existence of God.

Any proofs of God's existence have lost any validity they once had, mostly because valid proofs depend upon an acceptance of the revelations of God which tell us He exists apart from this universe but there are also some technical problems. For example, modern understandings of infinity and of the physical universe leave open certain possibilities that were considered impossible by Aristotle and his followers, including St. Thomas Aquinas within this context.

Nearly all of the arguments for the existence of God based on the Aristotelian assumption that an infinity cannot be realized look to be invalid. Arguments depending upon the impossibility of a regression to infinity could be validly reconstructed by allowing for the richness of different sizes of infinities, but this points to the problem – God is God and He's a Creator as well as being a Shaper of a particular universe. We should be wary of any arguments that depend upon a definition, a limitation, of God's Being or

bombing raids, believing them to be immoral but also telling his superiors that those attacks on civilian targets were hurting the effort to defeat the Nazis as soon as possible. That raises the likelihood that our civilian leaders were murdering civilians as a terrorist activity, to break down the will of conquered people and conquering people alike so that the American government could reshape them after the war.

His Powers. In a phrase: it doesn't seem to be all that hard to conceive of God creating an universe infinite in time or space. Modern physics, in the equations of the theory of general relativity, allows for an infinite universe though it's far from clear that such would be consistent with the known properties of our universe. But I'm not about to bet my faith in God on Aristotle's opinion that an infinity could not be realized in the physical world.

But, there's a stronger possibility of an infinity of sorts being realized in this universe. There's some reason to believe that physical constants are truly and absolutely random – having an infinite stream of digits with no patterns. This is not to say that we can ever prove such a speculation but the values of the most important fundamental constants, such as those in the equations describing gravitational force or electromagnetic force, show no signs of patterns and have to be calculated digit by digit by rigorous and highly disciplined experimentation. There's no reason at this time to believe that these streams of digits come to an end. We could never be sure if this is true though it could be proved false by the unlikely event of scientists finding finite values for all the important physical constants. Even without knowing for sure if those physical constants are truly random, doubt has been cast upon the Aristotelian claim that an infinity cannot be realized and a doubtful claim is not a good basis for any sort of proof. But I think the basic proofs could be usefully restated by consideration of the nature of absolute infinity. The construction of such proofs would require a man educated in both theology and transfinite set theory.[6]

But, from the Christian point-of-view, the main problem with the various proofs of God's existence is that such abstract proofs are meaningless because God is not simply a possibility, a being who could or could not exist. Nor is God simply one of a set of possible gods, the one who happens to exist. Outside of the context of a worldview founded upon God's self-revelations, proofs of God's existence are rather odd.

The strongest and most coherent versions of the classic proofs of God's existence are found in the writings of Aquinas and are firmly embedded in a Catholic Christian viewpoint. The obvious question is: Why develop proofs that God exists if they really can't be used to prove any such thing? Moreover, they can be dangerous out of context. A well-intentioned Christian

---

[6]See the next section for a very brief discussion of transfinite set theory in this context.

theologian can set out to prove God exists by use of his finite and fallible mental operations, but this opens up the possibility that we can prove that God doesn't exist. This has actually happened as Michael Buckley has discussed in his work on the development of modern atheism. In retrospect, we have to wonder how any Christian could come to believe God's existence could be proved, or disproved, by way of abstract arguments or by way of proofs from the physical world.

All of this comes together in the vision of a fragmented human being moving fitfully around the marketplaces of the modern world, except now we can see those marketplaces are typically in climate-controlled buildings which impress us with the accomplishments of human architects and engineers and steel-workers. Arguably, this fragmentation is part and parcel of Protestantism. In that form of Christianity, there will inevitably be regions of God's Creation from which the Lord Himself is excluded, most politely. This creates pressures towards Deism even on the part of those many Protestants who have struggled to hold on to an orthodox belief in the Holy Trinity and the human and divine natures of Christ. Such scandalous beliefs could be taken seriously only when revealed to us by God and by way of a story in which only an incarnate Person of God could participate, but that story has to be taken in its concrete wholeness. We don't have a Lord who simply created a human body directly from the elements but rather a Lord who drew His flesh from Mary, a Lord who developed in Mary's noble and immaculate womb, a Lord who suckled at her holy breasts, a Lord whose human moral character was formed under the guidance of St. Mary and St. Joseph. These are not incidental details such as the color of clothes He wore.

Some would suggest God could have instead provided us with a theological treatise revealing His Triune nature, but we're story-tellers when it comes to the great truths and theologians or philosophers work only to settle some background issues or to fill in some detail. This is exactly what one might expect if all truth issues out of the God who is three Persons in one Divine Nature. That is, though we human beings are born with natures and can only struggle towards person-hood, it would seem that person-hood is an ultimate truth of the greatest importance and greatest power. We can't ascend to God by way of Socratic dialogs – however useful those might be. Our ascension is itself a series of events to be narrated and God cleared the path for that ascension by the events of the earthly life of His Son.

The incarnation of Christ was not an invasion of the divine into enemy territory but rather an act by which the Son of God, already present with the Father and the Holy Spirit, took on a particular creaturely nature. The Bible makes this clear as do the traditional creeds. The Protestant Fathers fragmented human society into a religious realm, a political realm, a private family realm, and a commercial realm. This fragmentation led quickly to the idea that this division of human society, hence of the human being's deepest parts, was inherently true rather than being a provisional and practical division of human responsibilities. In the eyes of many modern men, God is restricted to church sanctuaries and to His supposed home in Heaven. We modern Christians – even Catholics – talk as if God is more present in Heaven than He is on this earth. That's Deism and not Christianity.

God is necessarily fully present in any existent thing and even the empty places of our universe. If He were not fully present, that thing or that empty place would cease to exist. A compartmentalized human being sees himself as being, independent of God in at least some of his parts and, hence, he cannot gain a view of a true world, unified and coherent and complete, and usually has no motivation to even try to gain such a view. A Protestant, or a Protestantized Catholic – as many are, is not only allowed to serve God and mammon both, he is bound to do so by the fragmented nature of the human society he lives in.

At least as Aquinas presented them, proofs of the existence of God are valid only for those who have a view of a world which was created by an all-powerful God Who is still present in His Creation, present in an intimate way understood well by St. Augustine as a theologian and psychologist but not understood in philosophical terms until Aquinas developed his existentialist philosophy of being. In particular, Aquinas was very aware of the real presence of Christ in the Eucharist.

St. Thomas Aquinas wrote a number of hymns and poems to worship the Blessed Sacrament, the very Body of our Savior, Jesus Christ. Aquinas, one of the most powerful thinkers our race has produced, was a true priest of Jesus Christ as well as being a street-preacher, and he was devoted to the Blessed Sacrament. This devotion was not something that he put on when he left his writing desk, as if he was taking off a theologian's robe and putting on the garb of a simple believer. Aquinas was a simple believer, first and foremost, just as I try to be. The foundation of Thomism is the body of simple beliefs which are also held by those Portuguese widows in black dress, yes, the ones praying with their rosary beads. The foundation of the thought expressed in this book is that same body of simple beliefs which I claim to be the foundation of sciences which can understand the forces which shape galaxies and the protoplasm of our bodies. Those simple beliefs are held before understanding can begin, but that understanding covers all aspects of the world and not some imaginary sub-world of subjective beliefs as so many modern human beings would have it.

Lord, I believe. Help my unbelief.

John Paul II told us repeatedly, "Do not be afraid," and a believer in the real presence in the Eucharist has no reason to be afraid, though, we're weak and frail creatures indeed and will fear no matter how much we're reminded that God not only created the world but He's still creating it even to the point of turning bread and wine into the body and blood of the Son.

Do not be afraid even if scientists discover you're really an ape which puts on prideful airs.

Do not be afraid even if scientists have shown it highly probable that human beings have no mind-stuff or soul-stuff, at least none which does anything important or interesting.

Do not be afraid even if historians and Biblical exegetes find that the writing of Holy Scripture was a messy process in which the human element often seems to obscure the words of God.

Man is not inherently fragmented, though he is born only with a potential for unified, coherent, and complete being; man is truly and culpably fragmented when his being is structured by an inappropriate or inadequate moral order such as that of modern ideologies. Let me confuse many modern men with this strange claim:

> Of all human thinkers, partakers in the Eucharistic Rite are the ones who have most willingly and most enthusiastically accepted the constraints of a physical universe created by a God who is transcendental in His own being but has made Himself immanent in the acts-of-being by which He continually creates the universe.

Still, formal proofs of the philosophical type have a real value. Under the proper circumstances, they can help to clear up various abstract issues and can give us the confidence that our minds can deal with such powerful truths as the existence of God. It would be nice if we could recover a sense of coherence between human thought and the existence of the God of Jesus, but we're not in a position to guess at the form of proofs of God's existence which can be set in a new Christian worldview which is founded upon revealed truths and also considers the mountains of empirical data and the knowledge which has come from mapping out those mountains. But the most important point is: we cannot prove to ourselves or others that the God of Jesus Christ lives unless we struggle to live as Christians in the most ordinary aspects of our lives, unless we pray and worship as Christians. We even have to learn how to die as Christians instead of allowing ourselves to be treated as targets for various exploiters, many of them well-intentioned for whatever that's worth.

I'm trying to give some hints about the sorts of thinking which might be involved if Christians were to regain their intellectual confidence and their spiritual energy and move forward to remind their fellow-men that this is a world and it's a world created by the God of Jesus, the most holy Trinity.

I believe that I might understand.

Can We Even Speak of God?

It could be of some interest to speak about some particular idea from modern intellectual developments which might play into our understanding of God. In a somewhat playful way, I'll choose an unprovable principle of a modern field of mathematics called transfinite set theory.

Transfinite set theory is, very roughly speaking, the study of numbers which can be big even by the standards of modern mathematicians. By those standards, ordinary infinity is pretty small and easily manageable by well-established techniques.

The biggest boy on the transfinite block is called absolute infinity. In *Infinity and the Mind*, the set-theorist Rudy Rucker pointed out a dangerous but interesting analogy between absolute infinity and the views of God held by the negative theologians of Christianity, including Aquinas. The analogy comes out most clearly in an unprovable principle, the reflection principle of transfinite set theory. That principle says that you can never prove any statement which truly refers to absolute infinity – anything you can say or prove about absolute infinity will be true of some lesser infinity and cannot be part of a unique description of absolute infinity. Taken literally as an analogy, the implication is that any property we can ascribe to God, even the most superlative, could refer to a creature He could have made.

This would seem also to imply that we cannot say anything uniquely true about God, but remember that mathematics says nothing about existence. Since God is His own act of existence, then mathematics says nothing about God, but it may say something about all that we can perceive, all the effects of God which are actual or which are conceptually possible to the human mind. We imagine all that's conceivable to us and God is still greater than that, but God is not conceivable as such. This seems similar to the claims of the negative theologians of Christian thought, including Aquinas and Augustine.

Mathematics can be used to discuss formal relationships even about such concrete matters as relationships inside a human community. God's existence, the Supreme Act-of-being, is beyond any mathematical proof. It would seem reasonable to believe that His existence is beyond any proof. It's when Christian theologians forgot that Aquinas started with his faith in the God of Jesus Christ that they engaged in activities that led to the development of modern forms of skepticism and disbelief. Equivalently, they forgot that God, from a creaturely viewpoint, is the Supreme Act-of-Being, a being of necessary existence. Forgetting this, they spoke and thought of God primarily as an essence, allowing them to deal with God as if He were a creature Whose existence could be verified by a safari into the deepest jungle of all.

Given that God is a community of Persons with a shared Act-of-being, He can speak to us, sometimes as Father or Son or Holy Spirit, and sometimes as a communion of the three Persons. This means that, unlike a mathematical concept, the Triune God can reveal truths about Himself which are unreachable to the human mind, starting with the truth of His very existence.

It seems contradictory to talk about concepts that are fully and literally beyond the reach of the human mind. Yet, transfinite set theorists posit the existence of absolute infinity though it can't be defined. It's the number of which nothing greater can be thought. Those who have wandered about the obscure byways of Christian thought will realize that I've stated this in a manner analogical to St. Anselm's vague and strange description of God in his ontological proof.

Anselm's proof involves a sophisticated version of the claim that if a valid concept is described by the phrase, "Of which nothing greater can be conceived," then God exists. Anselm's claim was that we could not conceive of this inconceivable entity, God, unless He truly exists. I doubt he intended it as a proof which would be convincing to a human being who didn't already believe in God, at least in a tentative and piously speculative way.

Anselm did not say anything more outrageous than modern mathematicians are saying in proposing the concept of absolute infinity and then saying, essentially, it's far beyond human mental powers but we can still speak of its existence without being able to say anything that would define it. If mathematicians are right that absolute infinity exists, then it becomes a known truth that cannot be proved by human mental effort, cannot be captured by any meaningful system of axioms.

I think that Anselm's proof might work in the context of a properly perceived world. Before you can have a concept, "Of which nothing greater can be conceived," you have to have a good understanding of the sorts of things and ideas which can be conceived. Within a worldview, it makes sense to speak of what lies outside and – so to speak – encompasses all that lies within the worldview proper. The sense of such a proof would be lost if that worldview were to be lost.

Similar statements can be made about much of our scientific and mathematical knowledge including the concept of absolute infinity. In particular, absolute infinity can make some small amount of sense to those who have an understanding of the properties of simple sequential infinity (the limit of 1,2,3,...) and the reasons why mathematicians say there are infinities of different sizes. The required background knowledge for a more profound understanding of the insights of transfinite set theory is far greater than that, requiring years of difficult study and probably more years of practice and contemplation as a set theorist.

So, What is a Proof?

There are a lot of bad proofs around, and some of them have won some sort of limited fame for philosophers or economists or scientists or sundry lunatics. But matters are confused because proof means one thing in mathematics and other things in other fields. To be sure, there are philosophers and theologians who have tried to prove various moral claims or even metaphysical claims by way of techniques which ape those of mathematics.

I'm arguing, both directly and in the very way I'm writing this book, that the best proofs might sometimes be narrative proofs where an entire worldview is the proof of its constituent beliefs. Of course, a narrative is always a rendering of real events or at least real possibilities and, thus, any narrative proof of the existence of the God of Jesus Christ implies and is implied by a concrete Christian life of witness to that God.

This oneness of belief and practice is an established truth of Christianity which can be learned from the lives of the saints and from the concrete rules for the traditional Christian religious orders: the Rule of St. Benedict, the Rule of St. Francis, etc. Most importantly, it can be experienced by participation in an active church community.

Our beliefs and our practices are one and that means that, given our concrete and biological nature, the most penetrating and meaningful proofs involve practice. Practice implies a worldview and is implied by a worldview. In most cases, they'll grow up side-by-side in a complex process which is invisible to most of those who are participating. Given this, I treat a Christian worldview as encapsulating a body of Christian practices. As a result, I regard a deeply held Christian worldview as being a narrative proof of the existence of the God of Jesus Christ. This narrative proof is valid only if it runs parallel to a life of corresponding practices, however imperfect that life might be.

I'm claiming that the best understanding of God and His Creation comes by way of a worldview intertwined with Christian practices. To a Christian, a worldview is a complex perception of the physical universe created by the God of Jesus. This physical universe takes on, in a provisional way, the properties of a world: unity and coherence and completeness. Such a world is perceived as the image of thoughts of a God who is fully unified and coherent and complete. That world is truly such a world only in the view of God, a personal God, a God of three Persons who has revealed His existence and His inner life, facts we could not reach by formal proof.

In the tradition of Christian thought, particularly the thought of St. Thomas Aquinas, we can understand God in an analogical manner through His effects, that is, through His actions in creating and sustaining this world. By understanding God's world, we're allowing into our minds thoughts which God manifested in that world, thoughts which God wished us to have. When they come together into a coherent whole, those thoughts form a worldview, as I've defined it.

A man who can bring a worldview into being, who can perceive a world where there was once chaos, can – by that very process – begin to particularize the properties of a world in his own being. He can become unified and coherent and complete – defectively so, but God can make up the difference. This transformation can happen just because the world we inhabit is an image of the thoughts of a God who is three Persons. We take the thoughts of those Persons into our being, reshaping our innermost selves and our behaviors alike to conform to those thoughts, and we become person-like.

To shape ourselves in this way is to shape ourselves in a manner analogical to Jesus of Nazareth, the human nature taken up and perfected by the Son of God – who is a true person. To hold a valid worldview is to carry out an act analogical to God's creation of this world, that act of creation being not possible to an abstract Deity or an impersonal Watchmaker but only to a God who is a Person of free-will. And we can attain a state of creaturely person-hood by imitating God in His acts of creating this world. A child comes to realize the nature of adult activities by imitating those he knows about. We can come to realize the nature of God's Creation by imitating His acts-of-being, by bringing God's world into view as best we can. By doing this, we restructure our own selves, gaining some measure of unity and coherence and completeness. We attain this higher state not by looking inwards as do the religions of the Orient but rather by looking out at our environments and struggling to see them as God's universe and then as His world.

To see this world created by God is to hold a very substantial body of thoughts which God wished us to have.

5 The Primordial Universe is Born

5.1 A Narrative

In the beginning God created the Primordial Universe and it was simple and beautiful. There was nothing but the Primordial Universe itself nor was there when for it was a homogeneously simple entity: a Universe with no things but only its own being, a realization of a metaphysical conception of a simple and beautiful entity. All was so symmetrical, so elegantly simple, that it had no parts and occupied no space. All had come into being as but one entity – the Primordial Universe.

The Primordial Universe had come to be and no time had passed, no time would pass for the perfection of symmetry was such that no change occurred.

And God said that it was good. It was beautiful and Father, Son, and Holy Spirit were one Creator taking pleasure in the embodiment of an image of a limited being, but one perfect within its limitations. There was no corruption because there was no change, no freedom for all was but one entity that had to be what it was once God had created it as an image of certain thoughts of His.

5.2 A Commentary

Let me remind the reader of the meaning of a few terms as I'll be using them:

Primordial Universe Not a collection of things and not even thing-like in its own being, the Primordial Universe is the basic entity which, in my tale, God created as a bridge between what-is-not and what-is. Unlike the concrete universe in which we live, this primordial entity is potentially eternal in that it is best imagined, at least by me, as timeless because it is so symmetrical, so sheerly homogeneous, that no changes would take place in it. It could also be shaped by God into the incorruptible and everlasting universe which the resurrected will inhabit. In fact, this other universe might be running parallel to ours. Scientifically, it makes no sense to speak of multiple universes since science is the study of particular, existing things, but metaphysics and theology allow the possibility of multiple universes coming at the same time from the Primordial Universe.

Universe The Particularized Universe as we know it has come into being as God imposed constraints of various sorts upon the Primordial Universe that it might become thing-like and capable of giving rise to other specific things, even living things. The universe, as it is commonly known, is what most people would associate with the term in normal talk, that is, it's the place where we and our planet and our galaxy are located. It's a collection of things, of galaxies and gas clouds and planets and black holes and maybe some strange things not yet observed. But it's primarily a thing in its own right, the primary thing created by God as He chose to shape a concrete universe from the Primordial Universe.

world A world is both the Primordial Universe and the concrete universe, viewed through a human mind by way of a moral structuring process. It's unified, coherent, and complete. A world may not in fact be true, but it has to be true to the human person who inhabits, or thinks he inhabits it, and it has to be true to all that he knows, or could be expected to know, about the universe, the Primordial Universe, and the worlds inhabited by those other human persons around him. Only God can see the world truly but He has chosen to create a universe where multiple provisional worlds would come into being. Presumably, He feels that human worldviewing enriches the world in its true unity and coherence and completeness – the world that only He sees.

No one can more than imagine if the Primordial Universe came into being as a stable entity – unified and coherent and complete and bereft of things and life. It's not even clear if that's a meaningful question from the human viewpoint as the Primordial Universe of my story is so symmetrical, so homogeneous, that nothing could have happened in it and, hence, no time could have passed. At least, no time could have passed so far as human beings can imagine or measure time.

The universe is a story told by God. At the same time, there's clearly a metaphysics underlying the concrete universe and the conjecture of a Primordial Universe is one way of cleanly separating that metaphysics that it might be more clearly imagined and analyzed. We should remember that the development of this universe can be imaginatively run in reverse, as cosmological physicists do all the time, and that reverse play does not point directly to God's creation of contingent being, but it does strongly imply the existence of an immediately earlier state of this universe which I've called the Primordial Universe. Yet, I'll mention here, and not again, that there might have been earlier states, perhaps of a nature beyond human imagination. And there might have been states in between the Primordial Universe and the Particularized Universe.

While God could have created any of an infinite number of concrete universes, it's harder to justify the possibility of other sorts of Primordial Universes. A different Primordial Universe would imply a different metaphysics. And that raises the related question which might be easier to deal with: Is there only one true mathematics possible? Since mathematics seems to be islands of order in an absolutely infinite sea of disorder – possibly the real-number line or perhaps something beyond human imagination, this raises the possibility that there are multiple possible true mathematics; a different group of islands might provide a different but workable mathematics. The reader, who is likely to be as confused as I am at this point, should be starting to understand why it is that a world has to be tentatively viewed and tested in one complex, recursive stream of processes. In practice, this stream has to be built up by way of trial-and-error in a manner analogous to the development of the universe.

So far as I can tell, the modern academic styles of philosophical and theological analysis will lead to abstractions of abstractions, constricting the human mind so that it can't perceive the self-revealed God in His concreteness rising above all creaturely possibilities including those of abstract reasoning. This strengthens the forces which fragment the human being in his mind and soul, which fragment all our views of the universe, preventing us from seeing a world. In other words, philosophy has been descending into the realm of dangerous, mind-destroying gobbledy-gook by following the methods of Descartes, Kant, and others who destroyed all coherent views of the universe by claiming that human beings can magically reach truth by ways other than explorations, empirical and contemplative, of what exists and, hence, what gives us truths, though not all truths. Truths which lie beyond the things of this universe can come to us only by revelation or by an active imaginative extrapolation from a world, that is, from the universe as a whole, with that universe being seen as subject to some plausible sort of moral order. Unless we first see a world, we cannot even see a valid metaphysics, a Primordial Universe as I'm telling this story. And to see this world, we must abstract but only by drawing out the truths we can perceive in the things of this universe, this phase of God's Creation in which we human beings were born and in which we develop.

We're more profoundly a part of this universe than most people, non-Christian and Christian alike, will wish to acknowledge. We're particular entities of the universe and cannot be on the outside looking in. Many modern thinkers would accept the view of William James that we cannot see a world because we see only individual things. James spoke of pluralities of worlds precisely because he could not imagine, or at least could not believe in, the possibility of one world visible to God. I speak of multiple worlds precisely because God seems to welcome the moral-ordering activities, as well as the universe-exploring activities, of creatures inhabiting a universe – ultimately a world, that He has created and that only He can see. We can see worlds because God has created a world that invites us to explore its richness and complexity and even to add to that richness and complexity.

We can see a world if we're truthful in accepting the best knowledge about the universe and if we have a plausible moral order through which to make sense of this knowledge. The Primordial Universe is another kettle of fish, as they used to say in Beantown. The Primordial Universe lies under, over, and within this universe and all the things it contains. We cannot view such an entity directly. We are made of this pure stuff which cannot be seen, which arguably cannot exist so far as the human senses are concerned, but I claim – along with many thinkers in history – that the pure being that lies between what-is-not and thing-like being can be seen by a well-disciplined and yet openly creative human imagination.

I'm not advocating a grandiose style of metaphysical reasoning but rather a modest style appropriate to our creaturely status and consistent with what we know of the concrete universe. Einstein's General Theory of

Relativity, extrapolated backward seems to move asymptotically towards a point where there's nothing but a homogeneous and symmetrical entity which is not matter nor energy nor field nor any combination of the three. It has no extension and endures no change so that it has no part of time.

There's a phase of creation which is absolutely beyond our direct observations and measurements. Then, God expanded something out of the Primordial Universe and imposed a particular order that a particular concrete universe might come into being. From there, the universe which God called very good, began to move along with some limited freedom and even gave rise to creatures with some limited moral freedom.

As St. Thomas Aquinas noted[1], the first science, metaphysics, uses the specific sciences, such as physics and biology. As I interpret his statement, a metaphysical system of thought based on defective or inadequate understandings of physics and biology would be defective. A metaphysical system appropriate for a human being living in this universe must be built from basic concepts consistent with what is known from the specific sciences – what we might call the empirical sciences. We have one universe to work from and modern physics seems to indicate a strange fact which would be more disturbing to modern scientists and philosophers if they were not so dedicated to keeping God out of His own universe:

> Modern physics indicates that the universe has an eerie tendency to collapse back to a chaotic and homogeneous state which I've called the Primordial Universe. The underlying particles of matter which make up particular things would collapse into each other, annihilating each other and melting the universe back to its primordial form, if not for behavior which seems to be imposed upon primordial being. This will be discussed in more detail in the next chapter, but I claim that our particular universe looks to be a result of imposing a particular set of ad-hoc rules upon the Primordial Universe.

Let me be more specific. Philosophers and scientists often debate various ways of viewing physical laws. A typical strategy in such a debate will involve an attack upon David Hume's view that physical laws have something of the characteristics of habit rather than law in the sense of being

[1]See Chapter 4, page 35 of the second volume of *Summa Contra Gentiles* in the edition referenced in the bibliography.

necessary and mathematically well-determined. Some people consider this a disturbing prospect. If laws cannot be derived from elementary principles usually statable as mathematical equations, then modern people seem to be on shaky ground. The particularized universe itself would be on shaky ground. So it would seem to some.

But that would be a wrong direction for our thoughts. If this universe has been created by a personal God and not just the God of the philosophers, then it'll reflect some of His preferences, even to His preference that human beings could have a chance to exist. Some of the principles shaping and constraining this universe might not be derivable from any set of mathematical axioms or elegant metaphysical principles though we Christians would be bound to believe they'll lead to the particularization of a world which can be seen to be orderly and rational. Many seek to protect their faith by seeing a God so radically separated from His universe that He stands outside it and manipulates it the way a machinist manipulates the lathes and hunks of steel in a metal fabrication shop. This is a very bad way to try to understand this world of order and disorder partly because it leaves most plausible the Jamesian suggestion that God is not all powerful. A Jamesian considering the existence of the Christian God has to see that Lord as working with materials which are not under His total control. He is then led to conjecture:

> We cannot really reconcile the belief that God is all-good with the belief that He is all-powerful.

We modern men are all Jamesians to some extent. If we were more orthodox in our Christian beliefs, we would fail to even understand the point being made by the likes of William James and his successors in this line of thought. Even in the decay we share with the neo-pagans around us, we still should be able to see a deep problem, though it might take some effort. With that effort, we can realize that we can't understand God's plans and His work without direct revelations. As soon as we have those direct revelations from the God of Jesus Christ, we can strengthen our faith, hoping that we will also understand more clearly.

How could we have ever imagined we have either the right or the mental capacity to judge God's world? Once we start down that road, we can only conclude that God is not fully competent in His power or not perfect in His goodness.

We need a faith that God is both all-good and all-powerful before we can even see the world let alone understand it, though our faith might be provisional in a psychological sense. God most certainly does not forbid us to ask tough questions of Him within the context of a living faith, though we must work all the harder to keep alive our faith if we do feel a call to ask those tough questions. Prayer and frequent attendance at community worship become still more necessary for those exploring God's world in light of the various difficulties which are to be encountered.

6 Between Perfect Order and a More Complex Order

6.1 Random Numbers and Other Facts

There are some misconceptions that some people have about mathematics and the role it plays in investigating empirical entities and empirical events. Such people are inclined to take mathematical descriptions as magic. This is true even of many people who have taken college courses in mathematics or the physical sciences. There is no magic. Mathematical equations express purely formal truths which are independent of context so far as the Particularized Universe goes but probably not independent of context so far as the Primordial Universe goes. A particular set of equations have to be chosen and then the context is supplied to the extent possible by way of setting the parameters and then setting various other values such as boundary values – starting values, such as starting positions. And then the equations have to be applied with seasoned judgment. Let's be rough and label all of this activity as the setting of initial conditions.

It is most certainly true that in all of these activities, men are making particular mathematical models in analogy to the Creator making a particular universe. There's no rhyme or reason to the current belief of cosmological physicists that the replacement of initial conditions by extraordinarily complex equations makes a Creator less necessary. As Stanley Jaki has argued for years, it's the particularity of the universe which points to a Creator. It's ultimately an empirical question as to the human model which can best help us to understand the creative work of God. That best human model might be an extremely complex mathematical model but that model would be just as particular as a simple model with many initial conditions. In fact, the nature of the physical constants would seem to indicate the proper model would be relatively simple but dependent upon initial conditions. A complete discussion of this profound issue is well beyond the scope of this book. The interested reader should read Jaki's book, *The Relevance of Physics* as well as his various books addressing the interaction of belief and empirical thought. Any reader, other than a professional physicist, who wishes to explore this area in depth should also read *The Great Design* by the physicist Robert Adair for a good review of real physics rather than the pseudo-philosophical discussions of exotic ideas which pass for physics in many popular science books.

In any case, I'll keep my discussions clean by assuming that a simple version of a Big Bang cosmology is valid, one using relatively simple mathematical models and depending heavily upon initial conditions. I'll not attempt a discussion of those models, discussing only particular observed facts or aspects common to a general version of those models as might be found in the introductory book by John Barrow and Joseph Silk – *The Left Hand of Creation*.

Without initial conditions, an equation is no more than an expression of a formal relationship, even if it has so strong a potential connection to physical reality as Newton's or Einstein's laws of motion.[1] With initial conditions, an equation becomes an expression of a formal, quantitative relationship within a specific context. The contextualized equation itself still cannot describe all aspects of concrete being. There's no real problem with the radical but rational idea that there are quantitative aspects even to our feelings of love, but those feelings are not just the mathematically describable interactions of organs and hormones. Nor is the simplest physical object, an electron perhaps, fully describable by its quantitative description. Quantitative properties don't exhaust any sort of concrete being.

We should not expect the basic building blocks of our universe to necessarily resemble the universe at our level of direct awareness. For example, our universe of time and space and matter might be built of physical components which don't have any aspects which are space-like or time-like. In terms of equations, it might be, for example, that there are very general sets

[1] In the general situation, there will actually be multiple families of equations which have to be chosen from and those families have general parameters and cannot be used directly. Those equations are parametrized and then initial conditions are set. This represents physical reality as if it were a set of problems in freshman physics, but that's not a bad way of approaching many problems so long as you always keep the real situation in the back of your mind.

of equations that describe some sort of pure created being missing many aspects of our universe, such as time- and space-like traits. Those traits were imposed by way of initial conditions and by the imposition of arbitrary properties as God shaped the Primordial Universe into the particularized entity which is our universe. It's reasonable to believe – and strongly implied by the Big Bang model of cosmological physics – that some of the ancient pagans as well as the authors of the book of Genesis were right in speaking as if God shaped our world from pre-existing being. A Christian should also believe that God created that pre-existing being. There are good reasons to keep the two processes of creation and shaping separate even if they might have been carried out in one step by God. One reason is that mathematics forces us to keep them separate just because mathematics can describe certain aspects of being, including the shaping that leads to particularity, but cannot describe the process of creation nor can it dictate the initial conditions imposed upon these processes.

However the process is started, it's likely we won't find time and space at the most basic levels of created stuff. I'll make a claim that largely relies on my interpretation of powerful arguments which Stanley Jaki has been making for years with few bothering to listen to him:

> It's a distortion of reason and of what's known of the physical world to see the Big Bang as being some sort of creation. If we follow the history of the universe back in time, we don't see a creation and could not possibly see such an event even if God were to try to reveal it to us. We can discuss such an event abstractly based largely upon contemplation of the nature of this universe, but we cannot locate it in time and space nor even at some alleged beginning of time. What do we see if we follow the history of the universe back in time? We see a process by which things disappear. Particularity evaporates at extremely high densities of energies, that is – high temperatures. Still moving back in time, we see the entire universe melting down into a homogeneous and chaotic form of being.[2]

But mathematics and physics, as conventionally defined, do not have any role in describing such a state of being in any detailed way. As philoso-

[2]Father George LeMaître, the Catholic priest who was a co-discoverer of the expansion of our universe, the Big Bang model, also considered that beginning of the expansion to be a shaping of a 'primeval atom' rather than a creation event.

phers have known since at least Pythagoras: mathematics and physics can provide useful terms and concepts for describing other states of being than the ones which we finite creatures can directly perceive. I even suggest at times in this book that mathematics, in its exploration of infinities far larger than the one we normally think about, and physics, in its exploration of the process of differentiation which produced this particular universe, overlap greatly with metaphysics. Modern mathematics and physics provide many tools and concepts for a generation of metaphysicians which has not yet been born, but that birthing process requires that we do what we can to start building bridges between realms of human knowledge which have been inappropriately split for ideological purposes. And I'll suggest again and again that it was St. Thomas Aquinas who understood that there are some absolutely unimpeachable truths of metaphysics (mostly very general principles such as the self-identity of being and its resistance to self-contradiction), but – this is a very big but – metaphysics, as a field of human knowledge, is dependent upon our knowledge of specific sciences, such as physics and biology but also history and other disciplined ways of studying some aspect of the universe. Where else could we physical creatures learn much of anything?

We can make sense of modern physics and evolutionary biology by using the Thomistic theory of knowledge as well as the Thomistic understanding of the nature of the act-of-being executed by the Supreme Act-of-being which is God. That is, St. Thomas Aquinas, though believing in the relatively static universe that could be seen by the Greek and Medieval scientists, provided us with a metaphysics that helps us to see a universe which itself develops and which contains particular things, and groupings of things, which develop over time.

To give the reader a better idea of what is going on and what will be addressed in the rest of this chapter, I'll suggest a journey of the imagination which is analogous to some aspects of the development of this universe:

> Imagine you and some companions are traveling down a very steep hill through a series of tunnels or open ruts. You can move uphill but it takes a great effort which is unsustainable for long though you might occasionally amuse yourself by tossing a rock uphill to see it roll back down.
>
> The tunnels and ruts which lie ahead have a very complex and complicated forking structure. you've an immense number

> of choices, but you notice something odd after some of your companions develop some instruments that are capable of seeing back through the tunnels and ruts you've traveled. Since you've taken only one path and since that path is what's seen by those instruments, it's possible to forget the number of choices you're making on an ongoing basis. It seems as if there's only one path you could have traveled though you can turn in the direction of your movement to see an immense and confusing variety of choices lying ahead.
>
> As you move forward, you not only risk losing an appreciation for the immense number of paths that were not taken, you also begin to think it strange that you can toss stones backwards to the path you have already traveled. Some of your companions begin to theorize that the down-slope is an illusion and there's really no inherent direction to your journey.

Be careful. Analogies and metaphors and allegories break down at some point, meaning they'll always eventually be in error in the context of human experience and human thought. But they're powerful tools. In this case, the analogy warns us not to think of the aspects of the concrete universe, not even its tendency to move in one direction of time, as being necessary. Time and space seem to be properties of particular concrete forms of being.

Do not apply metaphysical or theological reasoning directly to those aspects of physical reality which are imposed upon pure created being. Metaphysics says nothing specific about space and time as it says nothing specific about the behavior of electrons or the value of the gravitational constant. Theology speaks of God and not the particular aspects of His Creation. At the same time, you should realize that the ways in which you seek understanding of the world are set by your theological and metaphysical beliefs. For example, the Christian seeks to understand creaturely being at all levels as being a gift of a God who is inherently only His own Act-of-being, a God who becomes entangled with a world only if He freely chooses to create and to sustain that world.

Now, I'll reverse course and tell you that you should not fail to apply metaphysical and theological reasoning at the appropriate times. For example, while some physical events might involve backward jerks in time, this world is a story which God is telling from a time past to a time which we're anticipating. God is moving us forward in time, we might say relentlessly. Though it might well be theoretically possible, we don't need to fear our grandchildren will travel back to our time and kill us. A true Christian would consider the possibilities of time-travel to be meaningless even as entertainment just because the underlying events of Terminator movies and even *Back to the Future* are based on morally despicable assumptions about the world and its Author.

Time and space as we know them are properties imposed upon the universe as a whole, perhaps as a result of an unknown event during the shaping of the Primordial Universe. We would then see time and space as properties of a landscape over which we, and electrons, journey. Unusual events, such as jerks backwards in time, are possible, but – so far as anyone currently knows – they're so expensive in energy as to be rare and local in the universe in its current state of being which is cold enough to allow stable, living creatures to develop. Those properties which are imposed by the steep slope of the paths open to us should not be assumed to be properties of our own bodies or the objects we carry with us. When someone discovers that – with huge infusions of energy and under very specific conditions – elementary particles can move backwards in time, we should not think this to be a proof that reality is not what we see it to be. Reality is what we see it to be – however incomplete and defective our vision might be, but concrete reality, at the level of human perceptions, is necessarily a very specific reality which has come to be with very specific constraints, which constraints build upon metaphysical truths and aren't limited to those elegant sorts of truths. We're citizens of a universe which has properties, such as a tendency to move forward in time – relentlessly and steadily, and we should not be surprised if some of those properties are not to be found in the foundational components of that universe. We should not be surprised if these properties can be violated at times.

I'll jump to a claim which is in line with mathematical understandings of chance and probability and with modern understandings of what a random number is:

> Only God can make a random number.

Now, I'll make a claim equally obscure and possibly upsetting to many modern people.

> Randomness, as the term is commonly used, is a type of factuality viewed through superstitious eyes.

And I'll also claim:

> Any patterns in the world are small islands of order in the midst of tumultuous oceans of randomness or factuality which threaten to overwhelm us, physically and also spiritually.

Even the islands of order in this concrete and particularized universe are not protected against disorder. How could they be if they're emerging from the oceans of chaos and being pounded so that rock becomes soil with life then emerging?

Though our human natures are ideally to be fully ordered, they're being formed by energies and pressures generated by this struggle between the forces of order and the forces which would destroy all the particularized being of this universe. It's important to realize that this struggle, if lost, would not result in the birth of some sort of Satanic world. It would result in a collapse of the particularity of this universe and the things it contains, a collapse back into a homogeneous and undifferentiated form of being, quite good in itself and, in fact, necessary to our existence, and perfectly well-ordered in its own homogeneous way. The problem, as I've noted, is that a perfect, homogeneous order does not allow thing-like existence. We would fall out of existence if this universe fell back into that perfectly homogeneous state, and therefore I talk of that state as being a form of disorder.

It's only after we have been shaped in a world of this sort, with the struggle between order and disorder, that we can hope to be suited to life as the companions of God in a world which is so strongly ordered that this privation in being, in particularized being, is no longer our natural fate. The sculpting process is forming living statues and once those statues are formed the blow-torches and axes and knives can be put away for good. I've already claimed and will continue to claim that modern physics and evolutionary biology have given us a lot of knowledge about this process of forming those living statues which are us. I'll also claim that we can understand the process of both the creation of the Primordial Universe and the constraining of that entity into the thing-like universe by building upon the two foundational components of Thomism:

- The Thomistic theory of knowledge which tells us how the human mind is shaped and how it is that we can comprehend the universe and can even gain meaningful knowledge about God who is, in many ways, absolutely other than us and seemingly beyond any human knowledge at all.

- The Thomistic insight into the nature of the act-of-being as well as He Who is His own Act-of-being.

Modern mathematics, physics, and evolutionary biology have provided insights into a dynamic, evolving, physical reality. Those insights are not compatible with any idealistic worldview and, so far as I can tell, not compatible with any worldview but the one I've sketched out, a worldview built upon the two Thomistic insights listed above as well as the Christian doctrines of the Triune God and the God who became man that men might share in the life of God.

When we're trying to make sense of all of this, we should not forget to consider a major clue about our true situation: the thoughts of St. Thomas Aquinas are not those of an idealistic philosopher but rather those of a man living in the presence of God, a man who ate the Body of Christ and drank the Blood of Christ each and every day, a man who preached Christ's message to kings and peasants every day. It's my goal to make my own that simple faith which allowed Aquinas to become a saint before he could become such a great theologian, and I work towards that goal by bringing God's world into my view as well as by worshiping the God of Jesus Christ in a particular Catholic parish: St. John the Baptist in Ludlow, MA. It could not be otherwise. As Michael Polanyi told us even before he became a Christian: knowledge becomes truly such only when it becomes personal, becomes my knowledge, when it forms my insides and when it shapes my behavior.

6.2 The Interaction of Order and Disorder

In reading the rest of this book, you should always bear in mind that I'm claiming the concrete universe is the result of God's shaping that Primordial Universe to be the setting for a tale told by God and many tales told by us and God. We can hop from island to island, at times for real and at times in our imaginations, but we cannot entirely avoid the storms that blow in from those vast oceans nor can we avoid at least the occasional dunking. And though we must fear the ocean, or perhaps the kraken which lurks in its vastness, we can have faith that the same God created both infinite ocean and tiny islands. More than that, I'll argue that it's the oceans which give us our freedom. It's the oceans, crashing waves of facts in which no islands of order have arisen to the perception of the human mind, that give us the ability to move and sometimes to turn despite the heavy baggage of apish genetic inheritance and personal habits. At the same time, we should realize a heavily-laden ship can take a goodly distance and an agonizingly long time to turn. Ishmael might advise us to throw overboard all that's not needed for the voyage and to keep the ship in full sail through storm and calm alike. In no case should you ever go ashore, for there's where you'll find your life, your few options, and your many regrets, all pre-determined for you.

I should explain the jump from mathematics to an imaginative depiction of reality. Modern theorists working at very fundamental levels of mathematics seem to be telling us that what we think of as mathematics involves patterns over sets of numbers which sets are infinitesimally small compared to an infinite ocean, perhaps an absolutely infinite ocean, of random numbers. This is work which involves abstractions where there are infinities larger than other infinities – absolute infinity being unreachable by definition. This is also work which points to the insight that probability theory is just a subset of fully deterministic measure theory[3] with a little bit of mystification added, more for pedagogical purposes than for any other reason. A true randomness cannot be reached or even described by mathematics unless you consider the trivial truth that random numbers are those without enough structure to be part of mathematics. In a sense, mathematics defines randomness, or factuality, by what it excludes from its search for elegance and simplicity.

It makes more sense in light of recently discoveries to talk about randomness in terms of coding efficiency. A random number is random by some reasonable standard if it cannot be coded in fewer symbols according to that standard. For example, the number 0.333... where the threes go on forever can be coded in one of two simpler ways. We can restate it as the rational number, $(1 \div 3)$, or restate it in words such as "an infinite stream of threes after the decimal point." These are obviously shorter encodings for this number than a listing that goes on to infinity. A random number is one that's a fact, One application of this idea is to try to understand the nature

[3]It's sufficient to think of measure theory as a very rigorous theory of mathematical functions.

of the constants of physics. The gravitational constant is about $6.67^{-}11$, but, so far as anyone knows, this constant, written out as scientists calculate more and more digits, is absolutely random. That raises the rather odd possibility that some of the constants of physics are direct supernatural impositions upon our universe and yet their effects can be observed and measured, but never fully.

There are a number of fundamental constants in physics, though some might be derivable from others. They don't come from simple interaction of basic components which are fully and directly describable in terms of any mathematics accessible to the human mind. They're facts imposed upon the Primordial Universe as it expanded and fragmented to become the Particularized Universe, or simply the universe. It would be wrong to use this as a direct proof of God's existence and equally wrong to imagine, along with the atheologists in cosmological physics, that a system of equations can bootstrap its own parameters and constants, also actualizing what is described by those specific equations. The equation $1 + 1$ does not bring two apples into existence. We need to simply see reality as it is and then to try to make sense of it within the context of one tradition or another. If the physical universe makes sense within that tradition, that's as close as we can get to proving the validity of that tradition, whether it's a sophisticated Catholic theology developed by highly literate people or whether it's a simple animistic paganism developed by a simple, illiterate people who have never received Christian revelation. These traditions, being chewed up so fast by modern liberalism, help people to prove the validity of their ways of belief, their worldviews and theologies and sciences or superstitions. More importantly, those traditions help people to live meaningful lives and perhaps to serve God.

It's in the practice and the living that our best proofs are to be found. But mathematics and logic are important, almost necessary, to help us see the world once we have telescopes and copies of *National Geographic* on every coffee-table. More than that, I'm arguing that a full-blooded Christianity with priests and the Body and Blood of Christ on the altar provides a better way of understanding reality than do competing viewpoints such as Judaism, Islam, Protestantism, Deism, or Atheism.

Some scientists may wish to avoid the factual nature of our universe because there are those who wish to mis-use it as a direct proof of God's existence or even a direct proof that the universe was made for human beings (the strongest form of the so-called anthropic principle). This factual nature of our universe has to be taken into account in any worldview. And, it does provide a proof of God's existence, but only in the context of a worldview. It's not a proof in the mathematical or logical sense but rather a proof that the belief in God allows the construction of a reasonable worldview. If the physical universe can be perceived as being a world, unified and coherent and complete, under the assumption that it was created by the God of Jesus, then that's as good a proof of God's existence as we can get. So far as I can see, it's impossible to construct an atheistic or pantheistic worldview that takes proper account of what we know of stars and apes and mathematics.

There are also those who don't see the construction of worldviews as plausible or even desirable. This latter group would include many who follow one or another school of pragmatic philosophy and also the followers of Darwin's bulldog, T. H. Huxley, who saw man as being at war with the universe he was born into. A war-zone is not a world though it's clear that a world may contain war-zones. In fact, Huxley pretty much denied that a world in the sense of this book could be brought into human view, probably meant to deny any such world could even exist.

Remember what I had earlier stated:

> Only God can make a random number.

Equivalently, only God has a true free-will, and this is not only a theological claim. A non-believer can still accept the negative fact which this statement implies: creatures cannot act in a truly random way and that means they cannot have a free will in the strongest sense. To tie it back to the loose argument I just made: I can't really argue to a certainty that existing things imply a Creator, but a free Creation, factual and yet well-structured implies the existence of a Creator and one with a true free-will.

In a more limited way, in terms of a randomness defined in terms of coding efficiency or coding complexity,[4] creatures may be able to perform random acts, acts that are unpredictable at the scale of this universe though they might be fully predictable to a God's eye-view. Remember that randomness is more factual than mystical. Randomness on the part of creatures might be a sign of a misfiring brain-cell but it might also be a sign of

[4]The mathematician Gregory Chaitin, the major theorist in this field, uses the term 'algorithmic complexity theory' but I'd as soon avoid having to explain what an algorithm is. On the other hand, most people probably have at least a vague idea of what a code is.

real though limited freedom, and it might be hard to distinguish, even in principle. This doesn't cast any real doubt on the reality of human moral freedom, or the lesser moral freedom of elephants, but it does point to the truly random, that is – factual, basis of our freedom. And it points to the ambiguous status of our freedom, a problem which has resulted in extreme positions such as predestination and antinomianism.

God allows us to move with our limited freedom in our limited domain, and our freedom is a creaturely imitation of His divine freedom. Our freedom is analogically similar to the divine free-will which shows in God shaping this world to be so unbearably particular. Our freedom will not show up as some sort of magical ability to transcend physical reality. Rather does our freedom show up in the trail of facts we leave behind us as we move through space and time.

But God is omniscient and He can see past our freedom, so to speak, because His mind ranges over absolute infinity – He sees each point and each random number on the real number line. There are no discontinuities, no holes, no boundaries of knowledge to God who knows all facts and all possible facts. Our freedom is real from any conceivable creaturely standpoint and real to the extent that God has chosen to honor the constraints He imposed upon the Primordial Universe that this concrete universe might come into being.

One way to express all of this is to think of the universe as a giant computer running a program of self-exploration. Though this universal computer can know its own characteristics and behavioral possibilities, it cannot possibly know its own future because of the way that God constrained it at its formation. It would be like a pool table where there's uncertainty in the size of the billiards balls and in the forces being applied. Exact calculations of even purely physical events could not be made. This would seem definitely true if the physical constants, such as that of gravitation, are truly patternless, that is, factual. People get excited about the strange uncertainties of quantum physics and fail to realize that there are more basic reasons for a deep indeterminacy of physical events in our universe – from a creaturely viewpoint.[5]

[5]The real situation is still stranger than I've stated. Even under ideal conditions, a series of collisions on a billiard table soon reach an unpredictable state. Newtonian physics is not deterministic and the belief that it was so was a result of literalistically interpreting the simple equations which come from Newton's laws of motion. Yes, even those creatures of pure thought, physicists and evolutionary biologists, have been guilty of lit-

This indeterminacy, of many types and operating at various levels, breaks any possible line of reasoning which would explain either particular galaxies or particular human beings by way of physics and chemistry. We live in a world where complex entities are characters in stories. When we try to explain these complex entities in terms of the quantitative properties of their stuff, we're trying to use the chemical properties of ice and steel blades and protoplasm to predict the movements of a Bobby Orr. Even such a great athlete as Orr was limited by those properties, but he moved with an awful lot of freedom inside those limits. And we can move with a surprising amount of freedom within the limitations set by our DNA and our environments. At least we can do what is most important of all: to show our gratitude to our Creator.

We cannot rise above the universe to know all that God did to shape it, but we can know the laws which govern the movement of matter and we can understand the narrative flows of God's story. Sometimes we can even anticipate some future possibilities. Comprehension of the sort important to human beings does not necessarily include the power to determine the full value of the gravitational constant, whether it be absolutely random or whether it terminates at some point where further digits become irrelevant because of Heisenberg's Uncertainty Principle or some other constraint on physical reality. But those sorts of constraints are also factual and they're little different in principle from randomized physical constants. Only God the Creator can impose such constraints.

I hope that the above digression motivates the reader to think about these issues of mathematics and theoretical physics, but readers who have not taken college level mathematics, and those who have forgotten what they once had to learn, shouldn't worry about some of the terms I've been thrown around. It's sufficient at this stage to know the claims I'm making, based upon modern mathematical developments and upon the results of theoretical and experimental research in physics:

- Most modern people, including most scientists, talk as if there is some mystical source of random numbers or random causes, that source being beyond the reach of rationality. In fact, probability theory, includ-

eralistically interpreting the texts which they considered sacred. As Flannery O'Connor pointed out by way of some of her fictions, the intellectuals of the modern world are often entrapped more deeply in those ways of thought than are the Bible-thumping preachers who come down out of the hills of northern Georgia.

ing all conventional ideas of randomness, is not necessary to modern mathematics. All that's valid in probability theory can be stated in terms of a fully deterministic measure theory which is, roughly speaking, a very abstract and rigorous theory of functions, including probability functions. The concept of randomness doesn't appear in measure theory.

- An American high school student named Gregory Chaitin speculated during the 1960s that randomness is a matter of the efficiency of the coding of numbers. He went on to publish a proof around 1990 that all numbers are absolutely random except for a set of numbers with measure zero. In other words, that set of numbers with patterns is infinitesimally small compared to the set of random numbers. Random numbers in this proof were defined by the highest standard: infinite streams of digits with no patterns at all, not even for a short run of digits. It turns out that Gödel's theorem is a corollary of this simpler theorem.[6]

- A careful reading of reliable books about modern physics will tell us that the universe as we know it, at its most basic physical level, is not elegant in the way of something which is determined by simple sets of metaphysical principles or mathematical equations. It is, if you will, highly corrupted by facts. Only a Christian can accept this as a proof that God was a participant in those early stages of our universe, but it's consistent with that claim in a formal way that should be acknowledged by all thinkers. This sheer factuality of the universe has to be acknowledged and dealt with to construct any worldview no matter one's religious beliefs or philosophical predilections. Few have done this and nearly all modern people, including theologians and philosophers and scientists just wing it within the context of

[6]The conventional proof of Gödel's undecidability theorem is very complex but the most difficult part is the preliminary proof that his technique is valid. The proof of the undecidability theorem itself is not so complex by modern mathematical standards. Chaitin and others have presented easier proofs than Gödel's own proof. Gödel's proof of his own theorem is analogical to a story of a philosopher who said, "All philosophers always lie." The statement, if true, generates contradictions. If not true, then we have proof that a lie can be stated as clearly as a truth. Therefore, systems of statements at least as complex as that system we call 'arithmetic' cannot be both consistent and complete – according to current understandings of mathematics and logic.

the modern family of ideologies of which Adam Smith was the most brilliant expositor.

There's a pretty good way to generate physical events which are chaotic by some realistic and practical standard. The measurements of those events will be a stream of numbers random by some standard, sometimes quite high. You can simply put two independent systems in contact with each other and observe or measure what happens at the interface. That's all. It's a trick used in some of the simple experiments used to generate so-called chaotic motion. For example, take two pendulums with different periods of oscillation. Link the bobs of the pendulums and put one or both in motion. The two pendulums will clearly not be able to move as they would if each moved freely. In fact, the resulting motion will be chaotic, basically unpredictable. Equivalent experiments can be done with electronic components or even with simulations of the independent systems in software. There's nothing mystical involved in generating streams of physical events which are unpredictable or chaotic, generating numbers which are random by some low standard.

Chaotic motion can be visualized as an orbital path that never quite returns to the same point and is unpredictable beyond some length of time in the future or in the past. If you were to graph the orbits of such an object, and the orbiting earth is such an object, you would get a blur of orbits that lie close to each other and cross over often but no particular orbit is the same as any other. That sort of movement is patternless to human perception and measurement though usually staying within some tight boundaries. Physicists have shown by way of demanding computer simulations that "the orbital movement of planets in the solar system is chaotic... which makes practically impossible any precise prediction beyond a few tens of millions of years..."[7]

The early results of Professor Laskar's research (his first simulations of the solar system in 1989) indicate that a mere 15 meter error in measurement of the earth's current position makes it impossible to say if the earth's orbit will be stable 100 million years from now. Because the equations of dynamics are symmetrical in time, this means it's also impossible to prove

[7] I have taken a google.com translation of Professor Laskar's biography which can be found at:

http://www.academie-sciences.fr/membres/L/Laskar_Jacques_bio.html

the earth's orbit was stable more than 100 million years in the past, with that range of ignorance moving with us so far as the future goes and also moving with us so far as the past goes. A few years later, Gerald Sussman and Jack Wisdom of MIT showed that after only 4 million years it is not possible to predict the orbit of the earth, or any of the planets of the solar system, with any confidence.[8]

Undoubtedly, results will have been tightened up in the technical literature to which I have no access. But the principle is what's important.

In a sense, knowledge is constantly coming into view ahead of us and constantly disappearing behind us. To be more explicit, this means that, despite common sense, we cannot prove by mathematical means that the earth stayed in its orbit 4 million years ago. So far as the equations go, with initial conditions provided by the current state of the solar system, the earth might have crashed into the sun or gone shooting past Mars 4 million years ago. Common sense sometimes tells us things that mathematics cannot.

You shouldn't imagine that this situation occurs only at the level of planets like the earth. The sun itself is traveling a chaotic orbit around the center of the galaxy. Our galaxy, the Milky Way, is dancing around various gravitational centers of local clusters of galaxies and larger-scale clusters of galaxies.

There's a deep and fundamental lack of determination about the events in the universe, future events and past events alike. The strangeness of quantum mechanics does not really add much to this lack of determination, not in principle, though it's likely that it gives us a view of this looseness in reality on a different level. We're duty-bound to use this looseness in the chains of determinism to move towards God. We have a small but significant measure of physical freedom which we can use in making moral choices with some freedom.

There's a specific example of a chaotic or random stream of events that may be founded upon two interacting, independent physical systems which are largely well-determined – biological evolution. In the short-term and from the viewpoint of the individual organism, which is the entity being selected or otherwise acted upon, both genetic events and environmental events can be presented as well-determined, at least for the first stage of

[8]A short summary can be found at

http://www.aip.org/pnu/1992/split/pnu089-4.html

an analysis. The interaction of these two well-determined and independent systems produces a stream of unpredictable and under-determined events which are typically mis-labeled as 'random' by evolutionary biologists and popular science writers. Then again, they're random if we use the more recent redefinition of randomness to be factuality of a sort. They are random in the same way as the earth's orbit which doesn't quite repeat itself and is beyond the capabilities of human prediction, at least, given current understandings of what mathematics is.

Now let me state a principle that might help us move in the right direction away from the current confusion I've deliberately stirred up:

> Things which exist are infinitely richer than any possible description of those things in either human language or human mathematics.

Statements and equations can only cover specific aspects of things and usually those specific aspects will not be fully covered. Even if it were possible to know a thing has only ten aspects by some system of categorization, you would have to push Humpty Dumpty off the wall to get at those aspects. An equation describing the shell in all its surprising strength, a description of the genes in the yolk, and a philosophical discussion of the potential unity of these fragments and puddles of glop, won't get you Humpty Dumpty back again. No concrete thing can be broken up into sets of aspects which are non-overlapping but also cover the thing completely. Nor are we so good at dealing with aspects as some think. Again, it's St. Thomas Aquinas who had the better sense. While he defended the idea that the human mind could, in principle, comprehend all of this universe, he also noted that no actual human mind could fully understand so much as a flea.

William Blake added, in his powerful and poetic way, that a grain of sand assumes and encapsulates the Particularized Universe. This means we cannot understand the grain of sand any better than we understand the universe, nor can we understand the universe less well than we understand a grain of sand. Blake's phrase, "To see a world in a grain of sand," tells us much about the power and the limitations of the human mind, and it should tell us that we human beings are no more independent of God's world than that grain of sand is.

> We should always remember that God created a world, a concrete world. The Almighty didn't propose a set of equations.

Engineers design modern sound equipment so that the chips which identify and pass through (filter) the signals have a constant level of what is called white-noise. This static background leaves the chip in a state where it responds more quickly and more accurately than if it were 'cold', that is, not in some sort of motion. There's reason to believe the background rhythms of the human brain are this same sort of white-noise, chaos which leaves the brain in a state of readiness in a world which can present great opportunities and great dangers. It's that chaos which allows a fluid movement of the sort which can find pathways that lead to new domains, sometimes those domains being already known and sometimes being new areas. The mind which is too well-organized, overly specialized, is traveling the same ruts and wearing them quite deep. This isn't necessarily bad. Arguably, most serious and productive scientists and historians and theologians do exactly this for much of their professional lives. Such working methods allow for detailed exploration of a fellow's accustomed ruts but it doesn't allow him to solve problems which lie outside the scope of his accustomed ruts.

Material objects themselves and their relationships and interactions with each other are the source of all this randomness and chaos. More exactly, at least in my story, this confusion came about as a result of the ways in which God shaped the Primordial Universe that it become this concrete universe. There's no clean separation into science and theology and history and philosophy. Our esthetic and political views and our particular social situations do play a role in any substantial effort to understand the universe and to try to make a world of it. When I said that a world is the physical universe seen by way of a moral ordering process, I spoke a little bit misleadingly. The moral ordering process is more basic to the perception of the universe than any telescope. Few people realize how many metaphysical and theological assumptions underly our exploration of the physical universe. If we did not assume that something like a universe exists or that there's a story of the human race, our science would be entirely instrumentalist, devoted to solving immediate problems of health and comfort and material prosperity. In fact, it's likely that our scientific institutions are decaying in this atmosphere of moral disorder and theological confusion so that we're increasingly incapable of responding to the wonder that drives lines of research which are not self-centered.

It's the assumption that we have a universe, that it's capable of being defined explicitly as Einstein claimed and that the universe is a rational whole, that allows astronomers to look through a telescope and interpret those faint beams of light as the emissions of stars much like our sun. They assume those far-away stars are made of the same stuff as our sun and that the energy-producing processes are the same. The laws of motion and of gravity are also assumed to be the same. If not for these very strong assumptions, we would be living in an earthly environment which receives signals from the far-away regions of a chaotic assembly of environments. Cosmological physics is made possible by assumptions which were provided by a variety of sources, including Christian doctrines which made angels and spirits and demons merely contingent and optional entities, subject to proof or denial, just because it's God who creates. Most certainly, the Biblical tales of angels should be considered evidence on the matter, but we have no reason to believe we have final and rock-solid interpretations of those tales. And, I repeat: that process of creation was not a once and for all event but rather one which is continuous so long as any created entity exists. It's this constant creation which ultimately powers both the order and disorder allowing the universe to develop from a plasma to huge clouds of hot gas and then to galaxies surrounding voids and perhaps vast quantities of matter not yet detected. It's this constant creation which powers the order and disorder allowing life to come to be and then to evolve.

Unfortunately, far too few people see the ways in which their minds carry thoughts from one field of human endeavor to another. It's good that all is intertwined if we can toss away our ideological blinders and be honest about our true situation in this world created by God. If only some physicists could see they did not discover the world is made of only processes and not things; they inherited this idea from the ideologies of the modern world which teach us that human life is a stream of transactions. Some evolutionary biologists have learned from moral philosophies with non-biological understandings of human beings that 'an is cannot lead to an ought'. Unless those non-biologically oriented philosophers do have non-physical souls from another universe, it's hard to even guess where they got the idea that 'an is cannot lead to an ought'. From what non-fact, non-is, did they derive such an idea? Clearly, if we're physical creatures living in a physical world, is-ness, thing-ness in particular, shapes our views of reality, through evolutionary processes and through development of individual minds. Oughtness is generated by those issy things called brain-cells and by the things in the environments in which that brain developed. Still more bluntly: if Aquinas wasn't right in claiming truth to reside in things, then men can have no part of truth, because we first know things and then derive our concepts from those. This isn't a problem to a Christian who believes those things are images of certain thoughts of God. God's thoughts are true and, thus, things are true.

If man is truly a physical creature with no inborn supernatural components, as many early Christians believed, as I believe, as most biologists claim to believe, we better hope that truth is in things because our thoughts are shaped in that complex thing called a human brain and are a result of the properties of the brain and its fundamental stuff as well as being a result of the properties of things in the environments perceived by that brain. That brain and its organization reflects the nature of all things in the Particularized Universe and it reflects the nature of the Particularized Universe itself. We better hope that 'an is can lead to an ought' or else all of our oughts are illusions since they're derived from things and the relationships of things, both of which are as issy as you can get from a creaturely point of view.

I confess that I've a sense of living in the midst of rubble which resulted, roughly speaking, when the dismantling of tradition was followed by a period of mercenary activity, commercial and political, which was merrily conducted amidst all that rubble. The rebuilding cannot begin without endangering the modern ideologies and the political and commercial marketplaces in which they're at home. If we rebuilt homes and churches, even local pubs, people might leave the vast expanses of the public marketplaces to return to settings to which they're better suited and to which they're called by God.

The popular expositions of sociobiology often make the point that man is not adapted to his current world, certainly not to the urban societies he has built up, but rather to a New Stone Age world where he walked 30 to 40 miles a day to gather food, where he lived in small human communities with a lot of blood-ties, and where he had huge calorie needs along with irregular access to high-sugar and high-fat foods. Some of our health problems are due to the differences between our lifestyles and those for which our ancestors were selected, though we should remember that our ancestors had their own health problems. We're poorly adapted to our present situation, and I would question whether we should want to be well adapted to these sorts of societies which we have created and which we maintain.

Moral freedom is unlikely to develop in a creature which is perfectly adapted to his environment. Maybe I should weaken the claim to: "It's hard for a human being to see how moral freedom could develop in a creature which is perfectly adapted to his environment." Imperfect adaptation leaves open the struggle between order and disorder which can lead to further adaptation over generations but also leads to the struggle for order during the lifetime of a moral animal, such as a human being or a wolf. If we fit too well with our environment in the sense that our immediate desires are being met, our moral wills might never have developed. If we make our environment fit us too well, we might run into the same problem.

If we manage to conquer our environment so that we suffer from unrelieved prosperity, the pressures towards moral development will also cease. This doesn't mean it's impossible for a human being to develop his or her moral nature, but it seems to be the case that many, perhaps most, human beings will, in fact, not develop their moral nature if they're too comfortable. History indicates the situation will worsen if those prosperous people see their city or nation or ethnic group as being in and of itself some sort of bearer of moral truth.

For those who have not yet extrapolated from what I've said, I'll let you in on a secret: my worldview implies that this sometimes nasty world is exactly what we need that we be formed into the sorts of moral creatures who would be capable of living as God's companions in a world which does not have corruption or decay, a world in which grizzly bears and coyotes don't eat our children, a world in which there are no wars or plagues to kill millions of innocent people. A world of amoral processes would seem to have the odd result of forming moral creatures, not just human beings as I've repeatedly said.

In our attempts to secure all the forms of security and prosperity which the Bible warns us against, we're trying to build walls to protect us from exactly those struggles between order and disorder which can help us to develop into creatures suited to be God's companions. We're building environments in which human beings can have wings, in which men can become women, in which babies can be grown in artificial wombs.

A worldview demands that we take down many of the barriers we build in our all-too human efforts to justify ourselves and to hide our own natures from our own eyes. We need to destroy our attachment to the modern ideologies, the worship of the gods of the marketplace, but we need also to take down those barriers between different fields of knowledge. We need to see that there's no human practice, certainly not medicine, which is not subject to the demands of moral traditions, though profit-takers and exploiters would free themselves from those demands as they've tried through the centuries. It's a worldview that allows us to see a world, unified and coherent and complete and it's a worldview that takes away this pretense that medicine and biological research and farming and retailing are morally neutral activities. Adam Smith lied to us when he told a story in which the marketplace acts of those Glasgow Presbyterians were morally neutral. It's a very convenient belief and allows us to pretend that we can create moral order by way of morally unguided or even morally disordered acts.

A Christian worldview wouldn't allow a modern American medical researcher to carry out specific acts similar to those for which Nazi doctors were hung and then say he's only trying to help out people with Parkinson's or with spinal injuries. It wouldn't allow an American soldier to obey criminal orders, even issuing ultimately from the President of the United States, and think that frees him from his obligations as a moral human being or the more specific obligations of a Christian. It's no coincidence that Adam Smith was the major prophet of specialization, that way of organizing human societies so that most men will allow themselves to be rendered stupid in return for promises of safety and security and other men will be rendered usefully smart in such ways that they lose their moral integrity and their souls. The gods of the marketplace must be served and they know that human persons, in their unity and coherence and completeness of being, will not serve them. Human beings must be fragmented that the Gross National Product can increase.

6.3 Initial Conditions

To make sure that I've made my case in the minds of readers at various levels of mathematical knowledge, I'm going to present a more detailed, but still elementary, discussion of what is meant by 'initial conditions'.

We can drop an object, from a roof or an airplane, so that it enters free-fall in the earth's gravitational field. If we ignore air resistance, there's an equation that tells us how far it'll fall in t seconds: $16 \times t^2$. So, in 2 seconds, a bowling ball, or a feather if there were no air resistance, would fall $16 \times 2 \times 2$ feet or 64 feet. The value of 16 is appropriate for the earth's surface and is pretty accurate for a good distance above the earth's surface as well. In the more powerful gravitational field of Jupiter, the value would be greater at the surface of that planet. It would be still greater at the surface of the sun. More than that, we have assumed another initial condition – that the starting time is 0. If we were to use an initial measurement time of 2 and want to know how far it travels in the next two seconds, we would have to calculate the distance at 4 seconds and subtract the distance at 2 seconds.

Don't worry about the physics or the mathematics. For the purposes of this discussion, it's important only to see what is involved when we take general equations or even qualitative descriptions and make them specific to a situation. We can set the initial conditions when we simply try to calculate the behavior of a natural system, a system over which we have no control or have chosen not to exercise control. We can also set the initial conditions by making or altering a system to meet specific requirements. For example, there might be an equation which estimates the load-bearing capacity of a structure built according to a certain geometric design. Clearly, the parameters of that equation will be different for spruce timber and for steel beams. By selecting building materials and construction techniques, the engineer and architect set some of the initial conditions which determine how extreme will be the conditions of collapse.

These decisions made when a building is first designed and constructed do not fully determine the future uses of the building, but they do place boundaries on the possible uses. A multi-storied building with a frame of spruce 2x4s over an open basement is not likely to ever be used to hold a manufacturing operation with heavy machinery. A 16 story building where each story is 50 yards square is unlikely to be useful as a warehouse for an appliance manufacturer. Still, a building can often be used for purposes far different than those foreseen by its original designers and builders. Some of the storage buildings down at the mill complex in my home-town have been fitted with freezers and are used by a nearby ice-cream maker though they were designed to be open spaces holding jute at various stages of its transformation into linen. The main manufacturing buildings hold some small machine-shops but also an athletic club and have held at least one furniture show-room. These are neither unusual or exotic re-uses of a building, but it brings out the point that a design limits the use of a building, or other artifact but does not fully pre-determine future uses.

Even at the level of human builders, let alone at the level of God shaping a universe, the setting of initial conditions is important and it can define possibilities without allowing a human being to foresee all the possibilities. I speak of the processes in a physical creation and of the human thought processes which are part of those and which can run parallel to the formation of a star system but probably cannot jump to possibilities truly outside those of this Particularized Universe. We can think of events or things impossible in our particular universe but not likely is it that we can have coherent thoughts of events or things impossible in the Primordial Universe, the pure created being which is the foundation of the concrete universe. Other possible Primordial Universes – if there are such – and the concrete universes to which they could have given birth are probably beyond our imaginations. This is a negative way of saying that our minds are formed by our environments to see the truths which are the things of this particular universe and the closely related truths which are in the relationships between those things. There are some truths, such as the law of non-contradiction, which will be true in any universe, but, on the whole, a universe will be a complex, complicated, and very particular entity. A particular universe will embody not only truths which are absolute and would be true in any universe, it also embodies particular truths.

The universe, the physical reality explorable by physicists and biologists and other scientists, does not conform fully to elegant mathematical equations nor to simple sets of principles. It's probably impossible for a physical world to be elegantly mathematical in this sense. For example, the equation which simplifies to $16 \times t^2$ for the distance traveled by a free-falling object near the earth's surface has several variables and one constant, the Gravitational Constant.[9] The variables vary inside of our universe but the Gravitational Constant is itself something not set by mathematical necessity, not something which could be determined necessarily for a physical world. Arbitrary conditions have to be imposed for a particular and concrete universe to exist. At any rate, it's nearly impossible for me to imagine a world which is mathematically or metaphysically elegant and which gives birth to creatures with anything describable as moral freedom. God knew what He was doing when He made a messy sort of universe.

While the universe was cooling down, matter and energy and fields as we know them appeared and they appeared with strange behavior imposed upon them, which behavior allows matter to be stable enough to form into things. I'll mention only the Pauli Exclusion Principle and will discuss it a little before actually defining it. First of all, note that physicists were

[9]We can generalize one more level and speak of parametrization where the setting parameters might lead to different forms of an equation. Setting the variables of an equation might correspond to setting its context within the universe. Changing the parameters might correspond to the exploration of the quantitative properties of a similar but different universe.

careful not to call it a law because it does not seem to be a law in the sense usually intended for science. Second of all, I'll re-state part of the discussion on the Primordial Universe:

> The Primordial Universe did not have electromagnetism nor electrons nor protons nor much of anything else besides pure physical being, which seems to include gravity. Maybe the Primordial Universe can even be regarded, quantitatively, as simply gravity. The Primordial Universe seems to be pure created being, unified and coherent and complete beyond human imagining. Gravity is the unifying force of our universe, so it's hard to imagine it passing out of existence or melting down to something more primordial unless that would be a more basic force of unity. Pure unity might have existed though there would have been no things as we know them to unify.

The Pauli Exclusion Principle seems to have been imposed upon all of this elegance and simplicity in a rather ad-hoc manner. Not ad-hoc in any bad sense, but ad-hoc in the sense that it was necessary that the Universe might become our particular universe but it doesn't seem to be logically or mathematically necessary.

But what is the Pauli Exclusion Principle?

> No two fermions can occupy the same quantum mechanical state.[10]

What are fermions? It suffices here to say that electrons, neutrons, and protons – the basic stuff of ordinary matter – are all fermions.

Why can no two fermions occupy the same quantum mechanical state?

I'll start with the general observation that much of the subject matter that's called quantum mechanics is an odd mixture of beautiful mathematics and imposed rules that seem more like the dicta of a king, or rather a King for those of us who believe in a Creator God.

---

[10]This definition as well as the list of examples came from the science reference site on the Internet: http://scienceworld.wolfram.com, run as a service by the Wolfram Research Company.

The Pauli Exclusion Principle is one such dictum.[11] It can be justified after the fact in the sense that it's part of an orderly and rational universe, but it's not part of any known set of necessary rules for physical being. It seems to be simply imposed on matter. It's not necessary, is not the sort of rule which could be necessary, and it has great consequences. Ordinary matter could not exist in a stable form unless its constituent particles behaved in a way consistent with this so-called principle which is really a statement of observed facts. It seems likely to me that we're seeing hints that Wittgenstein was right when he predicted that when we find the foundations, we'll see they're being supported by the rest of the structure. In other words, order imposed upon the Particularized Universe as a whole determines behavior of matter and energy and fields at their most basic level. It's generally assumed in modern science that the behavior of the physical universe can be built up from its 'smallest' components, but there's no reason that this must be so unless you ignore the global nature of many properties of those components. As homogeneous stuff was being shaped to particular stuff, those properties seem to have been imposed across the entire known universe in a coherent and rational manner.

The first and most important consequence of the Pauli Exclusion Principle is that matter is stable. If fermions could occupy the same quantum mechanical state, then carbon would not have its amazing properties that make life possible. In fact, matter as we know it would not have come to exist, but if it did come to exist by some miracle: it would quickly destroy itself in a grand catastrophe to warm the hearts of the most enthusiastic prophets of doom.

There's not so much reason as some physicists assume to believe that the Particularized Universe can be re-constructed, or even its strictly quantitative aspects, by human systems of thought working from some very small scale of space-time and building up in a monotonic fashion. There seem to be too many discontinuities, too many impositions of arbitrary initial conditions or even impositions of arbitrary behaviors. Most of this takes place at the level of the universe. Take an analogy to building a house. At first it seems the house can be viewed as being built from elementary pieces,

[11] In the language of quantum physics, wave-functions, this property of fermions corresponds to a certain anti-symmetry, but that's a modeling of a factual aspect of the world and not an explanation to anyone but a positivist with his blinders on. The sheer particularity of this and other properties of the stuff of this universe implies that arbitrary and personal decisions were made.

but second thought will lead to the realization that some of those elementary pieces are the result of industrial, biological, and geological processes on a scale much larger than the house itself. Like all analogies, this one is very much imperfect, but it still can indicate a problem in the thinking of modern scientists. To be repetitive, Wittgenstein was likely right in his prediction: when we find the foundations, we might find they're being held up by the rest of the structure. More bluntly: the universe itself is the primary created thing rather than just a collection of things moving through time and space.

Yet, for all the fun one can have as a physicist or philosopher, or an observer of those folk, the real problem remains beyond human understanding:

> How God could have created a world where living beings might have any real freedom from His overpowering presence and from the laws governing the physical stuff of their bodies?

It's our duty to try to understand, and I'm trying to provide some tools to help us understand in the best way possible for creatures such as ourselves: we must tell a plausible story about God's world.

7 Many Things Come to Be

7.1 A Narrative

In the beginning was the Word: the Word was with God and the Word was God. He was with God in the beginning. Through Him all things came into being. For His sake, Father and Holy Spirit spoke with Him as one God:

> Let there be many things.

God imposed many facts upon the Primordial Universe, causing it to expand out of its perfect unity. And the Holy Three in One erected hedges that the many things not collapse back to a state of perfect symmetry in which there was but one entity however much it surged and seethed in its own timeless way.

Symmetry was broken. Perfection was destroyed. Homogeneity and unity became many things and time came to be for there were events that left the Universe in a different state than it had been. Space was being rapidly created as the homogeneous stuff of the Universe began to coalesce into particular things, particles and bundles of energy and fields. Weak and strong nuclear forces appeared as the various nuclear particles coalesced out of the chaotic homogeneity of the primordial Universe. Electromagnetic fields appeared along as electrons coalesced out of the chaos.

And many things came to be in such a way that they could become other things.

7.2 A Commentary

Things are necessarily particular. A universe of things is particular almost beyond human endurance. Things tie us down. Our own thing-like natures hold us back, not allowing us to sport wings, not allowing us to become men or women or centaurs at will. We flirt with disorder, thinking we can control it and use it to our advantage. At these edges of our natures, there's plenty of disorder for the flirting. There's plenty of disorder inside our natures. We are disorder. We are sin. And it couldn't be any other way so far as we know. It's that sin that allows us to shape our ordered selves. It's that sin that's the privation in us and in our environments, providing room for us to stretch out as we struggle to become true persons, well-ordered human animals.

And what has this to do with the electroweak force breaking down into electromagnetism and into the weak nuclear force which leads to the nuclear decay of power-plants and atomic bombs? What has this to do with the formation of stars and galaxies and black-holes from those particles of matter, those forces, those fields, which arose as perfect order and homogeneity and symmetry broke down?

We can see a world in a grain of sand but only so long as we see that world in our own minds. Of all the many things that assume and encapsulate the universe, only the human brain is capable of being formed as a self-aware image of the universe. This formation, which can be derailed or distorted, is one of the strongest possible ways of imitating the Son of God, our brother in flesh and blood and our Creator. In the very act of seeing that universe, we're applying at least a moral order assuming the existence of a rational Creator. With no rational Creator, there's no universe but only an incoherent collection of environments related, at best, to each other and to any possible totality of environments by infinite regressions of cause and effect.

In the eras after Einstein, we can see a universe first that we might see a world. At the same time, there are still some Christian believers who see a world without seeing that universe as defined by Einstein. But the number of such simple believers is dwindling with every TV documentary on the Big Bang and every newspaper report of another ape which might be an ancestor of man. This is no plot by Satan but rather the sign of a God impatient of Christian lack of faith as He was impatient of Israelite idolatry. We have preferred our human superstitions to the empirical truths of God's world and those empirical truths are images of thoughts of God, thoughts He wishes us to share.

Let us have the courage and confidence and faith to accept

> God's world without feeling a need to deform it to suit our preconceptions.

From a more perfect unity came a more ad-hoc unity in the form of this particular universe with its chaotic behavior. Remember what I said earlier about chaos. It's easily generated by linking two systems which move in ways independent of each other. Can there be two systems more independent of each other than the forces of order and disorder? It's in these complex interactions of order and disorder that complex entities, such as human beings, can evolve.

But we should be clear about the nature of that disorder. It's the source of evil. A disordered entity is not necessarily evil by intent, but it is evil. You could say it does evil or even that evil is inflicted upon it, but it's more direct and more to the point to say that it is evil. True enough it is that it's potential evil and the realization of that evil will result in that entity disappearing into the nothingness from which it arose, but it's usually better to speak directly. As St. Augustine said: We do not sin, we are sin. We are not disordered, we are disorder.

And we are order.

The same can be said of the stars of the Milky Way. They are disorder and they are order.

Some would say the disorder of the stars is not evil, but then why would the disorder of Mt. Etna be evil, natural or otherwise? Because it's nearer to us? That doesn't seem so good a criteria for dividing evil from good.

Then again, as I've been implying, we don't need to understand evil to define it, though we can often enough recognize it in some of its more extreme or grotesque forms. Flannery O'Connor thought of the grotesque, sometimes even the evil, as being good in formation. She knew St. Thomas Aquinas far better than I do. I suspect she was on to something of which I've only the slightest whiff. But I do have the whiff. And I think the answer lies in another claim of St. Augustine: The man who truly loves God can do as he will. And so we get to the heart of the matter:

> Love is the ultimate form of order.

I'm not talking about schmaltzy, sentimental love. And I'm certainly not talking about the sort of romantic love that typically leads to serial polygamy and shattered lives. I'm talking about the love which is one with a special sort of order that we Christians call peace. By peace Christians mean something very specific though we don't really know what it is just because we can only get hints of it in this world which is being born. And we're persons who are being born. Birth can be an ugly painful process in which the head gets squeezed into a non-human shape and the breath is cut off and the body gets covered with blood and gore.

We can say this much about the Christian concept of peace: even in the midst of this world's disorder, peace can come to us in an inner sense and in some, perhaps many, of our relationships which build local communities. Those who are resurrected will find themselves in a world which is fully ordered in all ways, though we can't say quite what that means since we have barely a clue as to the nature of that world or its underlying substance.

St. Thomas Aquinas wrapped up much of St. Augustine's thought in his more schematic writings in which the concepts of order are better developed. But I think there's much in St. Augustine that needs recovered, including his great appreciation for the importance of sin, disorder in general. It's not the case that we should ever nurture sin or disorder but rather that we should recognize that sin is a basic part of any creature in this universe. If St. Augustine had been able to more fully purge himself of his Neoplatonic ideas in his interpretation of his basic insight that we are sin, then Christians, and others in the West, might have avoided anthropological beliefs in conflict with empirical knowledge. Again, Augustine's basic insight was: "We do not sin, we are sin," and the concept of original sin was a way of expressing that so that it was an intelligible idea to those who accepted the pagan concept that man had fallen from a god-like state and the world had fallen from some sort of paradisaical state. I'll suggest another interpretation of the tale of the Garden of Eden:

> Our ancestors were moral animals which had evolved to an increasingly advanced state of rationality and self-awareness. The tale told in the book of Genesis about Adam and Eve reflected an intuition that man had risen from a state of animal innocence. Our apish ancestors might well have been brutal and aggressive creatures or they might have been relatively gentle. That doesn't matter so much as the realization that their moral crimes were not committed in a state of human self-awareness. Even as our ancestors were being selected for the moral habits necessary to a social ape with very slowly maturing children,

> those apish creatures did not deal directly with the sin and disorder which was a fundamental part of their apish nature and also a fundamental part of the environments they inhabited. Man is forced to deal with his natural tendencies to nurture disorder both in his being and in his environments, but he also has to deal with those sins which are due to his refusal to be found by the God who has spoken in human history.

An entity which develops or evolves rather than being created more or less complete will need disorder at least at its boundaries and probably inside of it. Else what could it expand into or use as the material of its ordered being? Our bodies are dependent upon a chain of life, starting with various sorts of bacteria which can take up nitrogen and convert it into a form usable by other living organism, plankton and plants which can absorb the high-entropy energy created by the nuclear processes of the sun, and various forms of life which can convert a variety of minerals into useful forms.

Life is a process by which energies and minerals, in an already degraded or high-entropic state, are organized by a self-sustaining entity in processes that increase the general state of degradation or entropy in the surrounding environment. Developing order depends upon disorder. Growth of that sort, perhaps of most sorts, needs raw materials, and those raw materials can be viewed as disordered. We turn disordered material into ordered material, sometimes ordered substance of our own being. But we also produce a greater disorder as a side-effect.

The moral ordering processes are at least analogous to these processes by which stars are born of great gas clouds collapsing under the force of gravity – gravity provides a sort of organizational force to create these massive nuclear furnaces, one of which is necessary to our existence. I'll not dwell on the physical organizational processes of this universe, many of which are quite interesting and are subject to active research and speculation. The bibliographical essays provide pointers to books which discuss what's known and what isn't known about the evolution of the physical universe.

Particular things – including living things, develop to their particularity by processes that need some sort of external disorder and probably internal disorder as well. Certainly, internal disorder is present in this universe, inside stars and galaxies as well as inside plankton and grizzly bears. Since I'm claiming that our underlying stuff, our only underlying stuff, is our flesh and blood, I'm bound to find our moral and spiritual natures in the physical processes by which we, as particular creatures, come to be. In a deep sense, which St. Augustine intuited but could not see more clearly because he knew not of genes nor of an expanding universe, we are disorder. If we're to become beings ordered by way of our partially free participation, morally well-structured persons capable of life with God and capable of enjoying that life, we need the disorder which surrounds us and which disrupts the most inward aspects of our being.

We need to grow into that disorder, conquer it in a sense, but taking into our own beings the stuff of that disorder, even the time and space which it stirs up. In my telling of the story of God's Creation, the good Lord created a Primordial Universe which was perfectly well-ordered, symmetrical and homogeneous. It was incapable of giving birth to particular things. That particular things might come to be, God had to break down that perfectly homogeneous entity, the Primordial Universe. A more particularized universe came to be, with an extremely chaotic balance between order and disorder. Our natures were formed at a boundary where order and disorder battled. Only by continuing that battle in the way commanded by Jesus Christ can we have any hope of achieving the higher state of person-hood, in imitation of the Lord Himself.

Disorder is not necessary for order. The Primordial Universe with its perfect homogeneity, perfect symmetry, perfect order, could have been maintained by God for time without end.

Evil is not necessary for good. Perhaps God can create truly good creatures, creatures made to be good and to be morally free from day one. Certainly, there was unbounded goodness in the lifeless perfection of the Primordial Universe.

Disorder is necessary for the sorts of particular creatures that we find on the earth, orcas and rattlesnakes as well as human beings. Evil is necessary that human beings might become good by the processes appropriate to the particular sorts of creatures which we are. Since the matter and energy and fields of this universe forms our stuff, our only stuff, I'm claiming we can see disorder and order as being evil and good viewed differently.

Why does disorder, specifically moral evil, exist? The answer is simple and was given to us in the Good News of Christianity, the Gospels:

> Before we were, God loved us.

These particular creatures we call human beings are the disorder as well as the order inherent in the processes by which the species evolved and the processes by which an individual human being develops. We do not sin but we are sin. I'm sure that St. Augustine was implying also: we do not do good but we are good. Rightfully, he emphasized not the battles already won but those which are still going on in our actions and our thoughts right to the instant of our deaths.

This is a point at which we can see the value of my revision of the Thomistic doctrine of the act-of-being so that it becomes a doctrine which respects the way in which contingent stuff comes into existence from nothingness and also respects the qualities of particular things made of that stuff. This slightly modified Thomistic form of existentialism can respect both the coming into existence which is emphasized in my discussion of the Primordial Universe and the consequent chaotic development which is emphasized in my discussion of the dynamic particularity of the Particularized Universe and the things it contains. As Gilson discusses in *Being and Some Philosophers*, most philosophers have been essentialists seeing existence as simply another quality possessed by stuff or particular things. There has also been a mistaken form of existentialism in which the act of ever coming into existence is emphasized in such a way as to etherealize things. In the case of Sartre, this was an explicit and conscious hatred of the particularity that prevented him from being what he wished to be. Sartre was very much a modern man, if more brutally honest than most.

The modern ideologies seem to me to combine the greatest errors of the essentialists and the existentialists who deny particularity. That is, they free Creation from God by seeing existence as an accidental quality of this collection of environments they mis-label as a universe and then imagine some sort of constant act-of-being that allows them to see the world as etherealized in such a way that things do not subsist but are constantly being brought to exist by our disordered desires. Human beings can choose their sex by allowing their bodies to be mutilated, and even more radical changes are on the way as our medical systems are more and more corrupted by magical thought. Human beings can separate themselves from their natural environment by way of climate control. Human beings can separate themselves from their local communities by joining the various virtual communities which form around the products and services of the public marketplaces.

We begin to see hints, but strong hints, as to why it is that a shaping of a human mind within the context of, for example, a small town in New England, prepares that mind for comprehending the universe as a whole, with all of its processes of star formation and nuclear synthesis. We can also see hints of the ways in which human beings are brainwashed so that they become worshipers of the gods of the marketplaces, creatures unsuited for everlasting life as companions to God. And this brainwashing moves forward in nearly all cases with the willing cooperation of the victim.

We also begin to see hints of a harsh implication of this more clear and less mystical way to view order and disorder or good and evil. We are sin and God will have mercy, but those who nurture their disordered or sinful tendencies will turn themselves into the sorts of creatures who could not possibly enjoy life with God even if He were to open the gates of Heaven to them. Such comments apply also to the way in which we raise our children. Unless we take this life as being meaningless in itself, we must consider the terrible prospect that God will not rescue those who turn their very selves into centers of disorder and sin rather than struggling to become good and to become ordered in that way that Jesus Christ offered when He blessed some and many: "My peace be with you." His peace is not of this world because it's the fulfillment of this world and thus lies beyond any possibilities of a world in which disorder is still present. But that peace will include the ordered human persons who emerge from this life, ordered to a Christ-like state which can be considered person-hood in a non-trivial sense.

I'll not presume on my own salvation nor that of any other particular people, though I've known some who seemed to have a foot in Heaven already, but I'll say that it seems unlikely that God will save those who nurture the disorder in their inner beings or in the outward activities of their lives. I can't imagine Jesus Christ ever willingly setting so much as a foot in DisneyWorld or in a modern pro sports stadium. We should be careful of appearances of order that mask a deeper disorder, often an explicit rebellion against human nature or against God's revelations of His purposes in creating this universe.

Other than the universe itself, there are two ordered entities that seem to be of particular concern to the God of Jesus: the individual human being and the Church. From a Christian viewpoint, certainly within the worldview developed in this book, there must be a basic truth in those concerns of God, a truth that will show up even in the physical natures of those who choose to be God's friends as well as the Church formed by those friends of God. It cannot be something He is imposing upon a world which otherwise belongs to Satan. I'll work my way back to that idea by first talking about wrongful sorts of order: parasitic order such as that of the nation-state and its servant – corporate capitalism.

Adam Smith was watching a society of morally well-structured Presbyterians interacting in such a way that they could take care of their own interests and still form a morally well-structured marketplace. As people began to value the marketplace activities for their own sake and not just as ways for Christians and other peoples to trade surplus goods of economies which were mostly local, then people, like Charles Darwin, began to beat paths away from the very source of order which had allowed them to develop their good character traits. Like animals that live by eating their own young, the inhabitants of modern societies began to exploit their own young in efforts to keep accelerating the already frenetic activities of the marketplaces. Mothers also came to be despised, to be considered useless unless they participated in public, taxable activities. Note that the word 'taxable' sneaked in to this current discussion. The nation-state is the master of corporate capitalism, passing legislation or making judicial decisions that allow corporations to enjoy hard-won human rights – as perverse a result as was ever celebrated by the liberal right.

There's a specific event which is a good symbol, and more than a symbol, of this deep relationship between the nation-state and corporate capitalism. A century and a half ago, the Illinois Central Railroad was granted a charter which allowed them to build railroads through Illinois. Some local communities protested when the railroad began to exercise governmental powers of land seizure. A young Illinois lawyer argued the railroad's case before the Illinois Supreme Court, securing the railroad the right to overrule the efforts of local communities to protect themselves from the predatory activities of state-chartered corporations. The name of that young lawyer was Abraham Lincoln and that case was a major precedent in the process by which the courts helped the legislature and the corporate lawyers to strip the local communities of any power or right to protect themselves against the unholy alliance of central governments and corporations. The state of Illinois was acting, in retrospect, as an agent of the emerging nation-state of which Lincoln himself would be the greatest prophet.

You cannot serve God and mammon both. You cannot be a loyal servant of a modern-nation state and a Christian both. You cannot be a loyal servant of corporate capitalism and a Christian both.

For generations, people were loyal Americans, or Englishmen or Italians, and also Christians in a way that justified the label. They were loyal employees of banks and car-manufacturers and also Christians. Because we ignored the signs that we were living inappropriate lives, living off the moral and spiritual inheritance which we were wasting, we have reached the point where the gods of the marketplaces, commercial and political alike, have even invaded our homes. They shape the minds and souls of our children, sometimes by way of mere background assumptions in movies or television shows which seem innocent enough. Recent surveys, published in *Science* magazine have indicated that American women dislike to raise their own children, preferring romantic activities and many sorts of work in the public marketplaces. Check out the movies, television shows, books, and music videos they watched while growing up. Young American women are being systematically purged of any maternal desires that they can spend more time working or consuming to the benefit of the corporate economy and the tax-collectors who are its greatest beneficiaries.

Human females are born with tendencies to develop the maternal inclinations that are so important to our species, for biological reasons and not because God imposed a vision of the Cleaver household upon us. Only human females are capable of properly raising human young, and those who gave birth to those young have brains which were restructured during the child-bearing and child-birthing processes. Their brains are altered so they're bonded to their children so intensely as to be beyond the imagination of a mere male. I raise this issue in this place to point out the extent to which we have allowed ourselves and our children to be shaped to the needs of the nation-state and corporations which value women as workers and consumers and act as if the people of the future can simply be imported from the same countries which build and design an increasing percentage of our cars and computers. Moral reform is impossible unless we manage to restore respect for the maternal natures of human females and manage to restore the confidence of young women in their own natures. As it is, we teach those young women that they should be either funny-shaped men or sluts, but I'll have more to say on that subject in the next chapter.

From here we can head in only one of two directions:

- We can trek back towards a proper order, which trek will force a generation or two of us to live in relative poverty while we're building a political system and economic system consistent with morally well-ordered flesh-and-blood human beings. Those sorts of creatures can only be morally well-ordered when they live in a situation where their social lives and inner selves can reflect each other and that reflection has to take on those characteristics I've often mentioned: unity, coherence, and completeness.

- We can accept the dictates of the gods of the marketplaces and march into a dark and dreary future of slavery.

We're born animals and we become more than that, even suited to be companions of God, by accepting God's gifts, including the gift of worshiping Him. It's clear that God gains nothing by our worship of Him, though it's His due. We're the ones who benefit. It's the gods of the marketplaces, especially the nation-states which gain when we are induced to worship them. We're the ones who lose. It's also clear that God gains nothing when we discipline our selves to His demands, including the demands implied by the social, moral natures He gave us. In both that worship and that disciplining of our selves, we move towards an ordered state which might prepare us for everlasting life as companions to God.

Disorder, even sin, can be our friends in the sense that we form ourselves by expanding into these regions of disorder and sin, inside of ourselves and in our external environments. We have this responsibility to bring order to these regions of disorder. In doing this, we enlarge ourselves in a sense, remaining minuscule creatures in an awfully large universe, but bringing into our own selves that which we need to become persons, that which we need to be suited for true life, life as companions of the Resurrected Lord and His Father and His Spirit. And they'll be our Father and our Spirit at that point, by Their adoption of us and not by our nature. For even our perfected selves, perfected on earth or in the flames of Purgatory, will be small entities, and our efforts no more than scribblings upon a wall. But our Father seems pleased enough with our childish efforts. We need to act in ways appropriate to this Christian teaching: what good we can do is very small indeed but it pleases God.

Yet that disorder will remain with us for all our lives on earth. I've known people who seemed to be already living in the Lord's peace to a shocking extent. Still that peace is mostly an inner peace and the person of even the most devout, cloistered monk is constantly assaulted by the disorder of this universe.

That disorder is usually present in our inner selves and always present in the universe in which we're embedded. This is another reason that only God can see the world truly: it's a world truly only over its entire existence including the times at which various purposes of God are fulfilled.

The apocalypse is ever present and ever threatening us, just as the Creation is ever with us. We should not look to the Big Bang for a vision of the moment of Creation. There's no such moment unless you imagine you can leave time to look at the universe from the absolute eternity which is not frozen timelessness but rather an everlasting explosion in which all instants of time are present at once. But only God can inhabit that region. For us, the creation is ongoing for the same reason that there are no edges to the Einsteinian universe. Every location in the universe is the center of the universe and no location inside the universe is privileged. Every instant in Creation is the instant of God's actions of creation, the acts-of-being which bring all contingent entities into existence.

Each and every one of us, each and every human community – Christian or otherwise, each gas cloud in deep space which is heading towards the collapse that leads to galactic formation, is a battleground on which forces of order and disorder struggle. This is not a matter of Satan fighting God for control but rather a matter of a world being born, of individual entities and particular human beings coming into existence and then forming, or failing to form, themselves appropriately. We can change, we can develop, the world can develop, species can evolve, not because of the actions of something called chance but rather because we're continually ceasing to exist and continually being brought into existence by God's acts-of-being. It is this process which provides not only the energy which drives the development of the universe forward but also the ice upon which we skate, the dangerously slippery surface which allows us to change direction, sometimes to even go up the side of a rut and into another rut. The process itself is neutral. We can use it travel to Heaven or to the permanent grave.

And it's the same process we should keep in mind when we modern people try to recover a sense of God's involvement in His own Creation. We, Christians as well as falling Christians, have pushed God away, exiling Him to the transcendent realms which we call Heaven when we wish to be in control. To the contrary, Mr. Christian and Mrs. Unitarian, God is so present that He is able to reconstitute ordinary bread and table wine into the Flesh and Blood of His own Son each Sunday in a variety of Sacramental Christian Churches and each and every day at nearly every Catholic church or chapel.

We are sin because sin is disorder, the lack of order, a privation in being, a privation which penetrates and surrounds our beings. And it's that privation which gives us the space and the disordered substance by which our animal beings can grow. It's growth, in size in some sense but certainly in order, that allows us to become persons. And it's that disorder impinging upon our beings that threatens to destroy us. A being which falls into disorder, into a willful state of sin, does not become evil in the glamorous way of modern-day horror stories. Dracula cannot live forever by drinking the blood of living human beings. Evil, a state of sin or disorder, is privation of being. That privation in our being suits the purposes of God as He welcomes us to become ordered creatures, creatures living in the peace of Christ, but we are to order that part of the substance of our bodies or the environments in which we live, bringing order to regions of disorder. If we nurture the disorder, then we're edging towards non-existence.

I'll conjecture that Satan does not literally exist. Movies and books which present Satan as a free-standing enemy of God are paganistic and are in conflict with the Christian understanding that all being comes from God, as well as the possibility of disordered or deprived being. But disordered being is in the process of passing out of existence. Disordered being does not rule any part of the universe because disorder cannot gain control over order – it can destroy order and produce death or even an explosion but that's pretty much it. The disorder itself fades into the universe even as it destroys.

If we extrapolate from our own nature and that of the only creatures we know and have studied, we can see that there's no immaterial will which is magically attached to some substance. There can be no creature, Satan or other, having an evil will but still being, in his substance, a creature of God and thus good in that substance. It's substance that's either ordered or disordered, good or evil. If a creature nurtures the disorder inside of itself and surrounding itself, that disorder begins to dissolve the substance of that creature. It's the opposite process by which good can form from the grotesque in ways explored in the novels of Flannery O'Connor, but a nurtured disorder will destroy any substance very quickly and substance is necessary for created beings.

The idea that human beings have some sort of will independent of our physical stuff is in conflict with Christian truths in light of modern understanding of what this universe is. Our wills are in the very intentions and habits of our bodies, our animal natures. This means that an evil will can't inhabit a good substance. An evil will is more a cancer chewing away at the substance of a self-aware moral creature and perhaps some which are not truly self-aware, such as bears or chimpanzees. We have no reason to believe there can be a creature corresponding to the traditional description of Satan: a creature of good substance and evil will. An evil will corresponds to the nurture of a disorder that will destroy any sort of good order. And we have no reason to believe that God would act to override that destruction of any creature which nurtures the disorder in itself or in the environments it inhabits.

Most Christians, for all their other good qualities, have been animistic pagans in some of their beliefs. That situation hasn't changed in the modern world for all of our pretenses to be hard-headed empirical thinkers. We should begin to move towards a Christian conception of the world, however austere it might seem to some compared to a world teeming with hosts of archangels and legions of demons. The basic problem is that we don't understand the dynamic nature of this stuff God created, this matter and energy and fields, this energy complex as some physicists say. We think of the world in terms similar to those of Plato and Aristotle but in a simpler and less rational way. We think the physical things of this world, including our bodies, are made of inert substances which cannot, in and of themselves, acquire the more dynamic and more ethereal qualities we associate – appropriately – with mind and soul. We have let the reductionistic and mindless materialists chase us out of God's universe and into a maze of superstitions.

To make up for what they thought to be lacking in the physical stuff made by God, philosophers and theologians and poets have often conjectured the existence of mind-stuff and soul-stuff. Those two sorts of stuff were defined in somewhat funny ways. Mind-stuff is stuff that has the properties necessary to provide abstract reasoning capabilities in a creature made of supposedly inert physical stuff. Soul-stuff is, very roughly speaking, what is needed to make us creatures capable of responding to God's call.

Only a generation or so before St. Augustine, another great Christian thinker – St. Athanasius, had attacked the idea of an immortal human soul as a pagan intrusion into Christian belief. It must be said that St. Athanasius was not so powerful or creative a thinker as St. Augustine, nor was he so concerned with the legitimate goal of making sense of the world in philosophical and historical terms. But St. Athanasius was the principle Christian warrior in a brutal fight to preserve the truth of the Incarnation: that Jesus Christ was the human nature taken up by the Son of God, God Himself. Jesus Christ was not a human person because the Son was a pre-existing Person. In his overview series on the writings of the early Fathers of the Church, Johannes Quasten wondered why Athanasius never spoke of the human soul of Jesus Christ in his writings which are so important to Christian orthodoxy. The reason is clear: St. Athanasius didn't believe that Jesus Christ has a human soul in the sense of a separable and immortal component. Nor did St. Athanasius believe that he, the Bishop of Alexandria, had any such component.

I think Athanasius to have been right but I don't wish to set Father up against Father. I'm pointing out that at least some of the orthodox Fathers denied the existence of the separable and immortal human soul on Christian grounds even when there seemed to be valid philosophical and scientific grounds to conjecture such a soul. Those who studied human beings in the ancient and Medieval world believed that matter, including our flesh and blood, is inert and can only be molded by the imposition of an immaterial form. And they couldn't see any signs that any human organ could mold itself in the plastic way which would allow us to develop abstract concepts from our perceptions of the particular things in our environments. Reasonably enough under those circumstances, pagan philosophers and some Christian thinkers conjectured soul-stuff or mind-stuff that could make up for what was lacking in the stuff of flesh and blood.

Now we know that the physical stuff of this universe is a very dynamic complex of a sort not yet fully understood though scientists have learned much about specific forms that complex takes in our currently cold universe: matter and energy and fields. They also understand some aspects of the physical stuff of this universe under other conditions, such as the extreme density and unimaginably high temperatures of the early seconds of the current expansionary phase of this universe – that is, the early seconds of the existence of what I've called the Particularized Universe. This universe created by God contains all the stuff that's necessary for forming the bodies of creatures capable of the highest and lowest of emotions and thoughts. The universe as a whole seems to have some sort of developmental inclinations, poorly understood and under active research, which lead to the birth of galaxies and their gathering into huge complexes which form arcs around still huger spaces which are void of observable matter. Are the evolutionary processes of life on earth related to those large-scale developmental inclinations? Maybe and maybe not, but economy of thought would probably lead us to first conjecture there's some profound lesson about the nature of this universe hidden in the histories of the birth and growth of galaxies and the birth and growth of life on earth. At a very general level:

> We live in a world which was not directly created by God, at least not in the best story I can tell using revealed truths and empirical knowledge. Rather does it seem the case that God made the basic stuff which underlies this universe and then He began to tell a tale starting with a very dense and hot state of matter and energy and fields and moving by way of developmental processes. Galaxies do not seem to be objects which can be fully modeled by equations so much as they are entities with a narrative history, that is, a factual history. Life on earth shares that narrative attribute with galaxies and, in fact, the entire universe.

In recent centuries, some fraudulently sophisticated lines of thought, honestly Deistic and dishonestly Christian, have converged in the belief that the universe is some sort of place independent of God. It seems as if we can view God as a one-time Creator who was nice enough to go away and let us take care of our affairs as we think proper. We push God out of the way, out of what used to be His universe, so that we can fix the general muddle He made of things with His inability to make our lives safe and comfortable and to make our pain and suffering go away. We know that God is well-intentioned but we have doubts about His competence because of all this unnecessary suffering He has allowed. As Melville claimed of Emerson, we believe that if we'd been present at the moment of Creation, we could have given God some good advice.

We inhabit a universe, or environments for far too many, in which we can misperceive signs of stability or signs of chaos, depending upon our moods. This is a form of disorder, of sin: to pretend to see a world of disorder, of too much evil. This is no less a sign of disorder, of sin: to pretend that evil has somehow creeped into a perfect world created by God. God created this world with its struggle between disorder and order, between sin and the peace of Christ. God created this world. I've done what I could in this book to tell a story which makes sense of it all, but such an effort is possible only for those who know beforehand that God is in charge and only God really understands what's going on. Yet, it seems clear that He wishes us to try to understand what He has done and even to understand to our limited abilities what His Son told us of the purposes of the Father.

We understand not once for all. If we somehow arrived at the best possible human understanding of what has happened so far in this universe made by God, that understanding would fall apart as new events passed by our eyes. To a large extent, the story is its own meaning. God loves us and He loves the world which is this story, though there's plenty of misery and sin and suffering in this tale. But He's telling the story and only He knows all the good that's being realized even now. God stays within His own guidelines so far as I can tell, but He can act in empirical history without necessarily making a big deal about it just because He's telling the story and He's continually creating the stuff which forms the characters and settings of that story.

Most metaphysical systems assume substances exist as a matter of course. Plato and Aristotle, Plotinus and St. Augustine, all emphasized substance and seemed to treat the act of creation as being a one-time event. After that, existence was simply an accident, as a philosopher would say, of a substance. The existence of a red ball is said to be as accidental as its redness. This is utterly wrong according to St. Thomas Aquinas who saw that God was His own Act-of-being and that we're the results of acts-of-being carried out by the same God. That model needs a small adjustment in my worldview. As I've already stated, I can add clarity to my telling of God's story if God's acts-of-being bring the Primordial Universe into existence as a primary act and the universe and its specific things as a secondary matter. I'm claiming that human story-telling is analogous to God's creation of particular thing-like being.

The difference is that it adds a second layer of contingency to specific things, including living creatures, in this world. This second layer seems to correspond better to what we now know about the development of galaxies and living creatures. In my story, this allows God to be continually creating the foundation of our being, the Primordial Universe, even as we and other particular things go about our activities, including those most directly involved in our development. And, yet, we must remember that God is going about those activities with us.

How can we make sense of this? Relentlessly, I suggest we make sense of this by way of the Thomistic theory of knowledge and the Thomistic understanding of the act-of-being and, most important of all, He who is His own Act-of-being. But I'm going to add a bit more to these ideas this time around. I'll start with the theory of knowledge:

> Our minds are shaped by our interaction with our environments, with the universe as a whole in some substantial sense, so long as all goes well. This shaping process is two-staged. The human mind, in its power and limitations, was shaped over the three billion years or more that living creatures have been evolving on earth. The individual human mind will develop some basic capacities but those capacities will develop to higher levels and other capacities will develop properly only when the child is nurtured, preferably by her own mother whose brain will have been partially restructured during pregnancy and child-birth, restructured in some general ways to make her a better mother and restructured in some specific ways to bond the mother strongly to that particular child.
>
> Our minds are shaped to form images of the physical universe. This can be seen very strongly in the tendency of boys to imitate animals, to imagine themselves to be elephants or gorillas or wolves. Males of the human species are naturally totemic. Our ancestral males, and many males around the world today, hunt animals of other species by becoming one with those animals. I imagine this remains true of the more specialized warriors of modern armies, that is, they're trained to put themselves in the place of the enemy soldiers from their different culture and their specific physical environment. I would even suggest strongly that a Shakespeare could think and feel in the place of his women characters much more effectively than even George Eliot (Marian Evans) could think in the place of her male characters.
>
> This all depends upon the physical brain. There's no generic human soul which is thrown into a male or female body. The brain is part of that body and the body is that human being. A human being with a properly developed mind is more than her body but that body remains the necessary foundation, the real stuff, of her thing-like being. A woman is not a generic

soul thrown into a body with a womb – she's a being of which a womb is an integral part.

I'll talk later about the way that modern human females have been deformed to better suit the purposes of the gods of the marketplaces, but I'll mention here that human males, particularly the creative boys, are also deformed by the way they're raised. The sort of free play in which young, totemic lads engage is not so profitable to computer manufacturers and software companies as computer games are, not so profitable to sporting goods manufacturers as little league, and so the more powerful sorts of masculine thought are destroyed as we exploit those young boys that the public marketplaces might grow. All of this is happening as knowledge of the developmental processes of the human brain grows. It's happening as we ignore the evidence that our ways of raising our children are evil – they're destructive of the natures of these children and destructive of family and church and local political community.

Knowledge is easily ignored when it tells us we should leave the public marketplaces. It's easy for us to ignore inconvenient knowledge because we're a people who have returned to magical attitudes. We're no longer a Christian people but we haven't become some sort of secularized scientific people. Science doesn't provide its own foundational beliefs, nor does any other empirical way of thought, not even engineering. We have returned to those days before Christianity drove magic underground where it increasingly became an esoteric and occult form of knowledge. Prior to the success of Christianity in imposing the attitudes of arts and sciences upon society, there was no substantial difference in methods or knowledge between magic and the arts and sciences. The real difference between magic and the arts and sciences lies in goals and motivation. Magic would control that which the wisdom of a Christian arts and sciences would see as being beyond our capability to control without destroying much that belongs to God.

A medical system corrupted so that it's magical doesn't need to invoke demons. Advanced surgical techniques and sophisticated chemicals work quite well to kill unwanted babies or elderly people. In fact, the witches of past centuries, such as the mother of Alexander the Great, used the best technology of their days to do their dirty work, though that knowledge was more a folklore knowledge of herbs, minerals, and the human body. So far as I know, that knowledge and those skills of witches were little different from those of more respectable medical doctors of the same eras. A medical system corrupted to a magical state doesn't help us to live a good life or die a good death – it experiments upon human babies to find ways to extend our miserables lives.

Our corporate businessmen and politicians are no different. They're turning themselves into magicians, creatures in rebellion against their Creator, creatures trying to gain control over that which belongs to God. There are conceivable futures where Christians will set up their own medical societies and have their own, morally well-ordered marketplaces, but there's little evidence that we'll be able to rescue ourselves within the next few generations. We collaborate with morally disordered societies which increasingly are replacing the moral order of our Christian ancestors with the perverse forms of order which come from magical ways of thought.[1] Moreover, I'll predict that science and medicine will increasingly become instrumentalist, reducing all human beings but those with great wealth or political power to materiel that can be used to meet the needs of the gods of the marketplaces. By that time, the needs of the gods of the marketplaces will be defined by the needs of the wealthy and powerful in our modern nation-states.

Now, those with ears to hear can understand a bit more clearly why it is that the order to be found in the institutions of the modern marketplaces, political and commercial, is not a proper order. It's not in tune with the evolving order of the universe. It's an order that's actually a rebellion against God, the Creator and King of the universe. Somewhere, Rousseau, a man who had an odd mixture of radical and traditionalist inclinations, predicted: when men come to believe they make laws rather than interpreting the laws of God and God's nature, then all hell will break loose on earth. We've reached that point. We're now in rebellion against our own biological natures and the natures of other creatures as well as being in rebellion against God Himself.

I've said that medical doctors, scientists, politicians, and businessmen are now magicians rather than practitioners of the arts and sciences of Western Civilization. Now, I'll extend that and say that any Christian who lets the television broadcasters or movie-makers mold his children, any Christian who allows himself to be molded in that way, any Christian who

[1]The discussion in terms of magic versus the arts and sciences is based upon insights found in *Of Masons, Magic, Monks, Medicine, and Marriage* by Hugh Barbour, O.Praem., prior of St. Michael's Abbey in Trabuco Canyon, CA. This article was published in *Chronicles: A Magazine of American Culture* in the March, 2005 issue.

accepts dubious medical procedures to gain himself a miserable few years of life or comfort, has gone over to the side of magic.

But there's more to all of this than simply human moral concerns. There's a God who's not only a one-time Creator but a Creator ever working, ever willing that the Primordial Universe and the universe come into being, else all created being would collapse into non-existence. Upon the scaffolding of the Primordial Universe and using the highly particular stuff of the universe, things are also created ever anew. More than that, things are participants in the story told by God, a complication that perhaps had escaped even Aquinas. This is my slightly modified version of Thomistic existentialism:

> God is His own act-of-being. We confuse matters when we speak of God as having essences or attributes as we know them, though we can gain some understanding of God by doing exactly this in an analogical manner. For example, God is not good because there's no substance as we know it to bear the property 'good'. Human beings become aware of God and perceive goodness as an attribute which is analogical to the creaturely attribute of goodness.
>
> Things are not simply molded out of substance as if we were dealing with the eternally existence matter of many pagan philosophers. Things are molded out of stuff that's continually being brought into existence. The things themselves in their particular qualities are also ever the objects of acts-of-being of God, but more in the manner of a story-teller whereas God's act-of-being for the underlying stuff of things is that of bringing into existence from nothing the pure being which can be shaped into many different worlds, or it can simply be left as it is.

Don't worry if this makes little sense or only vague sense at first. All of this has to be chewed upon, in quiet moments including times of silent prayer. I can assure you that much of my thought took place during such moments, even during the Mass when I was supposed to be concentrating upon the Lord and not fragile and provisional efforts to understand God and His Creation. Mea culpa.

The doctrine of "getting used to it" is our friend in matters such as this. Pray to God and think about what I'm saying in this book. If you have a different way, perhaps a better way, to bring God's world into view, and thus to bring God into view analogically, then Christians around the world need to hear of it. Christians need to think creatively, in analogy to God's true acts of creation. Rather than retreating from the world when empirical knowledge is in conflict with the provisional Christian worldviews of past centuries, we need to develop within ourselves the courage and the energy to creatively engage empirical knowledge that we might accept God's invitation to help Him tell the story of this His created world.

8 The Descent of an Ape

8.1 Narrative

Adam moved towards the sunlit grassfield but remained just in the shade of the trees, keeping his eyes upon the clumsier and stronger creatures who were so much like him and so different. Until recently, he'd joined in hunting parties with those creatures that he despised, though he didn't despise the wolves who also joined in the hunts, sharing the spoils. Adam didn't expect as much from the wolves as he did from creatures who seemed to be deformed versions of himself. Those knuckle-dragging creatures spoke in grunts that Adam could understand and speak, but they couldn't speak the words used in Adam's tribal group. And some of those words were used to make fun of those creatures, so slow in thought and clumsy in movement, so dull of eye, so wide and hunched-over. Those grunters couldn't even speak of the Great Spirit that walked the sky each day or the lesser spirits that ruled the night or roamed through the jungles. The grunters were lower than the animals just because they seemed at first to be higher.

Still remaining in the shade and out of view of his erstwhile allies, Adam began to move in the direction of his encampment, his tribe's home for the past few summer foraging seasons. Keeping his eyes upon the grunters, he saw that they had detected him and Adam snorted in disgust at the sight of the creatures lifting their noses up to catch the wind as if they were wolves or bears.

And their public parts were dangling in the wind as if they had no shame at all. Adam looked down at the triangular strip of leather which covered his parts now private. Eve had made such covers for the now private parts of all those in the tribe but the youngest of children. Since they had become private his parts had started to itch at times and to show white spots, but private they were and that was not something he regretted.

The first of his kind caught sight of a group foraging near his encampment. It was a mixed party of adults and children from his own tribe. He noticed Cain and Abel had caught sight of him. Even from a distance he could see Abel take a rapid skipping step and then run towards his father, anxious to hear the story of the hunt. Raising his right arm, Adam showed a leather thong to which nine rabbits were tied. It wasn't so exciting a catch as an elk or a boar, but it would make a good, tasty meal.

As he met Abel, he wondered why Cain had merely waved and then turned away. The boy was studying something growing in the tribe's trash pile. As Adam grew closer, he could see the boy was studying some plants which looked to be no more than grass. He wasn't sure why it interested Cain. Grass grew out of the trash-piles whenever they had foraged the nutty tasting seeds which grew on stalks in the sun-drenched meadows. He had noticed Eve foraging from those plants in the trash-pile but that just seemed natural. This business of studying...

Adam stared at his oldest son, wondering what was so fascinating about the grasses, but he was interrupted by a cry ahead of him. Suppressing his disgust, he forced himself to smile at his mother coming towards him, pointing she was at the rabbits and showing her pleasure with sounds that made her almost as one with the grunters that Adam had left behind him. Eve had been nagging at him when they were alone, telling him he should send his mother off to live with other grunters, like his brother who had joined another tribe after Eve had given him a leather breech-cloth to cover his private parts. Adam was glad that Cromag had wandered away and wished his mother Neander would follow.

8.2 Commentary

About a million years ago, the earth entered a cycle of severe ice ages every 100,000 years or so, with smaller glaciation periods in between as well as many cold periods without glaciation. Oddly enough, these cycles of glaciation events match up well with certain cycles of changes in the earth's orbit but it has been shown that the cyclical variations in energy reaching the earth's surface are not nearly great enough to cause these climate changes. Several years ago, when I was still keeping up with scientific discoveries, climate scientists seemed convinced that the earth's atmosphere had been put in a state where it was always near an ice age state because of the rising of the Himalayas. The cold air builds up in Siberia without mixing with the warm air to the south. The probable reason for the match-up with the earth's orbital cycles is that the atmosphere is unstable in the way of a sensitive drum-head. It's picking up the beat from the minor changes in energy level caused by the orbital changes.

And what has this to do with Adam? It sets the background for the evolution of the human race, though most of that evolution took place in Africa and it's far from certain how the climate in Africa was changed by the ice ages. But man was definitely affected by the minor glaciation event which ended a little more than 10,000 years ago. And those which occurred every 10,000 years or so before that. And man was also affected by the smaller ice ages such as that which began around 1400 and ended about 1900.

There's reason to believe that we're all descended from a single group of hunter-gathering people living in Africa about 60,000 years ago. This doesn't mean that there was no later mixing of Cro-magnon or Neanderthal blood into the lines of modern human beings. That mythical but real couple of Adam and Eve lived in comparatively recent times but still well before the time set by Biblical Literalists and a long time before man became a city-dwelling creature. I've also read that about 30,000 years ago, some humans seem to have migrated from modern-day Nigeria to the Near East. Those humans are likely the ancestors of most ethnic groups in Europe and some ethnic groups in parts of western Asia. It took another 20,000 years before the first city rose on the site of Jericho of Biblical fame. That city, perhaps the first in human history, rose near a work-camp of weapon- and tool-manufacturers that had been growing more and more permanent. During that same era, farmers in Asia Minor, modern-day Turkey, domesticated cattle and started farming in the modern sense.

But the modern human race did not come into existence at that time. It seems to have come into existence as early as 100,000 years ago. That early man would have been substantially the same at conception as he is now, but adult human beings might well have been a bit different from those of our age. For one thing, mothers might well have been passing on different genetic signals to the young embryos in their wombs.[1] In addition, the environments to which any human child would be exposed in its early

[1]The embryo in its earliest stages has no functioning DNA and is entirely dependent upon its mother to supply DNA that its cells can function. This means that mothers might have a greater effect upon the realization of a particular child than you might think

developmental phases would have been different from any that most modern human beings experience and perhaps even different from those experienced by members of the hunter-gathering peoples who have retained their traditional ways of life. In the context of this book, the most important issue would be that the very brains and minds of our ancestors might have been developed and organized in ways radically different from the brains and minds of a modern Brooklynite.

Another issue affecting the entire human body, including the brain, is the lack of food storage techniques which would have likely led to metabolic differences in our ancestors.[2] Since the brain draws heavily on bodily resources, brain development and brain activity might have been sacrificed in the bodies of many of our ancestors who were better adapted for famine than we are. All this is important, again in the context of this book, because we need to purge ourselves of this idea that human beings are autonomous beings simply cast into a world which is external to their natures.

Let me return to climatological issues to note that the first city was built during a period when the earth was warmer than it is now, a period very favorable to food production both natural and cultured. But the human race seems to have grown in numbers during a harsher period preceding that warmth. The timing of all of this is a little uncertain to be sure, but I feel confident in saying that the human race was already an aggressively opportunistic species that could expand into new regions and do well in those regions even during harsh times. It was man's opportunism that left him in a position to take full advantage of that warm period.

It was likely the opportunism of our line that brought about the extermination of Neanderthal man and maybe Cro-magnon man, though the latter might well be us. There's even a slight possibility that some of the Neanderthals bred into our line of descent. The species homo sapiens is not much like our surviving cousins in the family of apes. Chimpanzees, gorillas, all the rest, are niche creatures, no matter how intelligent they are by some measurements. We humans are more like wolves and bears in our opportunistic characteristics – this is an important point because it reintro-

---

from the standard high-school biology teaching that mother and father each contribute half an embryo's DNA. The mother might even have other effects upon the embryo developing in her womb even when that embryo has DNA which is fully functional.

[2]It's likely that famines will be common during ice ages, which are notably dry, for reasons which the interested reader can explore starting with *Climate History and the Modern World* by H. H. Lamb.

duces contextual and environmental factors and indicates they penetrate to the deepest regions of creatures which are presumed to be isolated individuals by the 'selfish gene' school of thought.[3] In fact, there's a phenomenon called 'convergent evolution', where unrelated species become very similar if they're adapted to similar ecological roles. The clearest case is that of the placental wolf and the Tasmanian wolf.

The placental wolf is the animal that most people intend when they say simply 'wolf'. The Tasmanian wolf is a marsupial more closely related to kangaroos and to koala bears than to the placental wolf. Yet, the two types of wolf look very similar and have very similar behaviors and capabilities because they both fill the ecological role of an opportunistic predator. The selection processes of evolution, and perhaps other processes, can cause very distantly related species to be so similar as to seem to be cousin species. This should tell us that context and environment are very important in this universe. Both the genocentric theorists of biology and the liberal theorists of economics and politics are incompetent in their understanding of the real world.

Human beings are the ultimate opportunistic species other than the usual suspects such as cockroaches, beetles, and bacteria. We can exploit almost any environment on earth. We expand and kill off species more by grabbing territory than by direct killing, though we have seen with whales that we're capable of more directly exterminating entire species when enough money is involved. It might well have been our ancestors who pushed the gorillas and chimpanzees more and more towards niches and the habits appropriate to such restricted living. It was not Daniel Boone who killed off the bears in Kentucky but all those who built towns and farms, leaving little wilderness. It was not the hunter Abel but the farmer Cain from whom descended those who built cities, eliminating vast expanses of natural habitat.

We are sin. In the terms I've chosen to use: we are disorder. We're also surrounded by disorder and all men, those who seek to order their selves and those who nurture their disorder, will try to bring their surrounding environment into a man-pleasing order.

---

[3]This isolation of organisms by an entire school of Darwinist thought is one of the clearest indications that scientistic thought has been driven by ideological considerations originating in political and economic thought. No sensible biologist – certainly not Charles Darwin at his naturalistic best – could separate an organism from its context, its environment, the way that various genocentric schools of thought have done.

Let's step back a little and think about how man evolved over the past few million years and how he became the dominant species on earth – other than those same usual suspects (cockroaches and friends).

The story is disturbingly complex and new discoveries of hominid species which lived during those few million years are occurring often enough to leave anthropology in turmoil. The brains of creatures in our line of descent grew at an explosive rate though no one can really say which of the many species are really our ancestors.

One anthropologist, Dean Falk, noted that changes to bone structure occur very slowly and are less likely than changes to soft tissue; therefore, she conjectured it would be likely our ancestral line is composed of those apish creatures with consistent and early development of sinus cavities which would allow a large and active brain to function without overheating. That leads to the humbling observation that we're the descendants of those apes with the largest and most plentiful holes in their heads.

Others have suggested that the most upright apes could use their hands most freely...

But for what? There's certainly the possibility that free hands could make man the spear-chucker a better fighter or hunter. But some have suggested that it's the increased grooming possibilities that tightened the bonds in human communities, encouraging the development of verbal skills. Thus we are may be descended from the apes which were the most talented gossips.

These are actually serious and well-grounded scientific proposals. I don't wish to make fun of those theories but I'm inclined to think we human beings should give up our prideful illusions. We're not fallen gods. We're apes which rose from our knuckles, which isn't so far a rise if you think about it.

From the Christian point of view, this is all right. It's God who can make us more than bipedal apes and He has promised to do so, but a realistic assessment of the human race in its current condition does not lead one to suspect we're anything but a race of apes who are more clever than wise.

Now I can get myself in real trouble by claiming that the modern ideologies bring a still greater threat than earlier collapses of moral order such as that which occurred when the Roman Republic decayed into the Roman Empire. I've already spoken of that greater threat, a serious threat indeed from the viewpoint of any Christian.

> The modern liberal societies are extremely effective at raising children to be the sorts of people who could not possibly be happy in any Heaven conceivable under Christian beliefs.

Is the United States the country of the anti-Christ though we imagine ourselves to be a Christian country, in fact, the most Christian country in history? This horrible suggestion first came to mind from two separate sources. I saw a quote on the Internet which was attributed to Mark Twain and it sounds like something he might have said. Though I can't track it down, I'm willing to mull it over as if he said it. My memory of the quote is: "Americans claim they wish to spend eternity in Heaven with God but they rarely choose to do things that might be part of a life in a Christian Heaven." A fellow in an Internet debate simplified and modernized it a little: Americans claim they wish to go to Heaven and live forever but the best use they can make of their short time on earth is to sit in front of the television.

The other quote was from Horkheimer, the German Neomarxist active in the middle third or so of the 20th century. He pointed out that the most brutal and competent of modern dictators could not destroy the family. The more they persecuted the family, the stronger some of those families grew. On the other hand, American businessmen have shown they can bribe people to freely and enthusiastically abandon their families. Is the sober, profitable evil of Walmart and Microsoft and the rational, benevolent evil of the Social Security Administration more effective than the sadistic, wasteful evil of the Soviet Politburo and bureaucracy? It seems that might be the case.

I'll seemingly digress here to let my readers know what is up with my interest in the moral role of the human family. After all, I'm speaking of God's universe and of God's offer of friendship to us, acceptance of that offer leading us towards the particular community of the Christian Church more than the community we call the family. Jesus Christ was not always a big advocate of the family, but He wants us to provide many children as members of His Body. Yet, the pilgrim Church on earth has far too often been more concerned with its institutional prerogatives and power and wealth than with the families which produce friends of God. At times, the family has prospered despite the hostility or indifference of the Church on earth – such as when the American leaders in the Catholic Church showed themselves to be mostly indifferent to the sacrifices being made by parents having lots of children during the Baby-boom era. In fact, the Catholic bishops in the United States supported, and still support, social programs that place heavy burdens upon large families, helping to produce major problems for themselves and other Catholics, including the loss of vocations in the Catholic Church.

God likes children as well as loving them. He said so in the Bible. Where else is He to find His human friends? I still can't tell you why an all-powerful God can find much pleasure in friendships with bipedal apes, but the very fact that He's a community of three Persons might give us some hint. To be sure, the family, as such, is fated to largely dissolve into the Church, though I don't know exactly what that means. I do know that morally well-ordered human beings will rarely arise outside of a traditional human family and that for reasons that can be derived from historical and biological knowledge without philosophical analysis or revelations from God. Moreover, peaceful and morally well-ordered communities, including local churches, are dependent upon those morally well-ordered human beings who are raised in traditional families. We could even say that it's in the bosom of the extended family that children are formed to be capable of being Christians. It's always possible to become a true Christian as an adult but conversions from a state of moral disorder into a state of Christian peace are usually quite painful.

The institutional Church, including its separated parts, helped to train their members not to have many children. Most of those members were happy to comply and to spend their money on fancy cars and their time on vacations in Cancun with their one or two children. More than that, American Catholics collaborated with the agents of the gods of the marketplaces in training parents to allow themselves and their children to be exploited by those agents – first of all, by allowing their very minds to be stunted and their souls to be deformed by various of anti-Christian and jingoistic propaganda. And still, the leaders of Christian churches – not just the Catholic Church, refuse to see that the gods of the marketplaces might be more effective enemies of the Church of Christ, of humanity in general, than the gods of war and destruction.[4] The reason for this effectiveness

[4]I should qualify that remark by noting that the Amish and other Anabaptist peoples are willing to organize their communities so that they serve God first and they don't seem to miss all the unnatural products and services that we're trained to consider necessities. There are also some Catholic communities of that sort, including the one at New Hope in Kentucky. It might be that this sort of community will be necessary to isolate children

is disturbing, and Horkheimer missed this important point: the businessmen to whom he referred are really just agents acting on the behalf of the American people. We vote with our pocketbooks and we have chosen to elect those who are most ruthless in tearing apart families to force all to live in the public marketplaces. We've all become enemies of God. But I'm most interested here in what is done to babies and children because it's at those early ages that human beings can be reshaped most effectively, forming creatures who would rather be in DisneyWorld than in any Heaven conceivable under Christian beliefs.

The embryonic human brain has many cells but few of them are actually doing anything though the human baby six months after conception has more brain-cells than it'll ever again have. In fact, a human baby at birth is an embryo and not nearly as well-developed as a chimpanzee newborn, let alone the young mammals – such as horses – which are capable of running rapidly within hours of birth. Human babies take weeks to develop to the point where they fully realize that thing that sometimes hits them in the face is part of their own body – their hand. At birth, the human baby's brain is only beginning to form its specialized cells and there's still little sign of functional brain-regions. At that, much of the human baby's brain is a mass of undeveloped cells, not yet even specialized to become nerve cells or glia cells which provide structural support to allow nerve cells to migrate and form connections and also move nutrition into the blood-poor regions of the brain.

It's all marvelously complex though not well-designed or well-engineered in the way of a human construction project. Those who argue for God's existence by those lines of reasoning are very far off-base. Human babies have just the sorts of unformed brains that allow them to model the messiness in their environments, model it in the very shapes of their mind. Aquinas, and Aristotle centuries earlier, actually believed that matter was plastic enough that a form could be imposed upon it, but they didn't seem to consider the possibility that matter, or material organisms, were plastic enough in a dynamic way that they could develop over time in a complex process of many stages. Now we know that the human brain has a very dynamic plasticity through adolescence and some dynamic plasticity through the human life-span – barring disease or other damage. By our choices, or those of our parents, we're formed into specific human beings. As a first approximation:

---

from the corrupting forces of the marketplaces of the modern world.

any human newborn can be shaped into a friend or an enemy of God. True it is that God can bestow grace where He wills, but we human beings are not to presume this. We're bidden to do our part in raising children to become Christ-centered adults.

Let me summarize:

> St. Thomas Aquinas had no theological or Biblical reasons to propose that human beings have this separate component he called the 'rational soul'. That form of separable soul was proposed to answer a technical question in philosophical understandings of knowledge. Aristotle tried to figure out how human beings can derive the abstract idea of 'dog' from seeing particular instances of dogs. It's quite strange that a young child who has seen only Labrador retrievers and German shepherds will see a dachshund for the first time and realize it's a dog though she may study the strange creature for a while before seeming to accept her own conclusion.
>
> Aristotle and Aquinas made an assumption that I've already discussed to be false. They assumed matter to be plastic enough that form might be imposed upon it but basically matter was inert in their expressed thoughts. Aristotle and Aquinas didn't consider the possibility that a bodily organ could be so dynamically plastic in its development that it could shape itself to draw abstractions from particular knowledge.
>
> Given what St. Thomas Aquinas knew, this question of how the mind can reason in abstract matters leads to the apparently good answer that the human mind has to be immaterial. It was never a theological problem nor one of Biblical exegesis. It seems all but certain to me that, if Aquinas had known much about modern biology, he would never have proposed even the rational soul, a soul which is, at that, a far more restricted entity than the soul that many modern Christians claim to believe in. The rational soul of Aquinas is a dry-as-dust entity, an unembodied Mr. Spock, which is only capable of abstract thought and does not love or have faith or hope. Modern knowledge about embryological development and brain development after birth does not shoot down the answer of Aquinas, the rational soul, so much as it redirects the question towards biological investiga-

tion and towards a philosophical and theological understanding of the best available answers that modern biology can provide.

Aristotle and Aquinas had no microscopes and no knowledge of brain development or even basic cellular processes. They had no reason to even guess that the brain develops in the way it does, even to the development of abstract reasoning skills in specific regions. Because modern brain-scientists have microscopes and a lot of knowledge of basic cellular processes, because they've been able to map out the brain's development and activity, they simply have no reason to even consider the possibility of an immaterial component to the human being, not mind and not soul. It is, in fact, quite remarkable, and an indication of the staying power of ideas even after they seem to be unfounded, that a vast amount of energy and paper has been used by scientists and philosophers and theologians to deal with the question of an immaterial mind-stuff or soul-stuff. As I've said before, there are aspects of the human being that can be described by the terms 'mind' or 'soul', but that's a different matter – most intelligent non-reductionistic materialists will readily concede that. The question is whether a human being has any substance, any stuff, other than his flesh and his blood.

This is my take on the situation:

- The general capabilities of the human brain, and its mind, developed over the eons of evolution, going back more than three billion years.

- The proper development of those general capabilities, as well as the development of specific capabilities, takes place as a human child interacts with his environment, but remember that some of those specific capabilities only develop in response to the appropriate stimuli during the proper window of opportunity.

- There's growing reason to believe that the human mother plays a particularly important role in the development of her child.

Now I'll enhance this model of the development of the human mind just a bit by noting that Aristotle and Aquinas considered a rational being as one which could be all beings. A human being can place himself in the position of other creatures. I remember reading of some feminist sociologists who tested play patterns of young boys and girls in some Israeli kibbutzim and found that the girls played at many different adult roles, male and female, while boys preferred to play at being lions, tigers, and bears. Oh, my. Our modern ideologues are dull of perception as well as dull of mind, being also so hard of heart that they're projecting upon children their presuppositions as well as their exploitive cures. I fear the agents of the commercial marketplaces have succeeded where failed the agents of the political marketplaces – boys are likely to play at unhealthy roles they've learned from the trashy entertainment to which they're exposed. It's even likely that few boys nowadays have much free playtime, free of little league and television and computers, or the exposure to nature that would lead to healthy development of their totemic, and potentially creative, inclinations.

Anyone who has bothered to observe children at play, anyone who has read even a few serious works of anthropology, will know that the human male is totemic – he naturally tries to understand the animals in his environment by imaginatively making himself one of them. This natural tendency is but one of the reasons for the dominance of males at the levels of genius. Another feminist study, published in the journal *Science* years ago concluded that there are more smart women than smart men but males outnumber females by about seven to one at the genius levels of talent. There seems to be a general feeling this pattern holds in areas of talent other than abstract intelligence – there are more competent women but highly talented males outnumber highly talented females by good margins.

It'll do us no good in the end to build a play-house society in which we pretend to be what we are not and cannot be. We destroy masculine creativity and the development of masculine genius both because it works against the needs of the gods of the marketplaces and because it makes it harder to attract women into the public squares. Moreover, such males don't make good corporate widgets unless their creative urges are destroyed at a young age. One of the results is that American endeavors in creative fields are jokes of a rather tasteless and boring sort. This is not just a problem for those who would like the opportunity to enjoy a good, recent novel by an American. Creativity is needed to restate the messages of Christ, in the strongest words possible, and to carry that message to those who have not yet had the chance to listen or to turn away.

The maternal role in human societies has been destroyed even more thoroughly than the traditional male roles. I'm not pointing back to that farce of a family idealized in such perverse productions as *Father Knows Best*, but rather to the family that actually functioned as a social and economic unit. Women took on certain types of tasks because of the great demands of bearing and nurturing children and because of the psychological drives of her maternal nature. Morally well-structured mothers of earlier generations have told me they couldn't tolerate being away from their young children as is common with mothers of the current generation. Thus, a farm-wife took care of the children, cleaned the house, cooked, and likely took care of the small animals and the vegetable garden. The men would roam farther, plowing the fields, harvesting the grains in large fields and the trees in the woods scattered around the farm. Wendell Berry has explored these issues in many books that are readily available. At the same time, he has made it clear he has spoken of what he knows – the life of farmers. We need people to draw visions of more sustainable, more humane lives in our small towns and our cities. I don't know of any who have even started on this task.

Healthy, well-balanced human lives won't lead to bloated public marketplaces. Traditional ways of life involve a lot of freely offered services and encourages its adherents to live simpler lives in which many needs can be satisfied within the family or local community. It doesn't generate pressures that force so many to be constantly visiting malls and giant department stores. This is a problem to corporations which profit from flows of goods and services through the giant public marketplaces of the modern world and also a problem to nation-states which feed their bloated governmental bodies from the taxes on those goods and services as they pass through the public marketplaces. A mother who works at a hamburger joint for minimum wage and places her children in government-subsidized day-care is contributing to the growth in the GNP, to corporate revenues and governmental taxes, while a mother who stays at home to care for her young contributes nothing to the GNP, by which our standard-of-living is measured.[5] The more effectively we destroy the mother's role, the better

[5]I've already stated this, but it's perhaps necessary to remind the reader that mothers become cleaners and cooks because of their role as mothers. They need to carry out these tasks for their young children and it makes sense for them to also clean and cook for their older children and husbands or other adults in the households. Also, in correspondence to the organization of work on a farm, it typically makes sense for women to do the inside housework while the husband does the work requiring more muscle or a mechanical inclination. The problem in the modern world is that the work traditionally done by women became a target for corporate exploiters – their own husbands for nearly two centuries and now the women themselves.

off we are. So the economists and politicians tell us.

To a Christian, this is quite strange. Families don't exist to support the father as he climbs the corporate ladder, uprooting his wife and children every three or four years. They don't exist so the doctor husband and lawyer wife can share safe sex on nights when they have enough energy. Families exist so children can be brought into the world and nurtured to develop their individual talents in ways that glorify God and help support the family, church, and local community. Families also exist as components of those church communities and local political communities. Ultimately, a Christian must see all individuals and all relationships between those individuals as being subordinate to Christ and our relationships to Him. Individuals and their love for each other will survive the formation of the Body of Christ, but in that subordinate state.

Specific attributes can be an accident of evolution, but they're usually the result of strong and often painful pressures on a population of creatures. There was simply no pressures upon human females that they would be selected for those totemic mental skills that allow a male warrior to put himself in the place of a deer or bear, the same general skills that allowed the teenaged Einstein to begin his mental experiments of riding on a beam of light.

A healthy woman, one with high self-esteem and confidence in her feminine nature – including its dominant maternal aspects, has a sureness of being, a confidence in her own worth and the dignity of her own place that's alien even to self-assured males. Unhealthy women, those with low self-esteem will mostly be either funny-shaped and dysfunctional males, helpless victims, or whorish creatures.

I'm not trying to be reactionary in defense of some nostalgic view of the dominant male and the submissive female, though there's a lot of biologically grounded truth in that general idea. Steven Goldberg, a sociologist with a preference for the radical-liberal ideals of the 1960s, wrote a book with the politically incorrect title of *Why Men Rule: A Theory of Male Dominance* to argue that men have dominated in public life in all known societies and this can be economically explained by the sensitivity of the male body to testosterone which is the hormone of aggression for both males and females.[6] But the dominance of healthy men in a morally well-ordered

[6]Oddly enough, Margaret Mead, a radical advocate of some sort of androgyny in her earlier years, was just about the only major anthropologist willing to praise the

society would not mean that they over-power women. In fact, those men would dominate in order to better carry out their responsibilities to their families at the center of which are the mothers.

The family idealized by so many confused conservatives was invented by Wilberforce and the other evangelicals in the Clapham sect, as I mentioned earlier. To remind the reader, they invented the modern suburb and the family in which Mommy stayed home, pure of the corrupt world of corporate or industrial capitalism. Mommy was supposed to both raise the children to be true Christians and also heal Daddy as he came home from his daily grind in the corrupt world. It was a courageous effort but doomed from the start. It makes sense in retrospect that Daddy, once he was in his office, forgot his responsibilities at home and began to develop and market products and services that allowed his corporate master to invade that domain and destroy the family he was supposed to be protecting. As one direct result of that invasion, women were pressured to become consumer widgets as well as chauffeur widgets to drive their children around to various places that were absorbing one or another function of home or church or neighborhood. It's not surprising that women became bored with such a degrading role in life, though a surprising number held on for the sake of the children and sometimes out of a sense of duty to their husbands as they struggled to make good livings.

About the same time that a watered-down form of feminism was being popularized in a number of books and a self-centered and chic form of feminism in a variety of books and magazines, there was a surprising return to the Clapham model of the family. In the midst of aggressive corporate capitalist marketplaces, with the sword of the tax-collectors hovering over their heads, some young American couples, largely Catholic and Mormon, began to have lots of children for the sake of their faith. It was a heroic effort that taxed the strength and endurance of these couples and those few in their families or church communities who supported them in doing what God had commanded. As Allan Carlson tells the story, the American Catholic Church, its leaders and general membership, paid verbal tribute to these couples and their large families and did nothing to help them. The same was true of the Mormon church and its leaders and membership. I come from one of the unusual Protestant families which had eight children.

first version of Professor Goldberg's book, published under the title *The Inevitability of Patriarchy*.

I can testify that, during a period of increasing prosperity, those in large families had to eat more meatless meals, had to give more Christmas gifts to be shared, had to pass down all possible clothing. None of this is bad though some families with many children had more serious financial problems than a tight budget for treats. The real problem is that these families sacrificing material goods for the sake of children were surrounded by the families which were more prudent, or perhaps more selfish, and the children who were giving up luxuries for the sake of their siblings had friends who were enjoying the morally doubtful bounty of American life. Moreover, those children were being taught to enjoy the products of the mass-media – television and movies and recorded music – which preached the glories of marketplace life.

A child growing up in a society where his acquisitive desires were aggravated by every television commercial and by the life-styles displayed in movies and television series does not so easily understand why he can't have a more expensive baseball glove like his friends. That desire for the baseball glove reflects the values he's taught unless he's growing up in an Amish community. The leaders of the Catholic Church, Mormon Church, and all other religious groups were swimming in the material prosperity just as much as the politicians and businessmen even if they were, in most ways, using their share of the loot for purposes arguably devoted to God. They weren't about to attack the gods of the marketplaces nor were they going to divert any of their share of the loot to the suckers who were dumb enough to do what the Bible tells God-centered people to do.

By supporting the social security system and the welfare state in general, the leaders of those churches were helping to put still greater relative burdens upon parents who were having a good number of children. And they were pulling money out of extended families and local communities to place it under the control of the bureaucrats of the corporations and those of the central governments. The New Deal was not enacted to help American citizens in trouble but rather to make the United States safe for large corporations. Social Security and unemployment insurance and other social welfare programs were designed and implemented to free citizens from their attachments to extended families and churches and local communities so they could be forced or enticed to pick up roots and move where the corporations wanted them to be, so that – even if they remained in their communities – they could re-organize their lives around marketplace activities of labor and consumption.

The New Deal originating in the Roosevelt administration and supported by all American presidents since was a brutal and largely successful attack upon what was left of Christian moral structures in the United States. Those moral structures were embodied in the habits of a people still having extended families and close ties to neighbors and members of the local church. Roosevelt was able to carry out the Fascist dream of tearing individuals free from their traditional and human-scale attachments that they might become the play-things of corporations and government bureaucracies.

The modern age advances and we have reached the point where few enter the seminaries or the convents but many are anxious to find careers in charities run by the same techniques as General Motors. Nearly four decades ago, the political philosopher Kenneth Minogue pointed out that doing good is no longer a calling from God but rather a career opportunity. I would add that doing good has also become a way that we try to cleanse dirty money, ill-gotten gains, so that we might feel that we're righteous and pure as the driven snow. A good chunk of our gross national product comes from that entertainment industry that's preparing young women to abort inconvenient babies and to value romantic affairs over the mature, and often slowly developing, forms of love which make for better and more stable marriages. As upsetting as this claim might be for some: the Amish and the Hasidic Jews and the Catholics of New Hope teach us that it's possible to raise children to form good marriages and to be responsible, God-centered parents but only at the cost of some substantial withdrawal from American mainstream culture which is a culture of marketplaces.

In general, the institutions of modern Christianity, such as the Catholic dioceses of the United States, serve the gods of the marketplaces rather than serving the God of Jesus. The American bishops raise large amounts of cash for building programs and for modern-style charities for a variety of human beings around the world. Those bishops seem to miss the rather obvious fact that the American ability to raise these impressive amounts of cash is due to the organization of our society, in its political and economic aspects, to better serve the gods of the marketplaces. The true Christians of the United States are those like the Amish who are willing to withdraw from those marketplaces and to establish true Christian families and communities where resources are devoted first of all to raising children – lots of them by the current standards of Americans including Catholics. If they were to put the God of Jesus Christ ahead of the gods of the marketplaces, American

Catholics would be trying to find a new way of living where true Christian families form to bear and raise children for the glory of God and that He might have more friends, some of them being priests and monks and nuns in this life.

But we all want to have a share of the ill-gotten gains of a cash-rich economy and we wish to convince ourselves that we're good Christians even as we serve our favorite gods of the marketplaces. We American Catholics refuse to see that American forms of political and economic organization have gently and benevolently destroyed families, churches, and other local communities. We even take a small percentage of our ill-gotten gains and give it to our churches or various groups that serve Christ's brethren. We don't have any chance to end the abortion holocaust when our favorite weapon is cash generated by activities which depend upon destruction of the role of mothers and the deformation of the minds and souls of the children. We're little different from drug-dealers contributing cash to drug rehabilitation charities.

Can profits from evil activities be put on the altar of God without committing sacrilege? When we generate profits by deforming the minds and souls of children, those profits are still dirty money even if we send a small percentage to tsunami victims in Indonesia.

These are dark thoughts and I hate having them, yet, I find myself indicting all of us American Christians in the deaths of so many unborn children, in the abuse of science to impregnate women in unnatural ways, and in the ongoing efforts to torture human embryos brought to life in the laboratory.

See that 16 year-old girl sitting in the waiting room of the abortion clinic. She's crying and trying to forget all she'd heard in CCD and in the homilies of her parish priest and all that her mother and aunts and grandmothers had told her. She might even be telling herself she's on her way to Hell as she goes through with her elimination of the product of an earlier mistake probably made because she was formed to seek the sort of romantic relationship which is far from the Christian ideal, just as far from biological sanity.

Is she being inducted into the culture of death? No.

Was she inducted into the culture of death when a high school teacher slipped her the address of an abortion counselor? No.

She was inducted into the culture of death when her Catholic parents set her in front of a television set as an infant, allowing the agents of the marketplaces to start forming her mind and soul to the needs of their gods.

The culture of death is not something imposed upon our political and economic systems. It's part of those systems. If the goal is to boost corporate profits or government tax revenue now, then that mother is worth more as a minimum wage worker in a fast-food joint. That child is worth more as a dumbed-down consumer of ephemeral goods and services. All the pro-life literature and anti-abortion marches in the world don't absolve American Catholics and other Christians of their sins in failing to organize their lives and their communities so that they can produce children to the glory of God and raise them to be humble children of the Father, grateful brethren of the Son, and joyful friends of the Holy Spirit.

In secular terms, we've trashed our culture and become trashy human animals. We turn our children into trashy human animals. During that process, children are taught to despise mothers and clergymen and missionaries and all others who have low-paid or unpaid jobs to do. Girls are particularly susceptible because most of them anticipate spending at least part of their lives in the despised role of mother. Feminist sociobiologists long ago conjectured that low-esteem women, for plausible biological reasons, will tend to adopt – unconsciously for the most part – the reproductive strategy which we might bluntly term 'whoredom'. If they have no chance to live out the role nature prepared them for, then they'll tend to make themselves available for the best immediate opportunity.

Look at MTV and VH1 and see the type of women that a high percentage of American girls are taking as their role-models. See the whorish Barbie dolls who induct American girls into the culture of death. Our television series and movies teach American children that a worthwhile life requires a 3,000 square foot house and a sports-car and an SUV in the driveway. To live this life, women have to give up their natural role and enter the marketplaces from which William Wilberforce and his followers thought to save them by inventing the suburb and the modern nuclear family.

That 16 year-old girl in the waiting room of the abortion clinic was inducted into the culture of death during all those hours she spent in front of the television learning that real women are slender and they dress in expensive and revealing clothes. Real women also drive fancy red sports cars or take rides from some sexy male with a fancy silver sports car and lots of cash in his pocket. Real women go to Caribbean resorts with men they met a month earlier.

There are biological processes underlying all of these moral issues. I've alluded to them in the chapter on "Getting Used to It" and in many other parts of this book. We're not agents who come into this world ready to make decisions for God and against God, for life or against life. The decision-maker is shaped by his experiences and perceptions, even by the decisions he makes as he goes along. "We are sin," as St. Augustine said. I've generalized this principle a little by using results from modern science and mathematics in the light of Christian revelation: "We are disorder." My way of expressing the truth retains the Augustinian insight that evil is a privation and also allows me to say: "We are order." Most of us are likely more disorder than order, especially in this age when freedom is often taken to be the right to inflame our natural desires into a form that makes us better prey for the exploiters.

The moral disorder of us Americans is largely due to our wrongful ways of bringing spirit and matter back together. We desire to be magical spirits having total control over our own bodies, those of other creatures, and also the non-living matter of our universe. We'll not even see the possibilities of a moral order proper to us bipedal apes unless we return to sanity on basic biological issues, though some who turn to God are scoured and humbled so that they can begin to view themselves and the universe more honestly – this can be a more direct but also more painful process. Take my word for it. A spiritual purging preceded and motivated all my efforts to integrate empirical knowledge into a Christian worldview – not that my spiritual purging is yet complete.

This is all quite important to the re-establishment of moral and intellectual sanity. Christian worldviews, even in their most abstract philosophical forms, cannot be separated from Christian life. And a Christian life is possible only for those who can see themselves, their spouses, children, and friends for what they are – bipedal apes with particular characteristics.

The sociobiologists and the authors of the book of Genesis are both right, and the stories they tell are variations on the same story. Adam was cursed by his inborn desire to maximize his reproductive success, though such desires are, of course, only matters of as-if. Adam was in fact cursed by his strange desires to be with this one woman who gave him many types of pleasure, genital pleasure being not the least. He felt some desire to be with the family group and not roam freely as do male elephants or live without responsibilities for others – even his own offspring – as male chimpanzees do. One of the most difficult tasks in evolutionary biology is to go beyond direct cause-and-effect relationships, which are sometimes figments of the human imagination, so we can see the proxy relationships which indirectly drive animals to survive and to reproduce successfully. This problem is likely behind some, maybe most, of the self-deceptions which are so common in the human race – we really don't know the full meaning of our actions for that meaning is a matter of context and not just of the thoughts and desires of which we're aware.

Human females have more firmly defined roles than human males just because they pay a much larger price for each act of reproduction. A male can impregnate and disappear to find another opportunity, but that wasn't so effective a way to reproduce in a world where even a woman in a tribe does better with a male supporting her and her children. The slow maturing process which strongly ties women to their children for an extended period will also cause men to be inclined, but only inclined, to stick around to help raise those children.[7] It's this burden women pay in reproducing that has been the principle force in creating such great differences between the sexes and the burden is best shared in exactly those societies which have strong families where men are raised to have a strong sense of responsibility for wife and children. Since my early years were spent in an extended family that was on its last legs, I also know that childless couples in such extended families will often share the burden of raising the children of their luckier relatives rather than traveling around the world. Empty-nesters, especially Grandpa and Grandma, were also helping to raise the children in their extended families rather than heading down to Florida for the winter.

Human females are more specialized for reproducing and nurturing their young – they have to be. Not only is the period of gestation long. Not only are female human beings particularly vulnerable when pregnant. Not only is child-birth more painful than perhaps for any species because of the over-sized skull of the baby, despite its relative immaturity. Even more importantly, that relative immaturity of a human baby at birth makes possible the development of our specialized brain functions and it's the mother who has the instincts and potential skills for nurturing that development process. Understanding this knowledge that was implicit in traditional ways of life, is important for Christians. We maximize the chances of children being able to properly respond to Christ's call if we raise them to have healthy

---

[7] Aquinas, a hard-headed empiricist to the extent that the science of his time allowed, discussed this inclination of men to raise their own children as being a major part of the foundation of human morality – see Chapter 123 of Book III of *Summa Contra Gentiles* where Aquinas discusses the reasons why marriages should be indivisible.

human minds – the traditional, and biologically sane, human mother plays an essential role in the development of healthy minds in young children and an important role in the ongoing development. Mary was not just a source of an egg-cell and a convenient womb; she also said, "Yes," to playing an important role in shaping the human mind of Christ. Young women must be raised so that they'll respond to the needs of their own children as Mary responded to the needs of Jesus.

Human babies are born with greater mental potential than the young of other species, but they're also less mature in their physical and mental and emotional capabilities. This immaturity is generally explained this way:

> The human baby at birth is still embryonic. Even our cousins, the chimpanzees, produce babies which are relatively more robust and more complete in their faculties at birth. If human babies were as mature at birth as chimpanzee babies, then their skulls would be even larger and women might have even more painful child-births, plus they would need much wider hips.

It's useful to speak in purely biological terms because it allows us to see what's really at stake. Once human babies had to be born in an embryonic state, something interesting would have happened. That embryonic creature would be shot out into a more difficult but also much richer environment than the womb. Babies which finish their embryonic neurological development in the scary world instead of inside their mother's wombs would have been able to develop richer and more complex brain structures, richer and more complex emotional systems. In recent decades, neurobiologists have shown that the human brain is formed into a very basic condition where it's ready for further learning and that first stage of formation is carried out by genetic processes, but then the more advanced development processes occur in interaction with the baby's environment. An animal has arisen which can develop and sustain complex and abstract states inside of itself because it doesn't have a brain that's mostly formed at birth. Human beings have brains that develop in response to environments which are part of the story God is telling.

Just a few days ago as I write this, I read in one of the newsletters of the Dana Foundation for Brain Initiatives about maternal traits to which I've already referred: scientists have shown that the brains of both human and rat females are altered when they give birth.[8] Among other effects, a human mother is able to distinguish the cry of her baby when it's one in a roomful of crying babies. Rats can be tested in ways that are impossible, or sometimes just unethical, when it comes to human beings, and the scientists were able to show that rat mothers become much faster and generally more effective at finding food that they might head back to their nest as soon as possible.

How can we once again view the world created by God as did Christians in past centuries? This is the same question as: How can we return our societies and ourselves to a Christian state of moral order? For most people, viewing a world is not an intellectual process, nor is it even a moral struggle in the abstract. It's plainly and simply living a life of moral order, a life which itself is a participation in the telling of that story of Christ and His Church.

So how can we live a life of moral order which is consistent with the Christian story?

There are many ways to answer that question, but I'm going to speak within the context of this chapter about man the apish creature born into environments but capable of seeing the universe and then a world which is that universe seen in its full moral order. In this context the answer is pretty straightforward.

> We need to re-establish respect for the human being as an embodied creature, a creature which has only the substance which is its body. And we need to re-establish respect for the human family centered around the human female specialized to be a mother to children still embryonic at birth. If we can do this, extended families will re-form and will re-build the local political communities and the church communities. At the same time, it's likely that these higher-level communities will have to begin functioning properly to help form those individuals and to help them to form proper Christian families. We're dealing with a complex human social system and not some sort of mechanical and linear system. There's a need to develop the smaller parts of this social system and the larger parts at the same time.

---

[8] See the November, 2004 issue of *Brain in the News*. The article *More than Mother's Intuition* is a reprint of an article by Alexandra Witze originally published in *The Dallas Morning News* on November 1, 2004.

At some point, likely when modern societies are still hostile to Christan ways of life, when serious sacrifices are still required, Catholic parents will have to start having more children and raising them apart from the marketplace economy and marketplace political system – to the extent possible. We should pray that such courageous Christian parents do appear, by the grace of God. We should also pray that, this time, the Pilgrim Church on Earth will support such families in multiple ways.

If we don't move towards Christian ways of life, we'll remain disordered human beings inhabiting disordered societies. Our society will then continue to be what it already substantially is: a complex system for deforming human beings into creatures who could not possibly be happy as God's companions in any Heaven conceivable under Christian beliefs.

Part III

Persons and Worlds

9 Where Do I Stand?

I'll remind the reader that I use the term 'Primordial Universe' to designate pure created being, the homogeneous and undifferentiated stuff which is not a thing and contains no things. I use 'universe' to designate where we are, the Particularized Universe which came about as dicta and initial conditions were imposed upon the Primordial Universe so that it becomes a particular thing and contains particular things. I use 'world' to mean the universe perceived through a process of moral ordering.

The moral structure we employ to see the universe as a world has to be consistent with empirical facts and plausible scientific theories, including not just those from the fields we moderns call 'scientific' but also the facts and plausible theories of history, economics, literary studies, and most certainly those implied by the human practices of our traditions including farming and carpentry and even acceptable ways of gossiping. In many cases, the moral criteria needs to be developed from an understanding of the empirical facts and empirically founded theories. The process is circular to a great extent, but necessarily so. Since we're particular physical animals who know only through our physical senses, it would seem that even revelation needs to be interpreted through our knowledge of the physical world, but that should not be upsetting to traditional Christians. God created this physical universe to be the place of our birth and our maturing. We become better images of God by taking as our own the thoughts of God which He manifested as this universe.

The careful reader will note another way in which this process is both circular and recursive. I was already returning to Christianity and was slowly making my way towards Rome when my interests in science and philosophy and literature were reviving – my mind and spirit were only half asleep when I was a thirteen year-old, but it was not long before I was enticed into a more complete state of submissive dormancy by the sheer mindlessness of American education and culture. I'm not denying my guilt in letting myself be enticed though I can provide a narrative excuse: when I was in fifth grade, I was involved in a conversation during an indoor recess and I realized I was going to have to start watching *The Monkees* and other TV programs if I was to be a part of such conversations. In high school, I can remember spending hours solving a problem only to find out the next day that it had been assigned as a mistake; modern students aren't supposed to apply themselves thus when *Laugh-in* was there to integrate them into American culture. Academically talented students are not the only victims of this cultural machine that grinds all down into widgets suited for marketplace life. Any who would be creative or any who would have hobbies which limit their marketplace activities are confronted by a massive brainwashing effort on the part of American culture, including peer pressure which is little different from the peer pressure which leads to drug use – and perhaps no less dangerous. The United States, and most other modern nation-states, need youth to spend their hours in front of the television or in front of the computer screen, preferably while listening to some pre-recorded music. Given the definition of prosperity in terms of Gross National Product, no nation-state has an interest in encouraging boys to rebuild cars or boats, little interest in encouraging boys or girls to play guitars or sing, no more interest in encouraging boys or girls to draw or to make wood furniture with Grandpa. Of course, Grandpa probably has no time for little Becky or Billy since he's spending his time traveling to vacation hot-spots with the woman he met after Grandma died – they say they need time together before deciding if marriage is right for them. Churches, however well-intentioned their leaders, are not allowed to interfere with the deformation of modern children into marketplace widgets.

During those years of adolescence during which a human being's abstract reasoning develops – or not – I was held captive by the missionaries of the gods of the marketplaces. Still, my mind remained somewhat alive, even after a horrible four years of further decay in a modern university. I was occasionally reading books of science and philosophy and creative works of literature and was more regularly reading books in history, social science, theology, and mathematics.

If I describe my final intellectual and spiritual state, I have to declare my Catholic doctrinal beliefs as absolutely foundational: The Father and the Son and the Holy Spirit are not just one of many possibilities which happens to have been realized. The Triune God is the most basic reality of all, the source of truths and not one possible truth, the source of beings and not one possible being. Believing is a matter of finding a way to live in the Presence of the God of Jesus and Jesus Himself told us that this is possible only for those who are members of His Body, the Church. I found my way into the Catholic Church when I admitted the absurdity from a creaturely viewpoint of Christian beliefs as found, for example, in the simple *Apostle's Creed.* It occurred to me that such absurd beliefs could have survived and could be plausible only if witnessed to by an easily identifiable authority. The Catholic Church was the only contender for this role.

> I most certainly do not intend to deny the validity of the Eastern Orthodox churches nor the more limited validity of many other churches out of communion with Rome, but history tells us that the Catholic Church, with its biggest church being the Roman Catholic Church, is where the main action is over the long haul – so to speak. Once you're ready to admit that Rome, with all its prudential mistakes over the years, is truly the center of Christianity, then it's time to consider the claims of the Bishop of Rome to be the heir to the powers which Christ gave to Peter.

After nearly 20 years of a self-directed recovery of sorts, I set out to write a book which reflects both the Catholic Christian beliefs which I came to accept and the emergence of those beliefs. Empirical reality came to make sense for me in the context of, and only in the context of, a full-blooded and courageous belief in the incarnated Son and His Father and Their Spirit. We can begin to understand this when we accept the Thomistic insights into the nature of human knowledge and the nature of being as existential, including even He who is His own Act-of-being. In a series of processes messier, far messier, that what can be seen in the final form of this book, I alternately sharpened my Christian beliefs, acquired empirical knowledge, purged myself of ideological corruptions, and wasted large amounts of time in mulling over the meaning of it all.

I found myself to be attracted to something I couldn't identify in the thought of St. Thomas Aquinas at the same time I was repelled by the obvious contradictions between modern science and much of the superstructure of that body of thought. It now seems to me that absolute truths, revealed or metaphysical, can be well-supported by provisional structures of human knowledge, though those structures will eventually be seen as defective or incomplete or both.

We're creatures of this universe, endowed by complex and messy evolutionary processes with ranges of characteristics and potential bundles of skills which suit us for life in particular environments on the surface of a particular planet circling a particular star in a particular universe of physical stuff which can manifest a variety of immaterial aspects. The specifics of our human beings are shaped, within the possibilities given by genetic and somatic heritage, to meet and cope with peculiar opportunities and specific challenges. We are what we are, including our thoughts and those complex thought-processes we call memories, as a result of interacting with our immediate environments. If all goes well, we find ourselves interacting with various pieces of the universe, many of them invisible because of large or small size or because they're really abstractions, and then we can begin to build a worldview. No matter how much empirical knowledge of a scientific sort enters into this process, it's essentially a moral process from beginning to end.

For example, it's a matter of faith that the world is essentially rational for all of the disorder and confusion, all of the suffering and seeming lack of purpose, which often hits us where we hurt or where our loved ones hurt.

Where in the world does that faith come from? In this context, I'm not speaking of a specific religious faith but rather a general faith that the universe is rationally ordered. In past centuries, even the most powerful of thinkers, say Aristotle and St. Thomas Aquinas and Sir Isaac Newton, had to accept this rational order on a very general basis indeed. Einstein, with the general theory of relativity, was the first man who provided a way to bring the universe into view as a potential world, a potential manifestation of a certain unity and coherence and completeness. The principle that matter shapes space and space then tells matter how to move is unexpectedly simple though the mathematics of general relativity is complex and you need a number of years of background study to deal with that mathematics. The simple example is: we fall towards the earth because the earth is massive enough to make space slope down towards it. The relatively massive earth shapes space in its immediate vicinity and that space 'tells' our less massive bodies how to move so far as free fall goes – free fall being the state of weightlessness we have all experienced in an elevator when it starts to descend. Our free fall is interrupted by the earth's surface but it's our bodies' efforts to fall freely towards the center of the earth which leads to that phenomenon we call 'weight'.

Simplistically speaking, the universe is a certain collection of matter, energy, and fields – most prominently the universal gravitational field. That energy complex, as some physicists term it, expands into space and moves along through time, creating space and time in that very expansion.[1] So far as anyone knows, all local time flows, including the possible backwards glitches, are but swirls inside of a river of steadily flowing universal time. If the philosophers and scientists before Einstein had developed even an intuitive feeling for the universe as being self-contained in all that we can observe or measure, then it's unlikely that Christianity would have been so thoroughly invaded by the pagan concept of immortal souls separable from the human body. All the dynamic properties attributed to gods or spirits inhabiting the sun or the planets are to be found in matter and energy and fields.

By way of an abstraction that is a theory of physical reality, Einstein provided a definition of 'universe' which is not simply hand-waving. And he opened up the possibility of a variety of questions that could be bothersome to some branches of traditional religious thought and also to a lot of modern thinkers, skeptical and neo-pagan alike.

For now, I wish to explore the ways in which human beings, when so inclined, make what I call 'worlds'. Einstein's universe, though more coherent, unified, and complete than any which had emerged from philosophical contemplation or even the mighty imagination of Newton, is still limited to the perceivable aspects of physical reality – Einstein saw only a universe and not a world. This is interesting in that Einstein imagined the universe into being only as part of an incomplete worldview he held, one with more than just objective content, one which held a view of physical reality which had been reworked by his sometimes ill-structured but always powerful moral imagination. He was right on target in setting his goal at understanding how the Old One thinks about His Creation though he had not the right view of that Old One. It's a moral duty of men to deal with our relationship

[1]At this point, the language becomes problematical because English doesn't have words reserved for God's primary acts of creation as opposed to those acts of physical creation which are really transformations of stuff or things that already exist. Though God is always here, bringing stuff and things into existence and providing energy to move into the future, He does manage to let the universe and its creatures enjoy enough freedom that we can speak of these creations which are really transformations as being natural events without much distortion.

with God, and Einstein made it easier in some ways to deal even with the moral aspects of a worldview, to come to a coherent and unified and complete understanding, however much the word 'provisional' remains lit up in stadium sized neon-orange letters. In principle, as St. Thomas Aquinas argued, the individual human mind – though incapable of understanding so much as a flea – is the right sort of entity to be able to comprehend all of this universe. He was right and one way to think of his point is to re-phrase it:

> The universe is a manifestation of thoughts which God wished us to take as our own.

There are a few important points to make about this. First of all, the universe is particular and concrete. Many constraints had to be imposed upon abstract created being that it form a particular universe. As I've earlier phrased it, God imposed dicta and initial conditions upon the Universe. Another point is an emphasis of an earlier claim: St. Thomas Aquinas, partly because the best physics of his day was grossly inadequate, had a view of the universe which was not nearly so coherent, complete, and unified as that which Einstein has made possible. On the other hand, he had a view of a plausible morally structured world and he even left behind a case study of how to construct a provisional but well-structured analysis of a world as seen by way of such a worldview. It's time for us to redo what Aquinas did, this time using the empirical knowledge which has accumulated over the past six centuries.

We should be humble enough to recognize that man exists as part of Creation as should be obvious to any one who believes in the revelations of the Bible. Creation can give rise to more than one universe, this Particularized Universe and the new universe of the resurrection are obvious examples to a Christian, but man remains part of Creation even if resurrected into a new universe, one perfected and incorruptible. More than that, it seems likely that man is a part of but one universe at a time, which implies that human nature is founded fully upon the human body, flesh and blood.[2]

---

[2]We could speculate on the nature of stuff in the New Creation. What will that stuff be so that it makes up a human body that doesn't age or decay? We're dancing on thin air at this point, but it does raise the insight that human beings will still have to be made of some stuff.

10 A God-centered Materialism

The major problem I've had since I've been struggling with the mind-body problem and the matter-soul problem is that I'm not sure why people have automatically concluded that there's some better stuff out there than the matter which God has created for this Particularized Universe. I'm not sure why I once thought I might be better than an animal by possession of a soul, but I now know that I'm better than a chimpanzee only because my Savior died on the Cross to offer me something better than an immortal soul.

There are purely theoretical arguments for the existence of the separable and immortal human soul and purely theoretical arguments against the existence of that soul. Those arguments had nothing to do with the contents of the Bible or other sources of revealed truth; those arguments were addressed to important technical questions raised by the pagan philosophers of Greece. For example, Aristotle knew the human mind formed itself in response to the surrounding environment. He believed matter to be plastic enough to accept a form but it never seems to have occurred to him that a physical organ could be dynamically plastic enough to be the foundational stuff of mind.

Aquinas accepted Aristotle's assumption of the relative inertness of created matter and thus was forced to also conjecture that there's some immaterial mind-stuff, which he called the 'rational soul'. That is, neither Aristotle nor Aquinas conceived of a physical entity being capable of developing by way of internal processes. And why should they have jumped to such an idea which would have been a wild speculation given what they knew? Newton also did not guess at the dynamically plastic and self-organizing nature of matter and energy, and he didn't even quite realize that there's such an entity as a field. Why should we expect Aquinas to know in the thirteenth century what was still unknown in the seventeenth century by Newton, arguably the greatest of scientists?

We now know that God created not inert matter but rather a very dynamic complex of matter and energy and fields, matter being a low-temperature form of this stuff. The brain is plastic enough to be the underlying organ of the human mind. Moreover, some scientists have made the attractive proposal that the fields generated by the brain, electromagnetic and perhaps quantum, might play a role in forming our minds. That conjecture is attractive since fields might form a good basis for the mind in its fluid and weightless aspects.

On the whole, empirical evidence is strongly aligned against the idea that our immaterial aspects are embedded in stuff different from ordinary matter, but the empirical evidence also casts doubt upon the idea that simple living creatures, let alone man, can be explained by simply building up layer upon layer of physical explanations starting with quarks, or whatever, and going to the metabolic level. Complex things are made of simple things and we have to realize that new properties can emerge by processes similar to those by which we build a house out of piles of brick, wood, and pipes. That house has properties not found in those underlying materials. The difference is that there's no explicit building process in the evolution of life but rather processes of energy and matter organizing themselves. No one has a clue how those self-sustaining processes of organizing were first started but it's potentially a solvable problem, the only barriers to solution being the fact that those processes were initiated under somewhat unknown and possibly non-duplicable conditions. Moreover, it might prove to be that the bootstrapping processes which lead to life are not likely to occur even when the optimal conditions exist. Still, some clever scientists might find their way around those very difficult problems.

So far as we know, the matter on a dead planet has the same properties as the matter in Earth's so-called bio-sphere but it's not organized properly because the conditions are not right for the unknown bootstrapping process from dead matter to living organism. It's also possible that simple life exists on Mars or other planets in our system or other systems but the conditions aren't right for the evolutionary processes which form larger life-forms. Other stranger possibilities remain (such as underground life on some of those planets), but those are purely speculative given what's now known.

We know this much: the earth has life and some lines of living organisms developed into moral and intelligent social creatures because God created a universe which contains matter that can cross the bridge to life, though the nature of that (most likely) short but all-important bridge is quite a mystery. But it's the sort of mystery that can be cleared up, in principle, by empirical investigation. There's no revelation that seems to clearly mean that God created life in a special way, distinct from His general activity as Creator and King of the universe, nor is there any revelation that tells us that man is separated from other forms of life by so much as the chasm that separates living and non-living matter.

On the other hand, we should be careful to retain the insight that God's general activity as Creator includes His ongoing activities which I've described as telling the story which is the world. We should also remember that God participates in this story He tells.

It's still a mystery how the human mind forms and even what it really is in objective terms. Everyone can recognize a creature with a mind when they meet one, though clever computer programs and responsive robots have confused us a little. The problem is coming up with a narrative of the formation of a human mind – in a general sense. A particular human mind cannot be fully understood even under Thomistic theories of knowledge since that mind is the product of unrecoverable historical processes – processes which necessarily involve complex interactions with environments. Still, neurobiologists have made a lot of progress and their work is generally supportive of the Aristotelian and Thomistic abstract description of how the human mind is formed. Unfortunately, few scientists can see past the mistake that Aristotle and St. Thomas made about an immaterial mind-stuff but I've also claimed this wasn't a mistake given what they knew of biology and other empirical sciences. In any case, modern brain-scientists tell us our brains are largely formed during the crucial windows of opportunity of our youth and adolescence. Unfortunately for those who idolize Charles Darwin, turning him into a deity in the modern pantheon, that Victorian gentleman was educated as a Biblical Literalist during those crucial years when his mind was forming.

Charles Darwin didn't know how to read the Bible properly nor how to think about God when he was an Evangelical Anglican and he didn't do any better when he gave up his irrational idea that the Bible can be read literalistically as a source of all truth. To a man with a mind formed in such a manner, the discovery that the Bible can't be read in such a manner might well lead him to conclude that God doesn't exist. And that is exactly what Darwin did, and there are still some who follow him down that irrational path of thought. I'll state it this way:

> Some human beings claim the Bible tells us God made the world 6,000 years ago and then made man in a special act of creation.
>
> Man is a genetic cousin of the chimpanzee and their common ancestor shuffled across the earth about 6 million years ago.
>
> Therefore, God doesn't exist.

The ideological Darwinists and the Creation Scientists seem to agree that the Bible can't be a source of revelation unless it's an accurate encoding of the past and future of this universe, but most of the time, people who are ideological Darwinists dispose of the Bible very quickly and move on to argue that God can't exist so long as they can spell the word 'random', though understanding the word 'random' is left as a future exercise. Even some mathematical physicists writing for the general press seem to have some sort of magical-pagan idea of randomness.

I feel a bit of sympathy for most of those who claim to line up behind the Creation Scientists or behind the ministers of Christian sects supporting some flavor of Biblical Literalism. Whatever political and moral and social sympathies you might have, it's clear that the world is changing rapidly. Even amongst those who assume the changes are mostly good, parents would have reasons to worry. It's not easy to raise children even in stable communities with blood ties and common cultural beliefs but few of those communities can stand the onslaught of cable television and radio. People with strong senses of responsibility towards their children will often try to associate with strong religious communities as a way of giving their children options beyond those offered by exploitive corporations and exploitive governments. I support efforts to protect human beings from exploitation, but there are far too many Christian communities which have strayed into strange territory, either to the left or the right of orthodoxy. Part of the goal for this unseemly act of publicly envisioning a worldview is simply to convince people that Christians don't have to fear Darwin or Einstein. Even those who don't have the time or background to follow through on the sorts of readings and contemplations that got me to this point might be comforted knowing that there's an intellectually respectable way to reconcile the discoveries and theories of modern science with a full-blooded form of Christian belief.

Alasdair MacIntyre has claimed that Christianity has been badly damaged by the belief that preachers, evangelists in general, do not have to be well-educated and intelligent. The modernist, Unitarian and Methodist and Catholic alike, feels it more important that a preacher be filled with the spirit, or even the Spirit. This general downgrading of the importance of the mind in Christian circles has widened the separation between Christian thought and disciplined thought in general. What's more frightening is the implication of Christian worldviews reduced to rubble – we have strayed far from the commandments of God and His prophets. Worldviews will come into being in any society which is morally well-structured and, as a matter of course, made up of citizens who are morally well-structured.

A collapse into ideology is a massive problem with intellectual and moral and spiritual aspects. I've been arguing that people under the spell of ideology cannot form into the sort of human being who is suited to life in any Heaven conceivable under Christian belief. Human beings with inadequate worldviews, perhaps tainted by various superstitions, don't necessarily have this problem. There are many God-centered Christians who hold more than a few beliefs from animistic paganism.

I'm not about to suggest that I can provide a program that points a way out of this field of rubble that we, and our forefathers, have made of Western Civilization. I'll be doing well to show that modern science can be reconciled to Christian truth, that the things of this world are true, as some lines of Christian thought have always maintained. I have, in fact, claimed the things of this world are true by claiming the world is a manifestation of thoughts of God.

Before we can regain our moral balance, we need to become more materialistic, in a manner of speaking. We need to regain respect for our own bodies, for those of other creatures, and for the simple non-living things of God's world. We need to regain enough respect for God Himself as a good and competent Creator. There are people walking around with T-shirts saying: "God made me and God doesn't make junk." True enough, but God made everything and we have to start respecting everything God made – each other, the non-human animals around us, and even our backyard soil. Perhaps most importantly, we need to start raising children so that their human nature is well-developed rather than being suppressed in the interests of a hectic life in the marketplaces.

I've claimed that Darwin, like Marx, borrowed much from Adam Smith. Some of Einstein's successors have definitely interpreted their work within the context of the dominant modern ideology. Good scientific work, in both biology and physics, is often presented in a confusing manner as processes are claimed to be the ultimate reality. Organisms and matter disappear, an act of prestidigitation made all the easier by the realization that not only are processes real but they occur at many levels, even at absurdly deep levels in matter itself. Things and even living creatures have disappeared, or perhaps survived as mere nodes in graphs that describe the meaningless progression of the processes. No longer are there any things affected by processes and engaging in processes. There are only the processes themselves including those measured in such morally despicable statistics as the Gross National Product.

Against the ideologies, I propose we return to a strong respect for the matter of creation. But let me return to the underlying reason for the traditional Christian respect for God's world – though there was clearly always a temptation to consider God's physical universe as the realm of Satan. Here are a couple of interesting quotations from the first volume of *The Christian Tradition* by Jaroslav Pelikan:

> It was not only the story of the resurrection of Christ that drew the fire of pagan critics as a fable or the report of a hysterical woman, but the significance attached to the resurrection by Christian theology. Nowhere is the significance more unequivocally expressed than in the polemic of some Christian theologians against the pagan doctrine of the immortal soul. "The soul is not in itself immortal, o Greeks, but mortal. Yet it is possible for it not to die." In these words, Tatian voiced the doctrine that life after death was not an accomplishment of man, much less his assured possession, but a gift from God in the resurrection of Christ. (page 30)

The next quotation hits the target still more strongly since it comes out of the efforts of St. Athanasius to defend and sharpen Christian views on the two natures and one person of Christ.

> The conflict with paganism had given prominence to the Christian insistence that the creatures had come into existence

> "out of nothing." The conflict with Arianism had made the insistence even more crucial. For "man is by nature mortal, since he is made out of what is not." He was therefore constantly being drawn back down into the non-being out of which he had been called by the creating power of the Logos. (page 204)

At this point, it should be clear that I don't claim and could not claim originality for the basic insights of this book. The humble status of creatures, our utter dependence upon our Creator even to exist moment to moment, is found in the writings of men who lived many centuries ago. I'm also not claiming that those who propose the existence of an immortal human soul are either irrational or heretics against Christian truth. Rather am I claiming that human beings, as creatures, are subject to empirical investigation and empirical understanding. God never told us we have immortal souls.

In past centuries, there were valid reasons for thinkers to conjecture the existence of an immaterial mind or soul, but it's interesting that some of the Fathers who relied on their faith and not their knowledge of pagan thought preached that there's no such entity as an immortal soul because of the conflict with Christian revelation, especially the promise of a bodily resurrection. Yet, I'll admit that the situation was more complex than I've presented it, far more confused than you might think from the smug, and incorrect, assumptions that Christians have always believed in a human soul which is separable from the human body and immortal to boot. It's true that many Christian thinkers even in the early years did advocate the view that human beings have a component with an existence separate from the body, which component was said to be immortal, but some of the Fathers saw the immortal soul or mind as being in conflict with God's promise of a bodily resurrection.

In the first volume of *The Christian Tradition*, Jaroslav Pelikan speaks of the complexity of the entire issue of determining a Christian position on the human soul, including the question as to its very existence as anything but an abstraction of certain aspects of the physical human animal. Let's let Professor Pelikan speak a little bit more on this messy historical topic:

> Indeed, the idea of the immortality of the soul came eventually to be identified with the biblical doctrine of the resurrection of the body, a doctrine one of whose original polemical targets

> was the immortality of the soul. The pagan or heretical equation of the soul with life and the claim of natural immortality apart from the action of God the Creator were rejected by Christian thinkers on the grounds that "the soul itself is not life, but participates in the life conferred upon it by God," by whose will alone the soul received the capacity to endure eternally. Therefore "the soul participates in life because God wills it to live; thus it will not even have any such participation when God no longer wills it to live." Tatian's statement that "in itself the soul is not immortal, but mortal" was based on his assumptions concerning the relation between time and eternity and between body, soul, and spirit. Yet it did give voice to the insistence on the doctrine of the resurrection in opposition to natural immortality. [page 51]

Yet, even some of those early Fathers of the Church who saw that an immortal soul was in conflict with Christian revelation made an error in leaving open the possibility of a soul separable from the human body. Knowing little of the true nature of matter and how the stuff of this universe can develop to very complex forms by identifiable processes, they thought too literalistically of a form being imposed upon matter. The human soul, even when acknowledged as being mortal, was posited as something which had to be imposed upon physical stuff for a human being to come into existence. We now understand, though not fully, how it is that a human being comes into existence by way of complex interactions involving at least:

- a partial set of genes contributed by a father;
- a partial set of genes contributed by the mother;
- soma contributed by the mother in the form of an egg-cell;
- working genes contributed by the mother prior to the DNA of the egg-cell being able to function; and
- miscellaneous environmental influences, some working upon the mother while she is still partially controlling the development of the embryo.

The concepts being explored under the label 'self-organization' seem to be a better description of this process than any concept involving the imposition of forms upon matter. We Christians have to remember that all of this is being powered by God's constant and ongoing acts-of-being which bring contingent stuff back into existence as it is falling back into non-being. And there are those other acts, a different sort of constant and ongoing act-of-being, by which God brings things and living creatures into being in the way of a narrative flow.

Only God, the Creator Himself, can bring anything across that infinite chasm between non-existence and existence, and it would seem that only God can move freely across the boundaries of different phases of His Creation. It also would seem that only God can transport things or living creatures across the barriers dividing our particular universe from any other – including the universe of the resurrected. Hypothetically speaking, we can guess that the New World, the world of the resurrected, will be a different phase of Creation, a new and perfectly well-ordered universe shaped by God from the Primordial Universe. God can bring us to a new birth of some sort, a resurrection, in that new phase of His Creation. We have no souls that can magically travel across the boundaries between different phases of Creation, from this universe to the universe of the resurrected. To be sure, this opens a different can of worms. How can we define what and who we are in order to believe that our resurrected selves are really the same entities as our selves in this world? This really isn't a new problem but rather one which has been obscured, perhaps by our assumption that our real selves are immaterial souls.

The neurobiologists and other biologists have gathered much information on the physical nature of human beings, but it's Einstein with his definition of a universe who has laid to rest the pagan ideas that human beings have separable and immaterial souls and that the physical world is moved along by hosts of angels and demons. With his powerful, totemic imagination, Einstein defined a physical universe which makes possible a human view of God's world in its unity and coherence and completeness. Modern physics makes it possible for Christians to tell a story which unites revealed truths with empirical facts so that God's world can be seen in its true glory. In return for this great possibility, we have to be willing to give up ideas which were plausible in earlier times with less adequate understandings of physical reality. But those sorts of plausible ideas become superstitions when we insist on holding them when they're no longer plausible.

God shaped a universe, which He alone sees in its full worldly characteristics, but we can understand it as a universe and see – however partially – its unity and coherence and completeness. Those characteristics, and His general competence as a Creator, argue against a universe radically fragmented in the sense of containing substances that areporous to creatures, a universe which angels enter and leave by their own powers. Either they are creatures inhabiting this world and made of its stuff or else they are outsiders sent in by God on specific missions. This sort of view was plausible in the Aristotelian Cosmos, but that was a pantheistic view of reality in which Heaven was simply what lies outside the orbit of the moon. Rather than a world under God, Aristotle saw a Cosmos which was all of being and ascension from the blood and dirt of the Earth led through Angelic realms into a realm which was not a far-distant region so much as it was the great Pan in all his purity.

Rather than accepting the Einsteinian universe as being a full description of reality, it seems possible to construct a way of viewing God's Creation in which entities co-exist with us where those entities are made of stuff differently shaped from the raw, metaphysical stuff of the Primordial Universe. This would be a difficult but not impossible task, since it is Creation as a whole which must be unified and coherent and complete in the strongest sense. This taks remains undone. There are many who are committed to views on souls or angels which are radically different from the ones I've argued for. They should get to work building a worldview which shows how such views are consistent with empirical facts and theories. Again, this is not an impossible task but it is a very difficult task and no one has taken it on. Souls and angels are currently accepted and defined in terms borrowed from pagan theologies. Neither hand-waving nor mixed Christian-pagan theologies will revive the faith of fallen Christians or those who are descended from Christians but were never even taught Christian beliefs of any sort.

So far as this world is concerned, there's no Heaven up there because there's no 'up there' in Einstein's universe. There is no terrestrial being versus ethereal being because all the universe which can be seen is made of the same stuff, the stuff which God shaped in the early stages of the current phase of Creation which I have called our world.

I've conjectured the world of the resurrected will be newly shaped by God from the Primordial Universe, though that's pure speculation. But it does seem the most plausible speculation available to us with our current understanding of the universe in the light of God's promises.

The point I'm driving towards is actually quite simple:

> Man is a creature which arose as a citizen of this Particularized Universe. Like other entities in this Particularized Universe, including that universe itself, man can be studied by empirical means. In other words, man is fully an empirical entity. There's nothing inherent to human nature that makes man a candidate for life after death. Whatever we get, in this life or the next, is a pure, unearned gift from God.

If an ape were offered a chance to be perfected and completed so that he became a person, if he were offered companionship with God for time without end, would he be so foolish as to ignore those offers in favor of the hectic activity of the marketplaces?

Unfortunately, it would appear that many would be so foolish, but God's grace is always available until the very time you pass into the grave from which there's no resurrection.

Appendices

A Suggested Readings

A.1 Introduction

This appendix on suggested readings has been one of the hardest sections of the book to write. Every time I set out to work on this appendix I would find myself moving towards an academic bibliographical essay. To counter this, I've used a more informal title and I've decided to go right to some creative works of fiction that might help the reader to climb out of the ruts of the modern ideological world. Writing about these creative works also helped to loosen up my mind and my writing style.

If I don't mention a specific edition of a work or list one in detail in the bibliography, that means it's widely available in various editions, sometimes different translations. For example, there have been many printings of *Don Quixote* in English.

A.2 Nourishing the Imagination

It's possible to purge your mind of the modern ideologies, at least to the extent where you can clearly see the ruts in which you're traveling. And it can be fun just because one possible first step in this purgation process is to feed healthy thoughts and images to your imagination. This is my suggested reading list for beginning such a mind-saving and soul-saving medical procedure:

The Life and Opinions of Tristram Shandy, Gentleman by Laurence Sterne

Sterne was an Anglican priest who never rose very high in his church's hierarchy, possibly because he was irreverent about all those parts of human life which we take too seriously, especially when we consider ourselves to be important and dignified. Apparently, he was in great discomfort most of his adult life due to some lung ailment. Perhaps for that reason, he developed a sense of humor which was more intelligently off-beat than that of any major author I've read. After quoting Horace's dictum that a story should begin in the middle of the action and never retreat from that action, Sterne's narrator, Tristram Shandy himself, goes off for a good half of the book before he returns to talk about his life. Many of those digressive pages are taken up by a small novel about Uncle Toby, one of the most attractive characters to be found in literature. This book is a masterpiece of the digressive style and the reader who tackles it with the right attitude will begin to purge himself of his techno-bureaucratic ways of thought. For good and bad, that reader might then have an unemployable foot in Heaven.

After all, life has convinced some of us that the story God is telling in this world has plenty of digressions. Only a people who've grown up on Hollywood's versions of the Bible and weekly episodes of *MASH* could possibly believe there's a single plot development to any worthwhile story.

Don Quixote by Miguel de Cervantes

Cervantes was a man who led a difficult life to say the least. A man of noble bearing, he couldn't convince the North African Moslem pirates who enslaved him for several years that he and his family were too poor to pay much ransom. They wouldn't let him go with the other poor people being ransomed by Christian missionaries for small amounts. He was also incompetent with numbers, including finances, and got himself in trouble with unaccounted moneys when he was a requisition agent for the Spanish Armada. Cervantes was wrote much drama but wasn't an innovator in that field. Surprisingly, he is said to have been a hide-bound conservative given to attacking all innovation. More the strange it's that he wrote such a powerful and creative novel. This is another digressive book. It includes a fairly long romance novel which has nothing to do with the rest of the book.

Moby Dick by Herman Melville

Melville seems to have set out to prove that an American can also write a powerful, digressive novel. Captain Ahab, who confesses himself to be competent in practical matters and insane in moral matters, was probably intended as something of a more courageous and more consistent Ralph Waldo Emerson. As I've already noted, that sage of Cambridge was seen by Melville and Nathaniel Hawthorne and Henry James, Sr. as a moral madman of sorts. All three feared that Emerson's moral insanity represented the mainstream of American thought. On the Internet at Melville.com, there are some quotes including a comment that Melville wrote into the margins of a book by Emerson: "God help the poor fellow who squares his life according to this." A good read of *Moby Dick* might lead you to fear that Americans in general have done exactly that. Pay particular attention to the philosophical discourses of Ahab and his mates and also to the horrible and brutal massacre of the mother whales and their calves when the *Pequod* and other whalers stumble on a nursing ground.

The Confidence-Man by Herman Melville

This is a very interesting, mind-stretching, and confusing book. It has some sections, including the third paragraph of Chapter 5, which seem to be experiments in producing prose which makes sense to a flexible and creative human mind but which can't be parsed by any explicit procedures. The reader will find it easier to understand this book if he realizes that Melville thought that Ralph Waldo Emerson's ideas and attitudes, and perhaps those of Americans in general, were founded on a spiritualized materialism that masked a nearly total lack of charity – love of others. As you might guess from what I wrote above, Hawthorne and Henry James, Sr. (father of the novelist and the philosopher/psychologist and a substantial thinker himself) agreed with Melville on this and were apparently worried by the good reception that Emerson received from the American public as well as from American intellectuals. I would recommend the Penguin Classics edition for which Stephen Matterson wrote a good introduction to set the work in context.

Wise Blood by Flannery O'Connor

Miss O'Connor was a highly intelligent and well-educated Georgia farm-girl who read St. Thomas Aquinas for pleasure. She took years in expanding a short story into this book which first seems to be a satirical look at a Southerner who has lost his Fundamentalist faith but was still acting in ways that would have made N'Yark innerlekchuals laugh at those dumb hillbillies. Begun as a student project at a well-known creative writing school, this book became nearly unpublishable when those N'Yarkers apparently realized she was really making fun of them. The protagonist of this book loses his faith while serving in the U.S. Army and returns to Atlanta to found the Church without Christ, an effort to keep some of the parts of Christianity he considered good while getting rid of that inconvenient figure of Christ. Some say it turned out to be an allegory of the intellectual and spiritual life of Nietzsche.

One Hundred Years of Solitude by Gabriel Garcia Marquez

So far as I can figure, this is just a fun book that stretches the imagination. As such, it probably can be considered as something of a comment upon the barren imaginations of well-conditioned citizens of the modern marketplace world. Just read it for fun. In fact, read all of the above books just for fun and then think about them on the second reading. All great books demand at least two readings, though there's not even enough time to read many of them once.

Other Suggested Sources of Nourishment

In this my book, I've described one way of morally structuring our view of the universe that a world might come into view. The novel was developed as a means of exploration of the moral nature of the human being, one result being the inward turn of the novel to explore inner moral spaces as the modern, bourgeois world developed. I don't really think that to have been a good trend on the whole, though many great novels emerged from the middle-class novelists of the past two centuries or so. *Don Quixote*, *Moby Dick*, and *One Hundred Years of Solitude* are examples of novels which don't fit into this middle-class mold.

Jane Austen wrote a number of great novels which do fit into that mold, though none of her characters are middle-class in an American sense. By way of deceptively simple romances, she explored a number of deep moral issues mostly from the viewpoint of those who were formed to the standards of the English country gentry. That viewpoint has little plausibility in our world, but her novels stand as examples of a certain moral order which was once plausible and more than simply decent. In any case, any examples of the interactions of morally well-ordered people should be of interest to those who would be morally well-ordered. But, as Lionel Trilling once advised, don't read Jane Austen's novels for just a sense of nostalgia before throwing yourselves back into a morally disordered society.[1] Instead, read those novels to gain a sense for what might be involved in bringing a different and appropriate moral order to our particular society.

George Eliot (Marian Evans) was one of the great narrators in human history and her novels, a generation after those of Jane Austen, show the moral disorder which is already creeping into the minds and souls of even people of the same sort as the typical character of, for example, Jane Austen's *Emma*. I'd recommend *Middlemarch* for sure, but there seems to be a general opinion that all of her novels are worth reading. The only novelist I've

[1] I would advise a good browse of *The Moral Obligation to Be Intelligent*, a collection of his essays selected by his friend Leon Wieseltier. Though I believe liberalism, right-wing and left-wing, to have been a mistake from the beginning, this collection reminds us that there was a time when some advocates of one variety or another of liberalism were intelligent men of great moral integrity and having serious insight into the human condition.

read who seems to me to be clearly superior to George Eliot in the ways of concrete narration is Leo Tolstoy. Tolstoy's moral sensibilities led him into strange ways of thought and behavior so that G. K. Chesterton described him as being a mixture of presumptuous barbarian and inhuman puritan. This development of his character is coming into view as early as *War and Peace* and has taken a brutally sharp form in *Anna Karenina.* That latter novel, about a wonderful woman who fell into sin, seems to me to close off the possibilities of grace for that fallen woman. It's hard to believe that the man who wrote that book could be considered as a great Christian thinker. True, he was willing to make great sacrifices, but no well-ordered Christian could ever close off the possibilities of grace to anyone, no matter how great their sins.

And, so, I'll refer the reader back to Flannery O'Connor's *Wise Blood* and to her other novels. It's clear that she's driving home that point: the possibility of accepting God's grace remains open at least to the moment of death, even for the protagonist of *The Violent Bear it Away*, an ex-Christian and anti-Christian. That Bible-thumping Fundamentalist become follower of Satan baptizes a young, retarded man and drowns the poor fellow in the process. Having accepted the truths of the Bible and then having deliberately turned away, that ex-Fundamentalist sees the world as clearly as a great saint. He accepts the judgment of the modern world that the life of a retarded man is not one worth living but he really doesn't think it necessary to condemn such a fellow to Hell. As for the liberals who have taught the world that only the sorts of lives they prefer are worth living? Well, they chose their own paths.

Grace is ever available if we have the courage and the sense of gratitude which will allow us to accept it. But there's that related question of our moral order, inside and outside. Sir V. S. Naipaul is the primary champion of those who would put the world into some sort of order without being able to pull it off – in my opinion, this happens partly because they cannot see the order which is already present. From this perspective, I would especially recommend *A House for Mr. Biswas*, *The Mimic Men*, and *The Enigma of Arrival.* There are varying hues of despair and the openness to something akin to grace as viewed by a Thomistic Catholic. He has continued to write and publish after winning a well-deserved Nobel Prize. You can read *Half a Life* as a more recent example of a tale of displaced people from ex-colonial regions, but I think that all of us in the modern world are displaced people of one sort or another.

Wallace Stegner explicitly believes that to be true of Americans, or at least true of those Americans who are ever ready to move across the continent to pursue a dream of making it big. I've read only two of his novels, *Big Rock Candy Mountain* and *The Angle of Repose.* I'd recommend both very highly, but I'd also suggest the reader consider a certain question. Professor Stegner was a man of moral courage but he confessed a certain moral disorder because of his upbringing as the son of one of those always looking for the gold-mine a thousand miles away (*Big Rock Candy Mountain* is apparently a fictionalized tale of his 'nuclear family'). I don't think he knew how to bring a novel to a true end and I suspect that's true just because of that moral disorder to which he confessed. In Christian societies, that moral order which allows great comedies assumes the possibility of grace. Dante's trip through Hell was a comedy for all the suffering he described; even more importantly, St. Augustine's *Confessions* would be considered a comedy if treated as fiction. The virtuous pagan societies which were far better at producing tragedies assumed a harsh moral code that drove a man towards a noble death in a world which seemed to be meaningless. Our post-Christian society has produced mostly confused literature which will likely be ephemeral even though some of it was produced by writers who could pen a more than adequate sentence. To put it in a more oracular manner: In the long run, no one really gives a damn about Holden Caulfield. To put it in more abstract terms: Christian comedies and pagan tragedies are both gibberish to us.

I'll end this digression into the art of literary imagination by mentioning Robert Louis Stevenson, famous for the adventure novels accessible to young adults and for the horrible botches Hollywood has made of *The Strange Case of Dr. Jekyll and Mr. Hyde*, a book in which is important though this highly disciplined author made one major technical error and some smaller ones as well. It was that major error, the use of drugs to effect the transition from Dr. Jekyll to Mr. Hyde, that makes this book attractive to semi-literate readers and illiterate makers and viewers of movies. Mr. Hyde might have been released by drugs, but Stevenson saw him as being created by Dr. Jekyll's moralism which led him to suppress his sinful tendencies rather than try to deal with them – as Jesus commanded. Access to a confessional booth could have killed off Mr. Hyde before he emerged to stomp that child into the ground. Read this short novel, or re-read it, knowing what Stevenson was really thinking as he wrote it. Once you know that he was a profound thinker, a keen observer, and a technically accomplished writer, you can move on to his other works and you might find riches even in his supposedly simple adventure novels.

A.3 Matters of Belief

A Christian or anyone interested in Christian thought, if only for academic reasons, should be reading the Bible steadily – though not necessarily constantly. I've read the Bible cover-to-cover about five times in the past 15 years, reading the Gospels once a year or so. When I read a work about the Bible or biblical times, I'll usually find it good to read at least one book of the Bible in parallel. Yet, despite the fact that my worldview is Christian, I'll start with a book about some very creative rabbis and how they dealt with the creation accounts in the book of Genesis.

The Rabbis Confront Creation

Confronting Creation: How Judaism Reads Genesis is a remarkable book about some rabbis who displayed astounding flexibility in their commentary upon the Torah and other holy works. In fact, the ease with which some of the ancient rabbis jumped from one verse of scripture to another seemingly unrelated, from one holy thought to another seemingly unrelated, puts them on the same level of imaginative talent as the likes of Cervantes and Sterne and Melville.

I think the rabbinical views of Creation as discussed in *Confronting Creation* can be, at the least, a useful antidote to a certain deadness of thought in the usual scientific views about the physical universe and a corresponding deadness of thought in Christian views about Creation. Often, that deadness takes the form of academic rigidity but it can also be a sort of Biblical Literalism (Jews are not immune to the attractions of this sort of fundamentalism) or a law-like rigidity such as the various distortions of

Catholic doctrine which come from ideological distortions of the works of St. Thomas Aquinas.

The Works of Raymond Brown

Raymond Brown was a Catholic priest who spent much of his career teaching at Union Seminary, the Protestant seminary in New York City. He has written an overview of the New Testament which is based upon his lecture notes for an introductory course at that school. He takes the position that such an introductory text can be written to be acceptable to all orthodox biblical Christians, Protestant or Catholic or Orthodox. *An Introduction to the New Testament* works well as a general introduction. Father Brown has published many other works on the Bible which are either scholarly or explicitly Catholic so far as I know. I feel safe in saying his name on a book is evidence of its trustworthiness, orthodoxy, and high quality.

I would recommend, to Protestants as well as Catholics, a more popular book he wrote, though some of the questions deal with Catholic viewpoints: *Responses to 101 Questions on the Bible.* Among other issues, he deals with the reliability of the major translations, endorsing both translations by Protestant scholars and also some of the slightly summarized versions of the Bible, including the Reader's Digest version. Part of his reason for endorsing the summarized versions is that some books of the Bible are hard enough for scholars and clergymen to deal with, such as the book of Revelation; other books in the Bible, especially some of the historical books of the Old Testament, are largely genealogies or other material of little value to the layman who is reading for either historical knowledge or spiritual renewal. It can also help greatly to pay attention to the homilies at Mass or the sermons at a Protestant service.

The Works of St. Thomas Aquinas

As part of the process of purging pagan thoughts, I'd suggest the reader tackle *Summa Contra Gentiles*, a few chapters at a time. Even if you read slowly and put in a few minutes of contemplation, it's a task that takes only fifteen minute a day. I recommend *Summa Contra Gentiles* rather than the other major summary of Aquinas, *Summa Theologica*, just because the prior work was written to appeal to people not holding a Catholic worldview. I'd also recommend reading some good commentaries upon Thomistic thought or histories covering his thought in parallel to reading St. Thomas' own works. I'd especially recommend a few works of Etienne Gilson discussed in the next section as well as Alasdair MacIntyre's *Three Rival Versions of Moral Enquiry* which deals with the difference between Thomistic moral teachings and those of modern philosophers. There are also many good discussions of Thomas' thought available in libraries and some are still in publication. Jacques Maritain wrote directly about Thomism at times and often about modern political and social issues from a Thomistic viewpoint.

Some of the most prominent modern commentators on the thoughts of St. Thomas might well disagree with my view of matters, especially my ways of extending the basic insights of St. Thomas. With that warning, I'll simply recommend two works by such thinkers before going on to discuss Gilson's works in some more detail: *Living the Truth* by Josef Pieper and *St. Thomas Aquinas* by Ralph McInerny. Chesterton's brief biography, *Saint Thomas Aquinas: The Dumb Ox* is also worth a read for a little flavor of St. Thomas as a concrete human being. Surprisingly little is actually known about the details of his life.

Etienne Gilson

Educated in modern philosophy, Etienne Gilson had an aha experience in which he decided that St. Thomas' insight into the nature of the act of being is of primary importance. He has written extensively on Medieval Christian philosophy, covering Christian, Islamic, Jewish, and pagan thinkers, especially those of importance in understanding the thoughts of St. Thomas Aquinas. I'm recommending the following books by Gilson:

- *Methodical Realism*
- *Thomist Realism and the Critique of Knowledge*
- *The Christian Philosophy of St. Thomas Aquinas*

- *Being and Some Philosophers*

These four books will give a good understanding of Gilson's views on Thomism and some understanding, from the fourth book, of some basic mistakes he sees in the thoughts of some major thinkers: some of the Islamic philosophers and St. Augustine on up the modern age where he acknowledges Kierkegaard's insight into the act of being but criticizes him for then losing sight of the particular substance which is brought into being. He also criticizes Sartre for similar but more serious errors.

Gilson is probably the best and most reliable modern expositor we have of Thomism. And that's important because the works of St. Thomas are easy to read and hard to understand in their totality, and it's in that totality that Thomism exists because that totality is glued together by his theory of knowledge and by his insights into the act-of-being, both of which remain true even though many of his specific proofs and teachings have been falsified by the advancement of empirical knowledge, including a better understanding of the history of the early Church and of the history of the Bible.

The Works of St. Augustine of Hippo

St. Augustine greatly taxes reading and thinking skills. He wrote many, many words. The priests in his Cathedral also wrote down many of his sermons and informal talks. You have to be very careful for more reasons than I'll be stating. First of all, he's engaged in a task far more speculative than mine: while I'm trying to pull together a Christian worldview in a landscape filled with useful rubble, he was making a similar effort in a world where most of the intellectual works were pagan. Second of all, I consider his earliest writings to be useful mostly for biographical and historical reasons because he was still trapped in the Neoplatonic or middle platonic viewpoint. Third of all, he had a sense of humor and a command of irony and other literary devices which finds few equals outside of creative fiction.

For the above reasons, I had considered ignoring St. Augustine in this bibliographical essay, but I couldn't just because I couldn't ignore him in the main text. The reader unacquainted with this extraordinarily fertile thinker would do well to learn about the man's life. I recommend Peter Brown's biography *Augustine of Hippo* for a sense of St. Augustine's movement from paganism to Christianity. I would also recommend Louis de Wohl's biographical novel, reprinted in recent years by Ignatius Press, for a good feeling of how eccentric and opinionated Augustine was. From both books, you'll also get a feeling for his profound charity, his love of his fellow-men and of God, and for his competence as a practical man. He was educated to be a very high-level lawyer arguing in front of the Imperial Court, as if a modern lawyer were educated from his early college years to argue in front of the Supreme Court. And he was so trusted as a judge that he was overworked during his years as a bishop. Under Roman law, parties in a dispute could choose to have their case tried in the local ecclesiastical court and, because of Augustine's honesty and competence, even pagan disputants often chose to have him decide their cases.

With that as background, I'll mention just three books by St. Augustine. *Confessions* can be usefully read just for its literary style and its psychological insights. In the context of this great man's thoughts, psychology is largely concerned with his discovery that God is not only a Transcendental God and Immanent Creator and Sustainer, but also a God who indwells in the deepest part of His human creatures. Augustine discusses his conversion in a way that indicates that the facts are less important than later contemplations that distilled certain events in his early life into a powerful narrative. The psychology of conversion experiences is explored with deep insight that shows up more in the arrangement of concrete events than in particular abstract insights. Don't take him at his literal word when he talks about events such as the stealing of the peaches. Instead, remember that insight of his that I repeated often in this book: we are sin.

Those who wish to get a taste of Augustine's early writings will do well to read a major translation of some of his earlier writings: the Westminster Press collection, *Augustine: Earlier Writings*. To me, the major lesson of those writings is that St. Augustine would have been a great pagan philosopher if he had not later become a dangerously creative Christian theologian.

I highly recommend *The Literal Meaning of Genesis*. Read after his earlier,

Neoplatonic writings, you'll see a radical turn towards an acceptance of the empirical world. In *From Dawn to Decadence*, Jacques Barzun tells us that St. Augustine eventually claimed that even our nail parings and hair clippings would be resurrected with us. Undoubtedly, he said that somewhat tongue-in-cheek but Barzun is right to conclude that St. Augustine became almost grotesquely physical as he became more and more Christian. Even a quick read of *The Literal Meaning of Genesis* will indicate that Augustine would have sided with Galileo and against Bellarmine in that famous confrontation.

The Works of Stanley L. Jaki

Stanley Jaki is a very learned Benedictine priest. He's a true authority on matters of theology, languages both modern and ancient, physics, history – especially the history of science, and philosophy. Unfortunately for his book-sales and for his reference-count in works of science and philosophy and history, he does not speak the lingo of the modern ideologies nor does he accept what passes for thought in those ideologies. With little recognition, certainly none at an appropriate level, he has worked diligently and steadily, brilliantly when brilliance was needed, to restore the physical universe to the status of a creation of God. Of course, the universe was always that – I speak of a restoration in human thought. More than that, he has argued for the particularity of this universe – a more important belief for both science and theology than most will acknowledge. Modern thought, formed to the needs of the gods of the marketplaces in my telling of the story, denies that the universe is a particular Creation because that would force men to give up the illusion of being autonomous, free-willed economic and political agents: men would have to acknowledge their status as fully particular creatures.

In *Genesis 1 Through the Ages*, Jaki convincingly shoots down the idea that these verses were intended as a cosmological account in the sense of modern physics or even Plato's *Timaeus*. *Bible and Science* is a rich discussion of the real and false conflicts between the Bible and modern, empirical science. There are no real conflicts which have any bearing on revealed Christian doctrine. Interestingly enough, he discusses Augustine's ability to see the important questions and his occasional, but important, failures to shed his prior prejudices to reach an insight which should have been dictated by his principles of exegesis.

Jaki's most important work on science is probably his first such work: *The Relevance of Physics*. This book argues coherently that physics is the primary science for not just historical reasons but for deeper reasons. I can't say if he would agree with my claim that the most speculative regions of theoretical physics can be seen as a quantitative metaphysics.

I'll also recommend two books dealing more specifically with the issues of cosmological physics: *God and the Cosmologists* and *Is There a Universe?*. Those books can help you see gobbledy-gook for what it is when a popular-science writer mangles rationality in his efforts to talk about the Big Bang.

The Works of Jaroslav Pelikan

Jaroslav Pelikan first become prominent as a translator and biographer of Martin Luther. From there he became a self-confessed follower of John Henry Newman as a historian of Christian doctrine, producing the premier overview work in that field as well as a number of works dealing with more specific topics, including histories dealing with aspects of pagan thought. I'm going to mention only two of his works, though one is a five-volume work: *The Christian Tradition: A History of the Development of Doctrine.* The serious Christian thinker should read all five volumes, but any well-educated Christian thinker should read at least the first volume on the doctrinal struggles in the early centuries of Christianity. The early Fathers of the Church retain their great importance even when they erred because of inadequate knowledge about empirical matters, including the history of the Bible itself as well as physics and biology. For example, the Biblical revelations about a great rupture between God and man, along with Neoplatonic myths of a time when the world was perfect, led to an understanding of the concept of original sin which conflicts with modern knowledge of human origins. As I've discussed in the book, the Biblical revelations, and common-sense observations of our sinful condition, force us to look for a doctrine in which man's sinful state is the result of our situation in this developing world created by God.

What Has Athens to Do with Jerusalem provides some reinforcement to the claims of Jaki and a few others that the Hebrews who wrote Genesis were not cosmologists and probably weren't even aware of the issues. The doctrine of creation from nothingness came from Plato, though by way of contemplations that converted a brilliant insight by a pagan into a Christian belief.

American Foundations of Atheism

There's a consensus view amongst historians of human thought that it was difficult to be an atheist in pre-modern times because the very language and cultural concepts of most societies assumed a world which was at least filled with gods and spirits if not always ruled by a single God. It took the will and mental discipline of a French Philosophe to clear away these pious assumptions. Nowadays, atheistic beliefs are often held in a casual way without any effort to think through the issues or to reject the existence of God or gods. How did this situation develop?

The historian James Turner wrote *Without God, Without Creed* to explain how so many Americans fell so readily into a state of disbelief. Turner's well-argued thesis is that Christianity in the United States was badly damaged by an attempt to convert it into a non-creedal religion, which attempt was made by the best and the brightest of the American Protestant clergymen. That effort reached what some of us would consider a low-point as the Congregationalists renounced any ties to a specific creed shortly after the War Between the States. Turner argues that history shows us that Christianity is a creedal religion and non-creedal Christians are merely on their way out of Christianity. A general theism might be held in a non-creedal way, but a religion centered on a God who entered the empirical world He had created is one with specific beliefs which need stated as creeds. As Charles Darwin's strange and brilliant grandfather, Erasmus Darwin noted: Deism is a feather-bed for the falling Christian. Deism is an early and lasting form of non-creedal Christianity, a Christianity without Christ. That is, in fact, how I remember the Congregationalism of my youth – a Christianity in which Jesus was not acknowledged explicitly as God. The Lord's divinity was never specifically denied so far as I can recall, but it's not exactly a fact natural to human thought, so it's being denied if it's not actively taught and preached.

Michael Buckley's work *Denying and Disclosing God* gives his latest views on the development of modern atheism, a development as difficult to understand as any other complex events in the history of ideas. His work, as he notes, is quite compatible with that of Turner but he deals more exclusively with the theologians who managed to turn God into a conclusion in abstract arguments. As I discussed in the main text of the book, using insights from Turner and Buckley and Hauerwas, such a move opens up the likelihood of plausible abstract arguments that God doesn't exist, at least not the God of Jesus.

A.4 First Steps Towards a Worldview

Alasdair MacIntyre

Before my views were at all coherent, I read *After Virtue* without understanding much, or so I see in hindsight. Then I read *Whose Justice, Which Rationality*. So far as explicit knowledge goes, I did manage to understand that the problems of the modern West are far deeper than many would-be reformers would have it. I reread those books after reading *A Short History of Ethics*, *Marxism and Christianity*, and *Against the Self-Images of the Day*. It was only with a reading of *Three Rival Versions of Moral Enquiry*, ten years after reading those other works, that I began to think in terms of a tradition and I could truly see the need for a tradition to provide the context for the entire range of a ideas and attitudes which a human being might experience. It was in this later book, a published version of MacIntyre's Gifford Lectures, that he makes a very strong claim that moral knowledge is less abstract knowledge and more a form of practice which must be learned in a tradition. This is a rediscovery of the nature of human knowledge and of the nature of truth: the schools of the ancient philosophers and the Medieval theologians were gatherings of masters and disciples rather than schools in the modern sense.

In a slightly different direction, *Dependent Rational Animals* bolstered my confidence in my emerging ideas and helped me to think through the possibility that man is a physical animal who neither possesses nor needs a separable soul of any sort, immortal or otherwise.

In addition to specific historical or conceptual insights, Professor MacIntyre has given us an example of a man who has pursued the truth in a sustained life-long effort which was mounted against the spirit of the age, which spirit I've named, in the plural as "the gods of the marketplaces."

Michael Oakeshotte

I've read some of Michael Oakeshotte's writings on history and on politics, but it's one of his earliest writings, *Experience and Its Modes* that put me well on the way to my insight that a tradition can be alive and effective only if it takes the form of a worldview, meaning literally that a tradition must bring a world into view where there was once a mere collection of things embedded in environments with some connections and similarities. Professor Oakeshotte had too many worlds and too few. He split the universe into realms of specialty knowledge – science and religion and practice with philosophy to rule and bind them. I propose that each God-centered human person, and perhaps a few others, have a worldview of some validity – no matter how simple it is. On the other hand, the worldview of even such a great thinker as St. Augustine of Hippo is provisional.

Oakeshotte's political and social writings are also worth a read. They helped to shape my ideas in those fields though I've gone a bit further than Professor Oakeshotte who was a rather moderate anti-corporatist and a relative optimist that national governments could avoid the corruptive ambition that leads to centralization of power. He was one of the very few true conservatives amongst the intellectuals of the 20th century and anyone reading all or parts of *Rationalism in Politics and Other Essays* will soon discover he has little in common with those who call themselves conservatives in American politics.

Stanley Hauerwas Boosts the Church

Stanley Hauerwas believes that the best proof of the existence of God is for the Christian Church to bear witness to God's presence in the world. Individual Christians as members of local churches must live as Christ commanded us to live. In the published version of his 2001 Gifford Lectures, *With the Grain of the Universe*, Hauerwas develops the argument by examining the cases of William James, Reinhold Niebuhr, and Karl Barth. He's sympathetic to all three and finds much to admire in the thought of all three, but it's Barth he sides with after showing that great theologian to have also taught that Christian practice is the best, perhaps the only, proof of the existence of the God of Jesus.

The interested reader can read samples of writings by Professor Hauerwas in *The Hauerwas Reader*, which samples are at different times of his career, addressing different issues.

John Howard Yoder Teaches Tough Thought to Christians

My mind works slowly when I encounter something substantial and I haven't yet comprehended the thoughts of John Howard Yoder but I've already been influenced by Yoder's willingness to ask the tough questions and to think outside of the lines. With the understanding that I have only a dim view of Yoder's teachings, I'll suggest that one of the basic insights of this book can be found in his writings. A Christian's response to Christ will bring into shape the moral structures through which he will envision a world. But, of course, it's a recursive process where moral structures are then altered by that initial vision of the world and then the world is seen anew.

These are three books by Yoder I've read so far and they've certainly stirred up thoughts:

- *The Politics of Jesus*
- *When War is Unjust*

- *The Christian Witness to the State*

In the book on war, resulting from a course he taught at the request of the ROTC commander at Notre Dame, Yoder steps partly outside of his own radically non-violent position to examine two questions:

1. Is the concept of just war intellectually coherent?
2. Is it possible to fight a just war under current political conditions?

For those who like to know how a story will end before reading it, Yoder's answers to those questions are "yes," and "no."

Read Yoder and let him challenge you. The experience will help to sharpen your thinking skills and you might even decide he's right in some of his radical conclusions.

A.5 Background Thoughts

Adam Smith the Whipping Boy

Besides a variety of works on the history of science and esthetic matters, Adam Smith left the two great and greatly dangerous works: *An Enquiry into the Nature and Causes of the Wealth of Nations* and *The Theory of Moral Sentiments.* Those two works are parts of a whole. There are some who think that Smith glorified selfishness in the *Wealth of Nations* and a soft form of morality in *Moral Sentiments*, but Smith was himself a benevolent and generous man and most certainly never intended to justify selfishness as such. In fact, I doubt he would have been able to justify to himself the radical individualism of his economic teachings if he had not thought that the moral order of the public squares of Scotland was brought about by an easing of physical hardships as modern prosperity came to the Glasgow and other Scottish cities. Those Scottish citizens of Glasgow were limiting their exploitations of others because of some very strong, inborn desire to be seen as nice and commercial prosperity allowed niceness to grow. He was clever enough to worry that there would be a softening of moral character in a commercial society, which softening could endanger the survival of that society, but being a modern man in his fragmentation, he never thought to wonder if that utilitarian concern might indicate a more profound error in his moral theories. In fact, experience indicates that modern styles of prosperity are a greater danger to the Pilgrim Church on Earth than Satan could have ever been.

Jacques Barzun

What can you say about a man who was active as a professor, university administrator, scholar in several fields, and writer of serious but accessibly well-written books for more than 70 years? In fact, the book that may be his magnum opus, *From Dawn to Decadence*, was published in 2000, more than 70 years after he joined the faculty at Columbia University. Professor Barzun maintains his scholarly persona through that book, though often writing with a tone of good-natured humor. He maintains that even tone though he is writing a history of the West over the past 500 years with the theme being the decay of literacy and the related abstract thinking skills over that period. Unfortunately, he supports all too well the prophecy of the last pages of the book where he predicts we're very near a collapse into a new dark age of ignorance.

Professor Barzun has written a number of substantial books which speak to our cultural conditions. I'll mention only two which are particularly pertinent to the main topics of this book.

In *Science: The Glorious Entertainment*, Professor Barzun pays proper respect to science for its accomplishment and for its important role in human thought as a whole. A proper respect leads him to deny that science is rightfully as dominant in human thought as it has sometimes been in recent centuries.

In *Darwin, Marx, Wagner*, he examines the ways in which ideologies grew from the thoughts of a insightful naturalist who produced garbled abstract thought, a powerful thinker who willfully confused himself, and a talented composer who thought he was a great prophet.

John Lukacs Tells Us Like It Is

John Lukacs writes history in the manner of a novelist, admitting he might have become a novelist if he'd not first studied history. He's also a man who places human values ahead of ideologies, leaving him in conflict with the modern world when, for example, his local community was about to be badly damaged by further growth on the part of a retail development – the King of Prussia mall complexes. I was there once and I found those malls to be interesting in the same way that I found gambling casinos interesting on my one trip to Atlantic City and my one trip to Reno. DisneyLand was also a fitting object for a pathological study of sorts on my one visit. Read *Confessions of an Original Sinner* and *The End of the Twentieth Century and the End of the Modern Age* for Lukacs' temperate but deeply biting analysis of the situation we've gotten ourselves into, partly because we tend to tolerate a non-stop succession of leaders who are morally disordered to a still greater extent than the average modern man. But those are the leaders we wanted and we even encouraged them to grow still worse once they grabbed hold of power.

You'll read why Lukacs had first proposed World War I as the true end of the 19th century. That war was the most criminal and destructive war in history, World War II being really the end of that first war. And you'll read why Lukacs thinks the modern age came to an end with the fall of the Berlin Wall, but he has a far more pessimistic and far more plausible understanding than most analysts of the true meaning of the end of the modern age.

If we'd had a president with the moral integrity or the moral imagination to choose a man like Lukacs as his Secretary of State or National Security Adviser instead of the likes of Henry Kissinger or Zbignew Brzezinski, we might have had a chance to return to political and moral sanity. It didn't happen and it ain't likely to happen unless we get ourselves an intelligent Caesar.

Mary Midgley on Evolutionary Theory

In *Beast and Man: The Roots of Human Nature*, Mary Midgley remains true to the title's implication and argues we shouldn't be ashamed or feel degraded at discovering we're animals, apes at that. As she was seeing matters then (late 1970s), the evolutionary biologists had made it clear that there's a well-defined and coherent set of characteristics which we can call human nature. Unfortunately, she chose to approach evolutionary biology by way of the crowd which was, loosely speaking, gathered around the Harvard ant-expert, E. O. Wilson. She was rebuffed by Wilson in particular who went on to claim traditional moral thought had no validity. He built a substitute moral code which I admit I haven't bothered to investigate since it's the sort of silliness to be barely tolerated on the part of of a self-righteous twelve year-old.

Anyway, the experience of dealing directly with Darwinists left Professor Midgley all too aware of the incompetence some scientists exhibit when they suddenly decide to engage in abstract reasoning outside of their training. In public, at that. Darwin had warned them, and us, by confessing he was incompetent at abstract reasoning. A high level of scientific competence, even some creative scientific genius, can be found in a man not capable of generalizing competently even from his own work.

What Biologists Don't Wish You to Read

The silly tomes on designer worlds which purport to shoot down Darwinism are not at issue. The book that professors of biology are said to have censored by way of silence is Gertrude Himmelfarb's biography: *Darwin and the Darwinian Revolution*. She presents, in greater biographical detail, a view of Darwin that's similar to that presented by Professor Barzun in *Darwin, Marx, Wagner*: Darwin was a decent man with some serious talent for understanding nature in its concrete aspects but he fell into mental confusion when he tried to think at a conceptual level. Read either book and weep at the ideological biases of scientists who have made a heroic genius of this fellow whose abstract thinking capacities were what you would expect knowing he'd been raised as a Biblical Literalist even while he was showing himself to be what we would now call a jock.

Sons of Gödel

I've spoken of recent mathematical advances in the understanding of what random numbers are, even the understanding of what numbers are. This is a difficult subject to discuss partly because this fundamental work is surprisingly irrelevant to the work of most practicing mathematicians and has, consequently, not been integrated into the basic knowledge taught in the classroom. In addition, I know of few philosophers outside of specialists in mathematics who seem to realize that a revolution in the understanding of this important line of human thought is ongoing – it didn't end with the publication of Gödel's work.

For those wishing to gain or refresh a basic understanding of mathematical thought, there are a number of options. The reprint house Dover Publications (www.doverpublications.com) sells a number of histories and overviews of mathematics in affordable reprint editions. Check out the books classified in their catalogs or on their web-site as either "History of Mathematics" or "Elementary and Popular Mathematics". Any large bookstore should also carry some of these books as well as some similar books printed by the first-run publishers. The British mathematician Ian Stewart has written a number of good works for the non-specialist reader, including the work on chaos theory which he co-authored with the embryologist Jack Cohen – this book is discussed below.

I'd recommend a browse through a book which is written at a simple level so far as mathematical reasoning goes, but it requires some effort and some high level of sophistication in general reasoning: *Gödel's Proof* by Ernest Nagel and James R. Newman. A reasonably accurate but simple statement of Gödel's famous theorem is: it's always possible to find a knowable but unprovable truth in any mathematical system at least as complex as arithmetic. It's also surprising to discover that Gödel carried out his proof by showing it's possible to map arithmetic onto arithmetic. All numbers and all arithmetic operations are coded by numbers. Proofs of theorems then become arithmetic operations, adding and subtracting. This, by the way, should let us know that even the most abstract and fundamental levels of mathematics are limited in the range of issues they can address, though analogies can always be seen by a disciplined and creative thinker.

If you wish to go still further, I'd recommend a playful and digressive work: *Infinity and the Mind* by Rudy Rucker, a mathematics professor specializing in logic and set theory and also inclined to writing science fiction. He points out that our apparent inability to say anything positive and unique about the absolute infinity of transfinite set theory bears a dangerous analogy to the similar claims about our knowledge of God which have been made by negative theologians.

And then there's the current master in this general field: Gregory Chaitin. As a teenager playing around with early computers (circa 1965) in a New York City high school, Chaitin had an intuition that the concept of 'random number' could be better defined by coding complexity than by any mystical belief in numbers coming from roulette wheels in some spiritual realm. The peak of Chaitin's mathematical efforts perhaps came in the late 1980s as he proved that all numbers, except a set with measure 0, are random. This means that the set of random numbers is so large that the infinity of numbers which are not random is small to the point of disappearance in comparison. Chaitin was able to show that Gödel's famous theorem was a corollary of this more general theorem.

I'd recommend a browse through his web-site. A reasonably fast mirror even by the standards of my dial-up system can be found at:

http://www.cs.auckland.ac.nz/DMTCS/chaitin/

You should first browse through the short articles that he and various magazines or publishers have generously made available for free downloads. A number of those articles look interesting and accessible, but I can certainly recommend the two articles originally published by *Scientific American*. They appeared before he finalized his proof but explain the basic ideas of randomness in a way that does not demand much mathematical knowledge. That web-site also includes a listing of all of Chaitin's books with descriptions of the contents. The collections of shorter writings published by World Scientific are quite good, though there's much overlap with the articles available for download. The final proof of Chaitin's main theorem is available as an undergraduate text in computer science: *Algorithmic Information Theory* and is published by Cambridge University Press.

It's interesting that Chaitin has a couple of quotes from Leibniz on the top of his home-page. The second is translated as:

> But when a rule is extremely complex, that which conforms to it passes for random.

It's also interesting that Chaitin's more recent works, which I haven't seen, let alone read, deal with the philosophical implications of his work and of that of Gödel, Turing, Post, and others who have explored the limits of mathematical proof in general and of algorithmic proof in particular. I would recommend exploration of those works on the part of readers well-versed in mathematics and philosophy just because Chaitin's prose style is so clear and easy-going for a thinker dealing with such profound and abstract matters.

Michael Polanyi

The book to read, as Jacques Barzun would write, is *Personal Knowledge.* I fear I'm underestimating the influence upon me of Polanyi's complex but concrete arguments that we can make the objective universe ours without involving ourselves in unhealthy forms of subjectivism or relativism. That misstates matters since Polanyi's writings tend to be more positive, simply telling us how we make personal our knowledge of objective reality in a way that retains the objective content. My idea of a worldview is plausible only if we can accept Polanyi's arguments that knowledge can be both personal and objective. When we absorb a tradition into our deepest thoughts and feelings, we make it our personal knowledge. An entire scheme, containing all of our theological and moral beliefs as well as our objective and empirical knowledge, is a worldview.

In fact, I've argued in the main text of this book that a human being can only become a human person in a non-trivial sense if she makes objective truth her truth to the deepest parts of her human nature.

Bertrand de Jouvenel

Bertrand de Jouvenel was a highly regarded French political scientist, an expert on American politics in particular. His judgments of American politics are sharp to the point of harshness. For example, he argues that American politics had already been dominated by machines for quite some time by the early 1960s. We've always imagined that our country is an honest country, not so corrupted as those old countries or the banana republics to the south of us. As Professor de Jouvenel points out, a political machine gains and retains its power by guaranteeing it can deliver votes in its clients' interests. Consequently, it strongly prefers its candidates be lacking in moral integrity and independence, else the machine's masters could not be sure those politicians will vote as directed.

I'll recommend four of de Jouvenel's books, starting with these three about the realities of modern concentrations of power:

- *Sovereignty: An Inquiry into the Public Good*
- *On Power: The Natural History of Its Growth*
- *The Pure Theory of Politics*

If you've any illusions that our modern political systems can be reformed, beware of reading these books. As I interpret these works and a few to follow, a squeaky clean national government would simply be more efficient at enforcing its will upon its own people and others whose resources or labor it needs. A people wishing to be free should not hope to use concentrations of power and wealth for the good; a people wishing to be free should work to prevent the concentration of power and wealth. It seems to me that this general insight can be drawn from the Bible.

Professor de Jouvenel agreed that the Bible is not neutral towards accumulations of wealth. He gave some lectures where he tried, with only partial success, to integrate his Biblical faith with the valid claim of some forms of liberalism that peace in society dictates a respect for private property ownership even when justice might seem to call for redistribution.[2] Despite its roughness, *The Ethics of Redistribution* was published and then was republished by Liberty Fund. In this book, he stated that a Christian has to recognize that the mere possession of wealth – even if gained by honest, hard work – is dangerous to the soul. It's interesting that de Jouvenel's good friend Milton Friedman, the radical individualist, vetted the economic arguments in a book which tried to make the greater moral argument that the mere possession of great wealth can endanger its possessor.

de Jasay and Hummel on Freedom

Anthony de Jasay has a bad attitude. He insists on reminding anyone who will listen that modern people tell themselves they're free when they're really no more than wealthy. He thinks there to be a fundamental difference between freedom and wealth. He also tends to think that institutions which hold great power, such as the governments of the modern nation-state, will serve their own interests and not those of the general populace. Read *The State* and *Justice and Its Surroundings*, both published by Liberty Fund, to discover why he believes that we're deluding ourselves as we forge our own chains.

Then you could read Jeffrey Rogers Hummel tell how we were tricked into enslaving ourselves in a war that was later billed as a struggle to liberate the black slaves of the south. Read *Emancipating Slaves, Enslaving Free Men*, a tale largely of the blunders of powerful men of strong belief and limited vision and how they badly damaged this country. Jefferson Davis enslaved the whites of the South in addition to the blacks as he created a national socialist state that anticipated Soviet Russia and Nazi Germany. Abraham Lincoln created an entangled mess of government agencies and large corporations whose growth was nurtured because they were needed, and are still needed, for the modern-style wars which destroy local communities and try to weld the resulting human fragments into massive nation-states.

[2] There's something funny when Christians, or others, espouse both non-violence and large-scale welfare programs. Do they not realize that tax collections are always backed up by threats of violence? Even such a man of integrity as George Washington, waged war on a body of ordinary citizens to settle tax issues.

Hannah Arendt Doesn't Admire Nice People

The first two books to read are *Eichmann in Jerusalem: A Report on the Banality of Evil* and *The Origins of Totalitarianism.* The lesson Hannah Arendt would have us learn is that the nice middle-class people of the modern world are the ones who actually executed the evil or greedy plans which led to so many innocent people being murdered or enslaved or dispossessed over the past two centuries. The dedicated Nazis could murder people in street fights and they could roar enthusiastically at party rallies. It took nice middle-class people, concerned about meeting their bills and advancing their careers, to round up the Jews, transport them, and have large work-camps and death-camps built and ready for their arrival. It had also taken such people to carry out the exploitation of African and Asian peoples as the British empire had expanded.

Another book to read to continue this depressing line of thought is *In Retrospect: The Tragedy and Lessons of Vietnam* by Robert S. McNamara and Brian VanDeMark. Pay attention to McNamara's realization that he and the other members of the Johnson Cabinet had all the figures showing the United States was fighting a large-scale criminal-war in Vietnam. Those figures were sitting in front of them during meetings where all went well. People crossed items off their to-do lists and they made progress towards their next promotion or their move to a big job in a private corporation. All those nicely dressed officials from the President's staff did their jobs in their nice offices and meeting-rooms so they could go home to the nice houses where they lived with their nice families and went to nice churches on Sunday, dressing in nice clothes and traveling in nice cars.

Here's my summary, including some information I've gained from talking to some who served in Vietnam:

> Those nice Americans decided in their Washington meetings that they were going to protect the freedom of those South Vietnamese people by moving them out of the rural areas and moving them into cities which might have well-defined and defensible boundaries. Many of those people were not interested in moving to inner-cities, especially after some moved there and saw their daughters become prostitutes and their sons become

> drug-addicts supporting themselves by procuring various illegal services or goods for American soldiers and other foreigners.
>
> Those people who remained in their villages were classified by American intelligence analysts as enemy sympathizers and American troops were sent in to find themselves fighting twelve year-old girls standing in front of their own houses. In case anyone missed the meaning of the revelations about Senator Bob Kerry's war-crimes, those American soldiers were also trained to lay down fire towards the ground as they melted back into the jungle – that fire would be sure to kill any babies or other human beings hiding on the floors or under the floors.

The lesson might be:

> Nice middle-class people think funny. And you better make sure you never get between them and their next promotion.

Soul and Mind in the History of Thought

The main book I relied upon for my understanding of how Christians came to imagine they had immaterial components was the first volume of Pelikan's *The Christian Tradition* discussed above. I also found a few other books useful, starting with Richard Rorty's *Philosophy and the Mirror of Nature*, a book almost calculated to raise the hackles on those many Christians who are going to defend the pagan idea of the immortal soul more strongly than they'll defend the doctrines of the Holy Trinity and the Incarnation of the Son of God. Rorty, a non-believer of the skeptical sort, simply pointed out that dualism is not necessarily a part of Christian beliefs and that, in any case, the likes of Aquinas held a form of dualism that acknowledged man's predominately physical, animal nature. Rorty's book also pointed me towards these two books which engage in what some might call archaeological philosophy:

- *Body, Soul, Spirit* by C. A. van Peurson; and
- *The Origins of European Thought* by R. B. Onians.

The first emphasizes the foundations of the concepts of 'body', 'soul', and 'spirit' in Christian thought, Jewish thought, and the thought of a few pagan cultures of great importance to the development of modern Christian belief. It would probably be more meaningful to most people than Onians' book which requires a knowledge of Greek and Latin to follow completely. Still, *The Origins of European Thought* is well worth a few winter's evenings which might otherwise be spent watching television shows. If you do read such books as these, you'll find those shows no longer make sense to you and that'll be a sign of impending sanity, both moral and intellectual.

A.6 Darwin's Dangerous Idea

In this section, the recommendations will not be for books which address the general reasoning of evolutionary biology, a form of reasoning which was in ferment when I was last reading the magazines *Science* and *Natural History*. Both magazines are worth a browse to get a feel for both recent information and for trends in interpreting that information. Along those same lines, *American Scientist* was also quite good when I was reading it regularly in the 1990s; it carried substantial, well-written articles as well as good columns and the occasional opinion piece on a controversial matter. I would hope that these three magazines would be found in the reading rooms of the public libraries even in small cities and you might be able to buy individual issues at a large bookstore. Stephen Jay Gould was a mindless sort of mainstream collectivist liberal on most political and social issues and he was also quite condescending towards religion – in a 'tolerant' way. Despite that, he wrote a number of clear and insightful articles for *Natural History*. He addressed such issues as the lack of determinism in natural selection (watch for misuse of 'random' and similar words as discussed in the main text of this book), the heavy cost of structural changes in lines of organisms as compared to soft-tissue changes, and the various ways in which changes in development patterns might result in a new species.

Most of the books I discuss below deal with the issue of human beings as creatures whose full foundational substance is flesh-and-blood though there are immaterial aspects to human beings as there are to chimpanzees and killer-whales. Our immaterial aspects, and those of other living creatures, come about in interaction with our environments – parts of God's world. If all goes well, human beings will also start interacting with God and our immaterial aspects will become far richer and more complex, but our substance will still be flesh-and-blood. It's that flesh and that blood which is of interest below.

What Are We?

The book *Why We Get Sick: The New Science of Darwinian Medicine* by the psychiatrist Randolph M. Neese and the evolutionary biologist George C. Williams will be an eye-opener to those who don't yet realize the extent to which modern medicine assumes, sloppily and half-heartedly, a view of man as a physical creature closely related to chimpanzees and related even to rats and pigs. In this book, Neese and Williams contribute to the effort to clean up those assumptions so that we can more explicitly deal with, for example, the joint problems – knees and hips and lower back in particular – which result from nature's 'recycling' of the body of a crouching animal. Read the book and realize that modern biological knowledge does not degrade human beings. Rather does it raise our appreciation for the improvised beauty of all living creatures and for the complexity of the environments, ultimately the world seen by God alone, into which we are born and in which we develop.

Jerome Kagan, a highly-regarded research psychologist has written a book which manages to be respectful of human beings while speaking of the ways in which our our evolutionary inheritance defines and limits our temperamental possibilities, that is, our general attitudinal and emotional frameworks. But *Galen's Prophecy: Temperment in Human Nature* does not by any means preach predestination or any other sort of fatalism. Professor Kagan leaves room for us to improve our situation within our limitations, just as the Bible and traditional Christian moral teachings do.

Martin E. P. Seligman is a clinical psychologist who was a professor at the University of Pennsylvania when he wrote the book, *What You Can Change and What You Can't.* In that book, Seligman provides similar information to Professor Kagan's book but in a context more oriented to help you make specific changes in your life, by sometimes changing your own self and sometimes realizing you'll have to change your context instead. The latter possibility will include those life-style changes that Christians would call 'avoiding occasions of sin'.

William H. Calvin was educated as a physicist before switching to the neurosciences. He has been involved in high-level research in the roles which various sorts of fields might play in forming the human mind or simply in the decisions about physical movements. I pointed out in the main text of this book that fields might provide the feel of an immaterial mind and, in fact, some of the real characteristics of that sort of mind. As yet, it's a matter of plausible and attractive speculation. Professor Calvin has written some interesting collections of essays of literary quality on matters such as the evolution of the brain and human consciousness. You can look for them in your favorite bookstore or your public library. I'm going to recommend a different sort of book here: *Conversations with Neil's Brain.* This book is an account, slightly fictionalized for reasons of privacy, of his role as a consultant for an operation to excise parts of the brain of a man who suffered from life-threatening epileptic seizures. We see in a concrete medical situation that many of our mental functions are not only tied to the brain, they're tied to very specific regions of the brain. People who believe our minds are made of some immaterial stuff better learn that some parts of their minds will go away with damage to very specific regions of their brains. Localized damage to a specific region of the brain might destroy your ability to remember the names of man-made objects without otherwise affecting your memory or your cognitive functions.

In *Descarte's Error*, the neurobiologist Antonio R. Damasio digs a little deeper in the localization of specific mental or emotional aspects of the human being. One of the cases he examines is that of a man whose brain was damaged when a blast of dynamite drove a metal rod right through his skull. After walking on his own to the doctor's office and seeming to be shockingly intact, the man's personality and capabilities changed dramatically. Professor Damasio adds to the richness of his discussion by exploring examples drawn from his own experience as a medical doctor who has consulted on some cases of exotic behavior change involving brain damage.

Semi Zeki has been heavily involved in researching the visual systems of men and monkeys, including the highly specialized regions for seeing color. His book *A Vision of the Brain* gives an overview of how we see, particularly emphasizing color vision. You might be surprised to learn that the primary-color business most of us learned in school has nothing to do with the way we see color. It's perhaps more surprising to learn that the 19th century physicists James Clerk Maxwell and Hermann von Helmholtz gave a clear and irrefutable argument why human vision could not possibly depend on mixing of primary colors or upon our perception of, for example, a ball being red under all conditions.[3] It was the MIT scientist, and founder of Polaroid, Edwin Land who nailed the issue with some brilliant experiments that required his unique (at the time) expertise in certain technologies. And you should be amazed at the complexity, and the ad-hoc nature, of the human color vision system.

For a worthwhile side-trip, read *Inner Vision: An Exploration of Art and the Brain*, also by Semir Zeki. It's a book written largely while he was a visiting fellow at the Getty art museum in California. Professor Zeki and other visual scientists have been receiving grants from that museum to explore various issues of human perception of art. *Inner Vision* has some interesting, and very preliminary results regarding the effects of different sorts of art on the human brain. As it turns out, art which implies a real story, such as the paintings of Vermeer, light up the human brain on noninvasive scan devices whereas formalistic and abstract art does not seem to stimulate the brain much at all.

Gerald M. Edelman is recognized as being a great neurobiologist even by those who have problems with some of his terminology and some of his interpretations of his own findings. I'll only mention his use of a term 'neural Darwinism' to describe the way in which brain-cells in the young human being, barely more than embryonic, develop by a selection process in response to environmental events. Some of Professor Edelman's critics claim he is introducing purpose into natural selection processes by using the term 'Darwinism' for purposive selective processes. That shows a great confusion on their part since brain-development processes are a result of ordinary evolutionary processes which form new species or different types within a species. If brain-development is purposive and comes about by

---

[3]It suffices to say that a red ball emits a different set of wavelengths of light when it's in the shade as opposed to when it's in the sun.

way of evolution over the past three billion years, then that indicates that self-organizing processes can become purposive, that is, goal-oriented.

Edelman's own position on brain development and related issues is summarized in a very readable manner in *Bright Air, Brilliant Fire: On the Matter of the Mind* where he reveals himself to be an intelligent and open-minded materialist of the non-reductionist type. More recently, Edelman wrote *A Universe of Consciousness: How Matter Becomes Imagination* with the neurobiologist Giulio Tononi. In that book, Edelman and Tononi take a more explicit Jamesian pragmatic stance. They're right that we live in environments in which much organization occurs from the bottom up, but they're wrong in denying that a true world can be perceived by human beings. All of that bottom-up self-organization is made possible by events which have taken place at the level of the entire universe.

In *Reinventing Darwin*, Niles Eldredge presents a realistic and complex view of Darwinism which is in a state of potentially fertile turmoil. There are great uncertainties about such suggestions as that of Eldredge and Gould that small changes build up gradually and then the actual separation of breeding populations, speciation, occurs very quickly – they called this 'punctuated equilibrium'. There are a variety of open questions that let us know we're far from having a solid theory of evolution though we have some important pieces. Then again, my arguments in the main text of this book imply that the evolution of life is a story and not something to be reduced to a theory.

Finally, I'll recommend a book by a distinguished neurobiologist which deals less with specific issues in that field and more with the difficulties and frustrations of actual scientific research. *The Making of Memory* by Steven Rose is based on journals he kept while carrying out a series of experiments which explored some finer points of simple memory formation in baby chickens. He covers the failed attempts, why they failed, and how he went on from there. Part of scientific practice involves the ability to deal with failure which produces interesting clues on where to head next and also failure which seems to indicate the efforts of recent weeks, or months or even years, were wasted. I think Professor Rose was right to publish such a book since most popular science books, good and bad alike, tend to discuss the eventual successes in such a way that non-scientists probably think scientists are relentlessly progressing in one direction. See the book *Voyage to the Great Attractor*, discussed below, for a similar, on-the-spot discussion of a complex astrophysics project.

DNA and Other Demons

Robert Shapiro was a chemist interested in various genetic issues, such as the line of descent of his own people, the Ashkenazim. It turns out, to the surprise of few, that the Ashkenazim are a mixture of Semitic and Slavic peoples. Shapiro explains the Human Genome Project in *The Human Blueprint*. The first stage of that project was finished years after this book was written, but I consider it to a good, informal guide to various issues about genes, including some of the motivations for a very complex project.

Read *The Great Human Diasporas* by Luca Cavalli-Sforza and Francesco Cavalli-Sforza as an attempt to reconstruct the great adventure of human dispersion through the world. A time-line can be developed in which the peoples of northwest Europe moved out first from the Near East and were not exterminated in the various social revolutions, beginning with the cultural conquest of Europe by the agricultural ways of life first developed in Asia Minor or modern-day Turkey. All the European peoples and the Caucasian peoples of North Africa and the western regions of Asia seem to be descended from a small population of black Africans who began migrating from the general vicinity of Nigeria millenia before the birth of human civilization in the Near East, where I use the true meaning of civilization – societies which build cities.

More recently, thc National Geographic Society and IBM have teamed up to collect genes from as many volunteers worldwide as they can get. The research team is headed by a geneticist and anthropologist, Spencer Wells, who has found good evidence that all modern human beings are descended from a single human being who lived in Africa about 60,000 years ago. The project goal is to map out the movement of the human race out of Africa and across the globe in some detail. You can find out more about this project as it moves along at the web-site:

http://news.nationalgeographic.com/

The Collapse of Chaos

The embryologist Jack Cohen and the mathematician Ian Stewart got together to write *The Collapse of Chaos* and the result should have encouraged more such efforts. This book makes a good amount of sense out of the current ideas on chaos by exploring the mathematics and the related physical phenomena in embryological development. The meeting point of these two fields of thought can be seen when we realize embryologists deal with complex systems of changing facts, systems that develop or evolve both in well-determined and under-determined ways. Professor Cohen makes some interesting comments on the importance of the mother to the process of truly making a baby. The processes in the movie *Jurassic Park* by which they grew a dinosaur from strands of DNA are impossible. You need a Mommy dinosaur to make a baby dinosaur. He also says that a modern-day elephant might be able to provide an adequate egg-cell and womb for growing a mammoth from the DNA of one of those frozen corpses which have surfaced sometimes in Siberia.[4]

A.7 Einstein's More Dangerous Idea

I've written above of Jaki's *The Relevance of Physics* which is a masterpiece of what might be called forensic philosophy: it places physics in a historical context and also in a philosophical context. Before you can understand the place of physics in human thought, you need to understand something of physics as a human practice. If you've any background in mathematics or physics at all, even decent high school courses in the calculus and basic

[4]On the other hand, I've read that Japanese scientists are working hard on an artificial womb, which development, if realized, would perversely make women unnecessary, at least to those who wish to grow their babies in glass tubes and I've no reason to believe that modern men would hesitate to do that if some aggressive corporation starts to market the idea or the governments of the nation-states push the idea as one which will keep more adults working and consuming in the public marketplaces without the bother of child-bearing. It seems likely to me that modern societies, so dedicated to life in the marketplaces, will increasingly favor barren life-styles, including homosexuality. Babies will be grown in the laboratory or purchased from countries without Walmarts or Social Security. After all, we should remember that modern people strongly believe that any potentially profitable idea which is possible will inevitably be realized.

physics, I would recommend a reading of Robert K. Adair's *The Great Design*. I'll even provide a quote from the book to show that there have been thoroughly sane books of popular science:

> It's important to understand that the description of virtual particles in terms of the Uncertainty Principle is not a primary argument in itself but a qualitative explanation of the results of well-defined calculations.

Read *The Great Design*, ideally with a pad and pencil at hand to work through some of the ideas. It'll give you some idea how physicists think and how they go about their work. There are also books available which tell how some of the great modern experiments were carried out. I've no specific recommendations, but it would be worthwhile for some to read such a book and find out how a mere human being can investigate and measure events to inhuman levels of precision and accuracy.

For a solid, no-nonsense overview of cosmological physics, less demanding than Professor Adair's book, give a good read to *The Left Hand of Creation* by John Barrow and Joseph Silk. Professor Silk's *Cosmic Enigmas* is also worth a read. By the standards of a fast-moving field, both of these books are a little dated, but Professor Silk has recently published *On the Shores of the Unknown* – which updates the state of cosmological physics to the end of 2004 or so. I hate to say this on a quick read, but I have a strong impression that cosmological physics has turned into a well-focused atheolgical effort.

For someone willing to read a book which presents arguments partially in the form of equations, I would highly recommend *Cosmology: A First Course* by Marc Lachieze-Rey. He is the only writer I've read, other than Stanley Jaki, to always speak of the "time at which the universe began its current expansionary phase" rather than a "time of creation." He refers the reader to the French philosopher Merleau-Ponty for a discussion of the general issues.

Robert Wald is one of the mainstream experts on relativity theory, having written the book titled *General Relativity* which was the standard introduction for graduate physics students, though it has more competition nowadays. I certainly wouldn't recommend it for the ordinary well-read layman, but it's worth browsing through if your local library or college library happens to have a copy. A quick browse will reveal lots of mathematical equations and a careful style of exposition geared to the formalisms of mathematical physics. You'll then know much better that no one can derive the meaning of life from those equations, nor can they tell us that time and space are just an illusion as some speculative theorists are inclined to do.

I strongly recommend Professor Wald's accessible book on special and general relativity theory: *Space, Time, and Gravity.* Just to give an idea of his no-nonsense attitude, he points out that while special relativity theory does show our ordinary ideas of time do not translate well to observers which are moving rapidly relative to each other, the best way to see what is going on to say that they'll disagree on the simultaneity of events which are moving at an appreciable percentage of the speed of light relative to at least one of the observers. This sounds like beating around the bush at first, but it's morally responsible speech. He also gives an accessible overview of the theory of general relativity which is quite a bit more complicated than the theory of special relativity.

And now I'll recommend a book which was controversial for its attempt to use exotic speculations in physics to solve the problem of human consciousness: *The Emperor's New Mind* by Roger Penrose. It's a magnificent survey of some of the most important aspects of quantum physics and cosmological physics. Recently, Professor Penrose's *The Road to Reality* was published in the United States, nearly a year after being published in England. It's said to be his magnum opus but I've only quickly browsed through it. I'm not sure what the target reading audience is since he seems to address some deep and difficult problems in mathematics and physics. If you're not truly mathematically literate, you might still wish to read it, skipping over the parts where you can't 'read the foreign languages' as I had to do with Onians classic *The Origins of European Thought.* I'm sure Professor Penrose has many important and interesting things to say regarding the meaning of mathematics and of physical reality. Though willing to go out on a limb at times, he seems to be always careful to let the reader know when he is speculating outside the mainstream of scientific thought.

As a last recommendation in the field of physics, I'm going to suggest that those interested in the ways of actual research should read *Voyage to the Great Attractor* by Alan Dressler. It's the story of a complex project to find out where our galaxy is headed. It turns out that the Milky Way and other nearby galaxies are streaming rapidly towards some sort of gravitational attractor. This book is very interesting for its discussions of the human elements of such a research project, such as the pressures on one of the astrophysicists to use his computer skills to support the other scientists, leaving him with little time to work on his own astrophysical projects.

A.8 More Advice for the Confused

I wish I had a better idea of what we could do to restore our societies, regrow our communities and families, nurse our own souls and minds back to health. I fear that worse times are coming. The time may be near when God-fearing people may have to refuse the benefits of an increasingly evil medical system. That will be only one of the more obvious problem as modern societies tend to hit bottom, reaching the minimum moral order for even a heavily-policed society and perhaps staying there if the more unscrupulous amongst us manage to hold others at the bottom as the speculators, bureaucrats, lawyers, and military leaders of ancient Rome maintained the enslaved state of the proletariat masses, developing systems of bread and circuses which maintained low levels of developed intelligence and moral integrity. Then again, maybe we already have that with MacDonalds and the Superbowl.

I'll refer the reader to just a few books that might give us some hope, books by two men who have looked into the eyes of the beast and have managed to retain some sense of what it means to be a moral person and not just a human animal of the degraded modern sort.

The Jewish psychotherapist Victor Frankl survived his time in a Nazi concentration camp while his wife didn't. He explains his struggle to learn how to love again after his wife's death in *The Search for Meaning*. While I'm not a fan of the psychotherapeutic way of treating human spiritual ailments, I'd have to say that this is one man who exhibits true wisdom.

Wendell Berry is a man who found his way to the path of wisdom by first leaving his academic career – he was in New York City at the time – and returning to his family farm in Kentucky. For nearly 40 years, he has run the farm, having to learn the hard way what he would have learned from his father and grandfather if he'd not left for his career as a writer and professor of English. He found a great store of wisdom in the traditions of the Amish, just one of the rediscoveries related in *The Unsettling of America*, where he examines generally the harm we have done to ourselves by destroying our farming class in the interests of efficiency.

Farmer Berry, also an accomplished poet, has done a lot of thinking outside of the lines of our culture and its various pseudo-dissident groups. He has considered our industrialized medical system, seen the good it can do in solving specific problems, and wondered if it's worth the cost we pay in allowing ourselves to become objects for manipulation by that medical system. He has looked at the way that we can regard human fetuses and cattle and the land as being no more than means to our ends. He has pointed out the harm in an educational system that works to destroy the attachments young people have to their families and local communities and traditional beliefs. He has tried to remind us that the earth and all the stars belong to God and were created to please God. We're in rebellion against God when we pay little respect to His creatures and His property. If you wish to read Farmer Berry's defense of the traditions of homemaking on the farm, you can start with these books:

- *What Are People For?*;
- *Another Turn of the Crank*; and
- *Life is a Miracle.*

You might even wish to sample a collection of Wendell Berry's poetry or one of his novels. They're available in higher-quality bookstores, and even in some of the warehouse bookstores.

Come to think of it, Farmer Berry's attitude towards animals and our relationship to them would lead us to the right sort of radical animal rights. It would be okay to let a head of cattle live a good life out on the range and then kill it humanely for food. It would not be okay to raise chickens so that they never see the sky or walk across real earth, nor does it seem okay to torture even rats to meet some sort of humane purpose – especially now that we've seen the results of training our scientists and doctors to torture dumb brutes. By the way, this might be one of those cases where we see a strong hint of the ultimate unity of utilitarian and idealistic concerns. From a utilitarian realization that all of our bodies are being turned into commodities for the use of the most ruthless and most powerful of our race comes a conjecture that it might have been wrong in moral principle to have tortured those poor brutes in the first place.

Visit a local Christian bookstore or browse the religious shelves of a better barn of books store. There's cruft on those shelves but also treasures. Read a little of both. Perhaps you'll have to read some at random to discover which are which in your opinion. It's most important that you should start reading the holy books of your tradition. I've been addressing my book to Christians, especially Catholic Christians, because that's where the fullness of God's revelation can be found. So, I'd steer those readers to the Bible and to the writings of the Catholic saints, but I've found much of value in the writings of other sorts of sacramental Christians as well as the writings of Protestants and Jews. Read the Bible numerous times, sometimes reading it as you would read a history book and sometimes reading it slowly while you talk to God.

Most of all, join a prayer group or Bible study group and go to Mass or other liturgies if you're not yet ready to become a Catholic. If you find yourself truly believing in the God of Jesus Christ, you'll be in trouble in practical terms because you'll be soon fleeing the clutches of the gods of the marketplaces.

Bibliography

This bibliography provides a short, standard listing for books referred to in the main text. The bibliographical essay which precedes this should be considered as the source of the more important information about these books and their relationship to the main text.

[Adair] Robert K. Adair *The Great Design: Particles, Fields, and Creation* Oxford University Press, 1987

[Aquinas1] Saint Thomas Aquinas *Summa Contra Gentiles, Book Two: Creation* Translated, with an Introduction and Notes by James F. Anderson University of Notre Dame Press, 1975

[Aquinas2] Saint Thomas Aquinas *Summa Contra Gentiles, Book Three: Providence, Part II* Translated, with an Introduction and Notes by Vernon J. Bourke University of Notre Dame Press, 1975

[Arendt1] Hannah Arendt *Eichmann in Jerusalem A Report on the Banality of Evil* Penguin Books, 1994

[Arendt2] Hannah Arendt *The Origins of Totalitarianism* Harcourt, Inc., 1985

[Augustine1] Saint Augustine of Hippo *Augustine: Earlier Writings* Translated by John H. S. Burleigh The Westminster Press, 1953

[Augustine1] Saint Augustine of Hippo *The Literal Meaning of Genesis Volume 1* Newman Press, 1982

[Augustine2] Saint Augustine of Hippo *The Literal Meaning of Genesis Volume 2* Newman Press, 1982

[Barbour] Hugh Barbour, O.Praem. *Of Masons, Magic, Monks, Medicine, and Marriage* *Chronicles: A Magazine of American Culture* March, 2005

[Barrow] John D. Barrow & Joseph Silk *The Left Hand of Creation The Origin and Evolution of the Expanding Universe* Oxford University Press, 1993

[Barzun1] Jacques Barzun *From Dawn to Decadence: 1500 to the Present* HarperCollins, 2000

[Barzun2] Jacques Barzun *Science: The Glorious Entertainment* Harper & Row, 1964

[Barzun3] Jacques Barzun *Darwin, Marx, Wagner* Little, Brown and Company, 1946

[Berry1] Wendell Berry *Life is a Miracle* Counterpoint, 2000

[Berry2] Wendell Berry *What Are People For* North Point Press, 1990

[Berry3] Wendell Berry *Another Turn of the Crank* Counterpoint, 1995

[Berry4] Wendell Berry *The Unsettling of America Culture and Agriculture* The Sierra Club, 1977

[HBrown] Hunter Brown *William James on Radical Empiricism and Religion* University of Toronto Press, 2000

[PBrown] Peter Brown *Augustine of Hippo: A Biography* The University of California Press, 2000

[RBrown1] Raymond E. Brown *Responses to 101 Questions on the Bible* Paulist Press, 1990

[RBrown2] Raymond E. Brown *An Introduction to the New Testament* Doubleday, 1997

[Buckley] Michael J. Buckley, S.J. *Denying and Disclosing God: The Ambiguous Progress of Modern Atheism* Yale University Press, 2004

[Calvin] William H. Calvin *Conversations with Neil's Brain* Addison-Wesley Publishing Company, 1994

[Carlson] Allan C. Carlson *From Cottage to Work Station The Family's Search for Social Harmony in the Industrial Age* Ignatius Press, 1993

[Cavalli-Sforza] Luca Cavalli-Sforza and Francesco Cavalli-Sforza *The Great Human Diasporas The History of Diversity and Evolution* Addison-Wesley Publishing Company, 1995

[Chaitin] *Mirror of WWW Homepage of Gregory Chaitin* http://www.cs.auckland.ac.nz/DMTCS/chaitin/

[Chesterton] G. K. Chesterton *Saint Thomas Aquinas: The Dumb Ox* Doubleday, 1956

[Cohen] Jack Cohen & Ian Stewart *The Collapse of Chaos Discovering Simplicity in a Complex World* Penguin, 1994

[Damasio] Antonio R. Damasio *Descarte's Error Emotion, Reason, and the Human Brain* G. P. Putnam's Sons, 1994

[Dressler] Alan Dressler *Voyage to the Great Attractor Exploring Intergalactic Space* Alfred A Knopf, 1994

[Edelman1] Gerald M. Edelman and Giulio Tononi *A Universe of Consciousness How Matter Becomes Imagination* Basic Books, 2000

[Edelman2] Gerald M. Edelman *Bright Air, Brilliant Fire On the Matter of the Mind* HarperCollins, 1992

[Eldredge] Niles Eldredge *Reinventing Darwin* John Wiley & Sons, 1995

[Falk] Dean Falk *Braindance: New Discoveries about Human Brain Evolution* Henry Holt and Company, 1994

[Frankl] Victor Frankl *Man's Search for Meaning* Simon & Schuster, 1985

[Gilson1] Etienne Gilson *Methodical Realism* Christendom Press, 1990

[Gilson2] Etienne Gilson *Thomist Realism and the Critique of Knowledge* Ignatius Press, 1986

[Gilson3] Etienne Gilson *The Christian Philosophy of St. Thomas Aquinas* University of Notre Dame Press, 1994

[Gilson4] Etienne Gilson *Being and Some Philosophers Second edition, corrected and enlarged* Pontifical Institute of Mediaeval Studies, 1952

[Goldberg] Steven Goldberg *Why Men Rule: A Theory of Male Dominance* Open Court, 1993

[Hauerwas1] Stanley Hauerwas *With the Grain of the Universe The Church's Witness and Natural Theology* Brazos Press, 2002

[Hauerwas2] Stanley Hauerwas *The Hauerwas Reader* Duke University Press, 2001

[Himmelfarb] Gertrude Himmelfarb *Darwin and the Darwinian Revolution* Ivan R. Dee Publisher, 1996

[Hummel] Jeffrey Rogers Hummel *Emancipating Slaves, Enslaving Free Men: A History of the American Civil War* Open Court, 1996

[Jaki1] Stanley L. Jaki *Genesis 1 Through the Ages* Thomas More Press, 1992

[Jaki2] Stanley L. Jaki *Bible and Science* Christendom Press, 1996

[Jaki3] Stanley L. Jaki *God and the Cosmologists* Scottish Academic Press, 1989

[Jaki4] Stanley L. Jaki *The Relevance of Physics* Scottish Academic Press, 1992

[Jaki5] Stanley L. Jaki *Is There a Universe* Wethersfield Institute, 1993

[Jasay1] Anthony de Jasay *The State* Liberty Fund, 1998

[Jasay2] Anthony de Jasay *Justice and Its Surroundings* Liberty Fund, 2002

[Jouvenel1] Bertrand de Jouvenel *Soverignty: An Inquiry into the Public Good* Liberty Fund, 1998

[Jouvenel2] Bertrand de Jouvenel *On Power: The Natural History of Its Growth* Liberty Fund, 1993

[Jouvenel3] Bertrand de Jouvenel *The Pure Theory of Politics* Liberty Fund, 2000

[Jouvenel4] Bertrand de Jouvenel *The Ethics of Redistribution* Liberty Fund, 1990

[Lachieze-Rey] Marc Lachieze-Rey *Cosmology: A First Course* Cambridge University Press, 1992

[Kagan] Jerome Kagan *Galen's Prophecy: Temperment in Human Nature* Basic Books, 1994

[Lamb] H. H. Lamb *Climate History and the Modern World* Routledge, 1995

[Lukacs1] John Lukacs *Confessions of an Original Sinner* Ticknor & Fields, 1990

[Lukacs1] John Lukacs *The End of the Twentieth Century and the End of the Modern Age* Ticknor & Fields, 1993

[MacIntyre1] Alasdair MacIntyre *Three Rival Versions of Moral Enquiry: Encyclopaedia, Genealogy, and Tradition* University of Notre Dame Press, 1990

[MacIntyre2] Alasdair MacIntyre *Dependent Rational Animals: Why Human Beings Need the Virtues* Open Court, 1999

[MacIntyre3] Alasdair MacIntyre *Against the Self-Images of the Age: Essays on Ideology and Philosophy* Duckworth, 1971

[MacIntyre4] Alasdair MacIntyre *A Short History of Ethics* Macmillan, 1966

[MacIntyre5] Alasdair MacIntyre *Marxism and Christianity* University of Notre Dame Press, 1984

[MacIntyre6] Alasdair MacIntyre *Whose Justice? Which Rationality* University of Notre Dame Press, 1988

[MacIntyre7] Alasdair MacIntyre *After Virtue: A Study in Moral Theory* University of Notre Dame Press, 1981

[McInerny] Ralph McInerny *St. Thomas Aquinas* University of Notre Dame Press, 1982

[Mcnamara1] Robert S. McNamara and Brian VanDeMark *In Retrospect: The Tragedy and Lessons of Vietnam* Vintage Books, 1996

[Melville] Herman Melville *The Confidence Man* Penguin, 1990

[Midgley1] Mary Midgley *Beast and Man: The Roots of Human Nature* Routledge, 1996

[Midgley2] Mary Midgley *Evolution as a Religion* Methuen, 1985

[Minogue] Kenneth Minogue *The Liberal Mind* Liberty Fund, 2000

[Nesse] Randolph M. Nesse, M.D. and George C. Williams, Ph.D. *Why We Get Sick: The New Science of Darwinian Medicine.* Times Books, 1995

[Neusner] Jacob Neusner *Confronting Creation How Judaism Reads Genesis* University of South Carolina Press, 1991

[Nagel] Ernest Nagel and James R. Newman *Gödel's Proof* New York University Press, 1958

[Oakeshotte1] Michael Oakeshotte *Experience and Its Modes* Cambridge University Press, 1985

[Oakeshotte2] Michael Oakeshotte *Rationalism in Politics and Other Essays* Liberty Fund, 1991

[Onians] R. B. Onians *The Origins of European Thought About the Body, the Mind, the Soul, the World, Time, and Fate* Cambridge University Press, 1988

[Patton] George S. Patton, Jr. *War as I Knew It* Bantam, 1980

[Pelikan1] Jaroslav Pelikan *The Christian Tradition: A History of the Development of Doctrine Volume 1: The Emergence of the Catholic Tradition (100-600)* The University of Chicago Press, 1971

[Pelikan2] Jaroslav Pelikan *What Has Athens to Do with Jerusalem Timaeus and Genesis in Counterpoint* The University of Michigan Press, 1997

[Penrose] Roger Penrose *The Emperor's New Mind* Oxford University Press, 1990

[Peurson] C. A. van Peurson *Body, Soul, Spirit: A Survey of the Body-Mind Problem* Oxford University Press, 1966

[Pieper1] Josef Pieper *Living the Truth* Ignatius Press, 1989

[Polanyi] Michael Polanyi *Personal Knowledge: Towards a Post-Critical Philosophy* The University of Chicago Press, 1962

[Ratzinger] Joseph Cardinal Ratzinger *Truth and Tolerance: Christian Belief and World Religions* Ignatius Press, 2003

[Quasten] Johannes Quasten *Patrology: Volumes I - IV* Christian Classics, 1983-1986

[Rorty] Richard Rorty *Philosophy and the Mirror of Nature* Princeton University Press, 1980

[Rose] Steven Rose *The Making of Memory* Anchor Books, 1993

[Rucker] *Infinity and the Mind The Science and Philosophy of the Infinite* Bantam Books, 1983

[Seligman] Martin E. P. Seligman *What You Can Change and What You Can't* Alfred A. Knopf, 1994

[Shapiro] Robert Shapiro *The Human Blueprint The Race to Unlock the Secrets of Our Genetic Code* Bantam Books, 1992

[Silk] Joseph Silk *Cosmic Enigmas: From the First Whispers of the Universe to Its Last Dark Secrets* AIP Press, 1994

[Silk] Joseph Silk *On the Shores of the Unknown: A Short History of the Universe* Cambridge University Press, 2005

[Smith1] Adam Smith *An Enquiry into the Nature and Causes of the Wealth of Nations* (in two volumes) Liberty Fund, 1981

[Smith2] Adam Smith *The Theory of Moral Sentiments* Liberty Fund, 1984

[Trilling] Lionel Trilling *The Moral Obligation to Be Intelligent: Selected Essays* Selected and Edited by Leon Wieseltier Farrar, Straus, Giroux, 2000

[Turner] James Turner *Without God, Without Creed The Origins of Unbelief in America* Johns Hopkins University Press, 1986

[Wald] *Space, Time, and Gravity The Theory of the Big Bang and Black Holes* The University of Chicago Press, 1992

[Yoder1] *The Politics of Jesus* William B. Eerdmans Publishing, 1994

[Yoder2] *When War is Unjust Being Honest in Just-war Thinking* Wipf and Stock Publishers, 2001

[Yoder3] *The Christian Witness to the State* Herald Press, 2002

[Zeki1] Semi Zeki *A Vision of the Brain* Blackwell Scientific Publications, 1993

[Zeki2] Semi Zeki *Inner Vision: An Exploration of Art and the Brain* Oxford University Press, 1999

Colophon

This manual was typeset using the LaTeX typesetting system created by Leslie Lamport and the memoir class. The body text is set 10/12pt on a 33pc measure with Computer Modern Roman designed by Donald Knuth. Other fonts include Sans, Smallcaps, Italic, Slanted and Typewriter, all from Knuth's Computer Modern family.